WOMEN AND JESUS
IN MARK

The Bible & Liberation

An Orbis Series in Biblical Studies

Norman K. Gottwald and Richard A. Horsley,
General Editors

The Bible & Liberation Series focuses on the emerging range of political, social, and contextual hermeneutics that are changing the face of biblical interpretation today. It brings to light the social struggles behind the biblical texts. At the same time it explores the ways that a "liberated Bible" may offer resources in the contemporary struggle for a more human world.

Already published:

The Bible and Liberation: Political and Social Hermeneutics (Revised edition), Norman K. Gottwald and Richard A. Horsley, Editors

Josiah's Passover: Sociology and the Liberating Bible, Shigeyuki Nakanose

The Psalms: Songs of Tragedy, Hope, and Justice, J. David Pleins

The Bible & Liberation Series

WOMEN AND JESUS IN MARK

A Japanese Feminist Perspective

Hisako Kinukawa

ORBIS BOOKS

Maryknoll, New York 10545

BS
2585.2
.K58
1994

The Catholic Foreign Mission Society of America (Maryknoll) recruits and trains people for overseas missionary service. Through Orbis Books, Maryknoll aims to foster the international dialogue that is essential to mission. The books published, however, reflect the opinions of their authors and are not meant to represent the official position of the society.

Published by Orbis Books, Maryknoll, NY 10545-0308
Manufactured in the United States of America

Library of Congress Cataloging-in-Publication Data

Kinukawa, Hisako.
    Women and Jesus in Mark : a Japanese feminist perspective / Hisako Kinukawa.
        p.   cm. — (The Bible & liberation series)
    Includes bibliographical references and index.
    ISBN 0-88344-945-5
    1. Bible. N.T. Mark — Feminist criticism.   2. Jesus Christ — Friends and associates.   3. Women in the Bible.   4. Feminist theology — Japan.   I. Title.   II. Series.
BS2585.2.K58   1994
226.3'07 — dc20   93-50075
                                                                       CIP

Contents

FOREWORD

Letty M. Russell

Hisako Kinukawa is an engaged feminist scholar and her engagement with the barrier breaking love of God is clearly seen in her critical presentation of *Women and Jesus in Mark*. Her Japanese perspective illuminates the culture of honor and shame, out of which the Gospel stories emerged, through comparison to a similar culture of shame in Japan. Her feminist perspective invites us to join in a hermeneutic of suspicion that looks at women as partners with Jesus in breaking down the barriers of patriarchy. None of this would yield such rich insight into the Markan texts, however, if it were not linked with careful, critical and comprehensive exegesis of the texts themselves. Hisako is to be congratulated for her achievement in bringing these elements together, and for her courageous retelling of the stories of women and Jesus from a Japanese feminist perspective!

As a New Testament scholar, Hisako Kinukawa has worked through each of the texts on women and Jesus in Mark presenting the exegetical scholarship that is available, as well as introducing her own critical perspective and contextual analysis. She makes use of the tools of historical criticism to make clear the textual, literary, form and redaction analysis, but she is particularly interested in the tool of critical rhetorical studies for social analysis of the ways the stories attempt to persuade the hearers and the later readers. Rhetorical criticism is particularly helpful in uncovering the patterns of patriarchy in the original story; in Mark's account to his church community; as well as in the later interpretations of the texts.

By examining the various layers of the story Hisako seeks to open up perspectives on the interaction between the women and Jesus in the stories.

Along the way, Hisako's critical feminist questions are particularly fascinating. For instance: Why doesn't Jesus speak to the poor widow in the temple rather than using her as an object lesson [Chapter 4]? Were women really equal to men as disciples and followers of Jesus [Chapter 6]? Why does Mark introduce the women as better examples of discipleship than the men [Chapter 9]? Her discussion of the ways women break the barriers of their own exclusion and oppression to reach out to Jesus is particularly provocative in maintaining that Jesus himself only broke the barriers of his patriarchal shame culture when he was challenged to do so by the women's courage and initiative. Speaking of these reciprocal interactions, Hisako Kinukawa says,

> The women led Jesus to become a responding "boundary breaker." Having spent his whole life in the culture of honor/shame, which was fully male-oriented and which expected women to bear all the shame, Jesus did not take initiative until the women prepared him by stages to break down the boundaries [p. 139].

Hisako Kinukawa's insights into the shame/honor culture of Mark's Gospel are heightened by examples from her own Japanese history and culture. She highlights the problems that arise from ethnic exclusivism, both for resident "aliens" such as the Koreans living in Japan who cannot become citizens, and for indigenous minority groups within Japan. Other problems of uncleanness, and projection of sin onto women are illustrated by reference to the forced prostitution of "Comfort Women" serving the Japanese soldiers in the World War II, and the ever expanding multinational tourist prostitution industry in Japan and Asia. The examples are even more telling because they serve the author's focus on Mark's Gospel. They join the many other insights of her book in inviting us to think through the issues of freedom and mutuality in a cross-cultural perspective.

This is a truly unique contribution to feminist biblical studies from one of the few Japanese women who are pioneering Christian feminists. I first met Hisako Kinukawa when I participated with the women who attended the Korea and Japan Annual Study Forum that was held in Korea in 1988. Since then I have been privileged to work with her in the programs of the Asian and Asian/American Women in Theology and Ministry and the programs of Advanced Pastoral Studies at San Francisco Theological Seminary. Currently we are sharing together in mentoring a Doctor of the Ministry Program in Asian Feminist Theologies, sponsored by San Francisco Seminary. I find that her teaching and ministry have the same integrity of scholarship connected with the struggle for justice that can be found in her writing. I rejoice that this book will be available for English readers in the United States and around the globe so that we can all benefit from this important cross cultural study of barrier breaking mutuality between women and Jesus.

PREFACE

Almost fifty years have passed since the Second World War put an end to Japanese imperial colonialism. But it has been only a few years since Asian women who had been horribly victimized during the war broke their long silence. They kept silent not because they had forgotten about their humiliating experiences, but because their cultural or religious circumstances made them feel ashamed of speaking about such experiences in public and also made them feel guilty, even though they had been intimidated into giving in against their will. These women had been drafted in the divine name of the Japanese emperor and enslaved for physically comforting Japanese soldiers at the battlefronts. Most of them were very young and from Korea and are now in their sixties and seventies. Many others were from other Asian countries colonized by the Japanese military government. Just recently several of these women have filed lawsuits in the courts in Japan and in the United Nations, demanding an official apology and reparation from the Japanese government.

What has troubled me about this issue is that, first of all, these women were treated as objects, raped, and deprived of their basic human rights in the name of the androcentric power struggle justified by the divine name of the emperor. Secondly, their dehumanization was intensified by traditional religious concepts, according to which they had defiled themselves against the teaching of purity. And their culture forced them to kill themselves after the war or to isolate themselves from any social or family life even after they went back home. They are the victims of racism, sexism, and power struggle in the form of militarism, imperialism, and colonialism. And most of all they are the victims of cultural conventions or religious traditions characteristic of almost all Asian countries. As a descendant of the people who dared to commit such barbarous crimes, and as a Christian woman, I feel called to search for the biblical foundation for explaining the crime and to offer a way for these women to recover their wholeness as human beings.

What has terrified me is that the Japanese government, which took advantage of these women's sensitive position, never admitted what had happened. The incident could have been hushed up forever if women who became concerned about the issue (at first Korean women and then women from different countries, including Japan) had not tenaciously investigated what had happened during the war. When these women dared to see the whole issue as a violation of human rights, the victimized women were empowered to speak up after their long period of silence.

The religious concept of purity that has demanded that women be chaste for the sake of men and punished women accused of impure behavior is not rare among world religions. It appears to be divinely rooted, but in fact it is patriarchal androcentrism legitimized under the guise of religious teaching.

My involvement and concern with such bitter issues as this have motivated me to engage in rereading biblical texts with a sharp eye in order to distinguish between sociocultural or political influence and authentic religious concepts. I have desired strongly to seek how the biblical texts could empower us to deal with women's painful circumstances such as this issue, in which women have been dehumanized in the name of hypocritical religious concepts.

Yet I, a woman in this patriarchal society, also had to wait for fifteen years before I could resume my studies and devote my time to this subject. When I married my husband, who taught mathematics at International Christian University, we decided to live on campus because we thought it was very important to have personal contact with our students. It was especially meaningful in the 1960s and 1970s when we had much student turmoil as well as student apathy. I learned to be in solidarity with students in pain who were seeking liberation during that period.

Meanwhile, we were blessed with two daughters to whom I devoted most of my time as they went through the competitive education peculiar to our country. It was also then that I learned another kind of pain and suffering mothers had to bear, caused by the devotion of their husbands to the economic growth of Japan and their seclusion from society.

As I continued to work part-time in the church, I noticed that teachings given at the churches appealed to men but did not necessarily vitalize women. Thus I spent fifteen years learning how Japanese society gained its growth at the sacrifice of the powerless sectors of the society, such as children, students, housewives, and less well paid laborers. When my younger daughter started high school, I went back to my own study of biblical interpretation. I began to formulate anew my perspective as a Japanese feminist theologian, based on my experiences since I had resigned my teaching position shortly after my marriage. I published the first and only book on biblical interpretation written by a Japanese woman from a Japanese feminist perspective and waited for an opportunity to deepen my concerns.

Sometimes our path of life takes a sudden turn and we may see a way to choose very clearly. I experienced this in 1988, on a beautiful spring day when the cherry trees were in full bloom. It was then that I met my future advisor, Dr. Antoinette Clark Wire, who gave a lecture on Corinthian women prophets at the International Christian University campus in Tokyo. Instantly I made up my mind to write my doctoral dissertation with her.

From that time on, and through my two stays in Berkeley (1989-90 and 1991-92), she has been most supportive in every sphere of my study life.

Well known for her deep commitment and strict care in scholarship, she has been a tough disciplinarian. The experience has been invaluable. I deeply appreciate her patience and sympathy as she tried to understand my perspective. I treasure numerous occasions on which we exchanged our thoughts and shared our experiences, and found differences arising from our respective cultural backgrounds as well as the common ground that we experienced as women struggling for liberation. Our discussions helped me greatly to clarify my thoughts, and her critical questions and insightful suggestions have reinforced my feminist theology. My heartfelt thanks for her efforts in both refining and in cherishing my foreign-accented English.

I am deeply grateful to Dr. Walt Davis, Director of Advanced Pastoral Studies at San Francisco Theological Seminary, and Dr. Warren Lee, Assistant Director, leaders of my Collegium group. They have been most encouraging to us students in developing a well-planned sequence of study for us, maintaining occasional contact through correspondence, and overwhelming us with their personal warmth. I thank each member of my Collegium group, which was characterized by its diversity and its deep concern about all forms of discrimination and injustice: Hmingi (from Burma), Jay (from Canada), Mawia (from India), Kevin (an African American), Hoong Yul (a Korean American), Virstin (a Chinese American), Gary, and Larry (both European American).

Many thanks also go to Ginger Johnston, who helped to refine my English, and to Pat Perry in the APS office.

I am thankful to women's groups in the USA: AAAWTM (Asian and Asian-American Women in Theology and Ministry); PACTS (Pacific and Asian American Center for Theology and Strategies); and CWR (Center for Women in Religion). Friends in these groups have been most empowering to me.

I am most grateful to all the Christian and non-Christian women in Japan with whom I have collaborated in building up women's networks and activities, and who have helped me develop my feminist theology in various ways.

I am grateful to Dr. Joanna Dewey who, having helped with my studies in Berkeley, encouraged me to publish my dissertation. I am also grateful to Dr. Letty M. Russell, who has supported me with her thoughtful wisdom all through these years. My deep appreciation goes to Robert Ellsberg of Orbis Books, who kindly read my dissertation and encouraged me to publish it as a book. Thanks to Susan Perry of Orbis Books and Dr. Shannon Clarkson, who devoted much energy to refining my English.

Probably I am most indebted to my husband, Masa, who stood by me and supported me all through my studies. I appreciate the support and concern offered by our two daughters, Tomomi and Akemi, who both have chosen to continue their studies in America.

1

INTRODUCTION

My main concern in this book is to elucidate the reciprocally influential relationships between women and Jesus and to determine the positions of women in the circles of Jesus' followers. I try to interpret Jesus' events through focusing on women's interactions with Jesus.

I read them from a Japanese feminist perspective in a contemporary context. Since the situations of Japanese women in their own society are unique, the questions and concerns become particular. Nevertheless, I believe particularity is always connected to universality. In addition, the feminist perspective will contribute to correcting the androcentric bias attached to biblical texts.

The trend of academic historical and theological scholarship has been to justify the status quo of the dominant political power structures. It has legitimized men as normative and served the social structures of oppression. The Christian tradition of assigning women subordinate positions only confirmed in the Japanese churches an inequality that was already deeply embedded in our patriarchal culture.

One of the reasons that motivated me to conduct this study is found in the fact that our knowledge of biblical texts had been androcentrically biased in many ways: (1) The texts that interest women or are important for understanding women have been neglected in churches, so that we have hardly known that such texts exist. (2) Even the texts referring to or suggesting equal relationships between women and men have been read only for male convenience. (3) Many original texts are translated into Japanese in such a way as to affirm the Japanese traditional patriarchal understanding of the relationship between women and men. The newest translation of the Bible in Japanese was a collaborative effort among seventy people representing both Protestant and Catholic churches. Though it has been said to be an epoch-making enterprise, it was a disappointment for women, since not only were there just three Catholic Sisters on the translation team, but also no Protestant woman was invited even for consultation. We have found words that are simply inappropriate for expressing what biblical texts try to communicate to us.

I became more strongly convinced that we urgently need to reread biblical texts from a feminist perspective in order that we may speak up in churches and liberate ourselves from our subservient mindset.

The following questions are my point of departure: (1) Who are the women depicted in the gospel? (2) How is their life changed by their experience? (3) What does being Jesus' disciple mean to them? (4) What influence do they have on Jesus? (5) What roles do they play in their communities? (6) What new vision do the women get concerning their relationship with men?

Thus I feel compelled to ask new questions based on the unique position of Japanese Christian women. First of all, Japanese Christians, who have never reached one percent of the total population in this multireligious society, are not in easy circumstances. And we Japanese Christian women need to become aware that we are in conflict with the patriarchal structure of our society and that we are called to struggle in churches as well as in the society. For that purpose, we need to be empowered with a concrete strategy. I would like to find our models in the interactions between Jesus and the women of his time. By studying how those women who were subjugated under patriarchy were transformed and empowered through their encounter with Jesus and involvement with his movement, we will also find a way for ourselves to be not only transformative but constructive.

Of course I realize that in trying to find the meaning of the biblical texts I cannot project whatever I want into the text. But I also realize that I cannot be free from my contemporary experiences and questions. The process is all the more difficult when I see that the biblical context may have similarities with my own. As Schüssler Fiorenza says, people must depend on some frame of reference when they discuss the available historical evidence and "the frame of reference is always determined by their own philosophical perspective and values."[1] For this I have come to hope that my experiential understanding of patriarchy may be a help rather than a hindrance in comprehending a patriarchal past.

I have chosen Mark's Gospel as my resource because it is the earliest record of Jesus and his followers and it was written in the earliest stage of the patriarchalization process of the church. However, in order to get a sharp picture of these women I have had to clear away layers of clouds that have obscured their images in the texts as well as throughout the history of the church.

Since the evangelist who portrays the women I deal with is male, we can easily assume that the entire process of collecting traditions and sources and molding them into a cohesive narrative structure has been done from a male perspective.

1. Elisabeth Schüssler Fiorenza, *In Memory of Her: A Feminist Theological Reconstruction of Christian Origins* (New York: Crossroad, 1983), xvii.

At the same time, most scholars consider that Mark depicts the male disciples of Jesus rather critically. Even though Jesus gives them special positions, encourages them with special instructions, and disciplines them severely, they still fail to comprehend Jesus' suffering messiahship and to respond to his call to suffering discipleship. The negative portrayal of male disciples, however, does not guarantee that we will find positive images of women. Women may still be introduced only when they are useful for the evangelist's purposes, and their images may be biased in favor of a male-centered framework of thinking.[2]

Most scholars agree that Mark wrote his Gospel because he believed that the resurrected Lord was activating his community of faith through the words, deeds, and life of Jesus of Nazareth. Mark's christological insight into Jesus' inevitable fate of suffering, execution, and death shapes a theology of suffering and death. Mark depicts a following of the Jesus who serves others as the core of discipleship and the basis of a discipleship of equals. This may suggest that Mark would have a favorable attitude toward women, because women, being so accustomed to following and serving are among those who could easily put the call into pratice. Yet at the same time, we may need to question the key concepts of discipleship—following and serving—because they still imply vertical relationships between the following-serving and the followed-served.

If we consider the possibility that Mark's Gospel and the letter to the Colossians may have been written at approximately the same time and that the latter clearly reflects the patriarchal household code adapting to the dominance/submission structure of the society of that time, we may conclude that the Markan ethos of discipleship is remarkable. Sailing against the current of the time, Mark may have tried to strengthen the faith and praxis of his community of faith with a theology of suffering and death. In this he exposed the need of understanding true discipleship, the anxiety about losing the spirit of true serving, and the weakness expressed in desiring power in his community. At least we may say that he made an effort to prevent his community from further adaptation to Roman society. In this sense, his Gospel may have distanced itself somewhat from a genuinely patriarchally-oriented framework of thinking.

In any case, we will not see early Christian women expressing themselves, since they hardly had any chance to write. When men such as Mark reconstructed early Christian history, their androcentric mindset, nurtured by the

---

2. Carol P. Christ, "Spiritual Quest and Women's Experience," in *Womanspirit Rising: A Feminist Reader in Religion*, ed. Carol P. Christ and Judith Plaskow (San Francisco: Harper & Row, 1979), 230. "Feminist studies therefore maintain that established scholarship is not *partial*, to the extent that it articulates male experience as human experience, but also biased, to the extent that its intellectual discourse and scholarly frameworks are determined only by male perspectives primarily of the dominant classes" (Elisabeth Schüssler Fiorenza, *Bread Not Stone: The Challenge of Feminist Biblical Interpretation* [Boston: Beacon Press, 1984], 107).

sociopolitical system of patriarchy, further silenced and marginalized women and other "nonpersons" and virtually eliminated them from the historical record. Therefore my task will be to reconstruct the reality and voice of the silenced and marginalized women from the androcentric primary records.

I start reading the Markan texts with the following premise:

> Androcentric language and male authored texts presuppose women's historical presence and agency but for the most part do not articulate it. Therefore, the relationship between androcentric text and historical reality cannot be construed as a mirror-image but must be decoded as a complex ideological construction.[3]

Since "historians shape their material not just in terms of a narrative framework, but also engage in selection of 'data,' periodization and ascription of significance,"[4] their mindset affects and controls their work of assessment as they respond to "historical reality." But such historical reconstruction as Mark's that is done with close attention to the "historical reality," even though with a male perspective, can sometimes help us to discern what is repressed or hidden if we carefully observe what is displayed in it. I believe that the Markan text, unconsciously or consciously, invisibly or visibly, witnesses to the existence of suppressed voices that constitute an inevitable part of the community of faith. Therefore I do not intend to distinguish the "canon within the canon" and discard the rest. Through the totally androcentric texts we are challenged to reconstruct the reality about which they keep silent.

Therefore we cannot locate the detached, objective truth of reality as a "transhistorical or universal human experience and essence."[5] As long as a writer is living with her or his own value system and presuppositions, the resulting descriptions cannot provide unbiased "pure facts" of history.

ONE APPROACH TO MARK

Mark's Relationship with Oral and Written Traditions

When we try to reconstruct the historical reality of interactions between women and Jesus using the Gospel of Mark as our guide, we need to observe, evaluate, and interpret Mark's relationship with oral traditions and written sources that had their own contextual environment and

3. Elisabeth Schüssler Fiorenza, "Text and Reality—Reality as Text: The Problem of a Feminist Historical and Social Reconstruction Based on Texts," *Studia Theologica* 43 (1989), 28.

4. Ibid., 23.

5. Ibid., 24.

reflected the reactions, evaluations, and interpretations of their carriers and hearers. Roughly speaking, only one generation elapsed between Jesus' crucifixion and Mark's writing. Many of those who were young when Jesus was crucified might still have been alive when Mark started writing his gospel narrative. Even Mark might have heard stories about Jesus during Jesus' actual ministry, if he was writing in mid-life or later. So we should not overestimate alterations in the tradition. It is equally possible that the original was maintained as that transformation occurred.

Form Criticism

There have been many historical-critical efforts to remove the strata of alterations and reveal the original forms of traditions. Form criticism, originated by Rudolf Bultmann and Martin Dibelius, pursues two basic goals: (1) to trace the historical process of the transformation of traditions backwards with close attention to the situation in which they were transmitted (*Sitz im Leben*), determining the typical forms of the traditions, and (2) to extract formative factors operating in the development of these units.[6]

Form criticism is interested in distinguishing literary genres by tracing similarities between traditions and connections between texts. The literary forms gained through this analysis are independent of time or history. Some call this part of the analysis synchronic.[7]

At the same time, form criticism is based on the hypothesis that traditions concerning Jesus' teaching and his life with his followers are transmitted in various kinds of "forms" that reveal the intentions of a community of faith. The continued transmission of traditions took place in the contexts of liturgy, mission, or instruction. Thus the *Sitz im Leben* of the traditions is found in concrete situations in the community. To pursue how this process developed is called the diachronic approach.[8]

Bultmann classified traditions into sayings of Jesus which include apothegms and dominical sayings, and narrative material, consists of miracle stories, historical stories, and legends. Each of these forms is related to various phases of worship, such as liturgy, admonition, proclamation, etc.[9] If the traditions are intentionally used for the mission of the community of faith, their forms are shaped for this particular purpose, and the contents are enriched according to their forms. Thus the "living traditions" are constantly corrected by the various elements of their community: the composition of the members, their social class identity, their issues, their values and worldview, and their cultural and religious background. This means

6. Martin Dibelius, *From Tradition To Gospel* (New York: Scribner, 1965), 4.

7. E.g., Gerd Theissen, *The Miracle Stories of the Early Christian Tradition* (Edinburgh: T. & T. Clark, 1983), 3-16.

8. Ibid., 17-24.

9. Rudolf K. Bultmann, *The History of the Synoptic Tradition*, trans. John Marsh (Oxford: Basil Blackwell, 1972).

that the transformed traditions with their *Sitz im Leben* reflect the constant interaction of their carriers and hearers.

But form criticism is limited to analyzing those traditions that were transmitted within the community of faith. It did not deal with those traditions or rumors that must have been formulated at the very early stage by those around Jesus who had not identified themselves with the community of faith.[10] My attempt to uncover the earliest stratum of the Jesus traditions takes me back before the stage of the community of faith as the transmitter.

It should also be pointed out that form criticism tends to stress sayings and other "words," components of tradition rather than the narrative texts in which historical characters seem to be more vividly depicted.[11] Although I am more interested in historical persons and their behavior, I am also helped by linguistic analysis and philology. I will refer to syntax and semantics when they help me for a picture of the original situations.

Redaction Criticism

In the process of collecting traditions, interpreting them and molding them into the Gospel from his own perspective, Mark worked within his particular horizon of experience and knowledge that formed his conceptual framework. Redaction criticism helps us pursue the writer's redactional process and intention. Our tasks are (1) to uncover the writer's particular perspective and reveal his understanding of Jesus; and (2) to distinguish the earlier tradition from the redactional process including changes and additions to the tradition, to set it in the context of his Gospel. Redaction criticism has developed in conjunction with form criticism, and they are not exclusive of each other.[12]

Sociology of Literature

Some scholars attempt to reach further backward beyond the limits of form and redaction criticism by using sociology of literature.[13] The analysis of the *Sitz im Leben* of religious traditions that helps us see the intentional development of certain forms of tradition also draws attention to the *Sitz im Leben* of the people who participated in shaping traditions in various ways. It examines behaviors of those who compose, transmit, and receive traditions.[14]

Tellers tell stories because they want to instruct, entertain or persuade. Hearers would not listen to them unless they thereby received lessons,

10. Sasagu Arai, *Iesu Kirisuto* (Jesus Christ) (Tokyo: Kodansha, 1979), 54-55. E. Schüssler Fiorenza, *In Memory of Her,* 41.

11. E. Schüssler Fiorenza, *In Memory of Her,* 152.

12. E. Schüssler Fiorenza, *In Memory of Her,* 384.

13. Theissen, *The Miracle Stories,* 28-40. Arai, *Iesu Kirisuto,* 55.

14. Theissen, *The Miracle Stories,* 28.

consolation, joy, empowerment, encouragement, or conviction. This is why sociology of literature defines texts as symbolic forms of interpersonal behavior. Socio-ecological, socio-economic and sociocultural factors are at work. The hypothesis is that traditions are shaped by their full historical life-contexts.[15]

Mark seems to have collected traditions carried by the people who socioecologically lived in rural areas, socio-economically belonged to the lower stratum of society, and socioculturally practiced norms and values that could attract them to Jesus' movement. The closer the symbolic interactions between tellers and hearers were to the interactions between Jesus and Jesus' followers, the more their forms of speech must have reflected the earliest versions of the stories.

It is said that the traditions adopted by Mark were mostly transmitted by the Galilean people, and that they belong to the early stage of transmission. Thus we may expect that the traditions would be comparatively close to the historical reality.[16]

If there were women tellers who kept remembering and relating the interactions between Jesus and his women followers, women hearers must have enjoyed hearing these stories and found them empowering. Undoubtedly women would have repeatedly told one another those stories and identified their own experiences with them. Mark might have received such traditions among his sources.

Mark's Relationship with His Community of Faith

Also necessary for reconstructing the historical reality of interactions between women and Jesus based on Mark's Gospel is to evaluate Mark's relationship with the community of faith to which he was related and for whom he wrote. This is the *Sitz im Leben* of Mark as the writer.

The community of faith consisted of multiple experiences of lives that produced diverse conceptual frameworks and horizons of expectation. If Mark wanted his Gospel to communicate something to the members of his community of faith, he must have been aware of the particular areas of contention in their faith as well as their broader value systems and worldviews. Mark had to see, all at once, the past he was writing about, the present he was writing for, and the future he hoped to shape.[17] He addressed this by trying to reconstruct a history that was in some tension with his motivation for writing. The tension was born out of his effort to join the present to the past and to let the past be meaningful in the present and toward the future.

Aware of certain concrete issues, Mark molded the Gospel for a certain

15. Ibid., 1-40.
16. Arai, *Iesu Kirisuto* 409-10.
17. Elisabeth Schüssler Fiorenza, *Bread Not Stone: The Challenge of Feminist Biblical Interpretation* (Boston: Beacon Press, 1984), 145-46.

group of people. For his rhetorical purpose, he must have chosen the literary form of the Gospel as opposed to a letter or apocalypse, as the most powerful and effective medium, and written the Gospel so that it would challenge, encourage, and sustain the community of faith.[18] Therefore we cannot get the proper sense of his Gospel without knowing the context of the social-historical world in which he lived and which evoked his intention for writing. With such a socio-literary perspective, we may get a view of the interactions between Mark and his readers. Through that process we hope to come closer to recovering interactions between women and Jesus, which, we must be aware, could be colored by the evangelist's rhetorical purposes.

In short, I want to touch the reality of life experienced by those women who interacted with Jesus. By "reality" I do not mean an inaccessible historical "factuality," but the reality that we may discern through the texts available to us. It is possible that the women depicted in Mark might not be real persons, and I am not interested in discerning whether they could be specified as individuals. But I would like to see certain aspects of women's experiences peculiar to those who encountered Jesus. Those experiences, I think, constitute the history behind Mark's Gospel.

Since we are dealing with the narrative Gospel written "for" some community, we must expect that our texts are situational and commitment-laden in a way that reflects Mark's horizon of experience and knowledge.

This requires us to critically evaluate and interpret how the texts were influenced both by Mark's dialogical interpretation of the issues in his community and by his value system. I will rely on textual, literary, form and redaction critical-historical analyses to the extent that they help clarify the meaning of the text in its social, political, religious, and historical situation. That is to say, I will use historical criticism to the extent that it can bring out the ideological character of androcentric texts and language.

Gender politics

We are always reminded of the fact that, from the early stage of the formation and transmission of both oral and written traditions to the stage of selection of traditions by Mark, the culture in which the traditions were embedded was patriarchal. And at the stage of redaction, Mark was facing the church in the process of patriarchalization. If these factors brought about the textual marginalization of women, a critical analysis of the theological dynamics and aims of a story must recover the history it obscures. For this purpose biblical interpretation must move to a critical evaluation of its own theological rhetoric.[19]

The experiences of the sexes might have been so different that the Gos-

18. Ibid., 145.
19. E. Schüssler Fiorenza, *Bread Not Stone,* 144, 111-12.

pel came to mean something else for women than it did for men, the rigid patriarchal structures taken into consideration.[20]

We need to read between lines of the texts, for we may read only the image of women that Mark wants to fashion. We should be sensitive and careful enough to distinguish the gender politics inscribed in androcentric texts.[21] Mark's women could be fictitiously colored figures with their historical truth hidden behind them.

Patriarchy has been the heuristic key for feminist critical analysis. I use it as a major basis on which to observe, describe and analyze male-dominant structures of society and to locate all kinds of oppressive forms of marginalization, dehumanization, and exploitation in different spheres of life in society. Elisabeth Schüssler Fiorenza understands patriarchy as "a socio-cultural system in which a few men have power over other men, women, children, slaves and colonized people."[22] She does not use "the widely accepted feminist understanding of patriarchy in terms of sexism or the sex-gender system, i.e., the 'manifestation and institutionalization of male dominance over women,' "[23] nor does she explain why she uses patriarchy in the sense of elite male domination. However, she does add that "patriarchy as a complex ideological and political-economic system of sex-race-class-cultural/religious domination affects women *differently*."[24] I agree with her that patriarchy is not simply "all men dominating all women equally,"[25] but I cannot limit the male-dominant pyramid to manipulation by a few elite men in power. My experiences of patriarchy in our country involve male domination within each social level, suggesting that her description may reflect her distinct social-cultural context.[26]

In Japan, "patriarchy," highlighted by emperor worship, was forced upon the people as the principle of national unity, of legitimizing all sorts of unscrupulous invasions, and of supporting paternal lineage. It penetrated deeply not only into the political and social life but into each family's life. And its influence and residue have been found in many places and occasions. I need to define what patriarchy means in my country. I also need to find out what "patriarchy" was in first-century Palestine in order to locate its influence on social, political, and religious aspects of the society.

According to Janice Capel Anderson, "Patriarchy is a controversial term.

20. Inger Marie Lindboe, "Recent Literature: Development and Perspectives in New Testament Research on Women," *Studia Theologica* 43 (1989), 161.

21. E. Schüssler Fiorenza, "Text and Reality—Reality as Text," 22; *Bread Not Stone*, 114.

22. Elisabeth Schüssler Fiorenza, *In Memory of Her*, 29. Also "Text and Reality—Reality as Text," 19-20. "I use patriarchy 'in the narrow sense' to signify the domination of *elite* Western man over his gendered, raced, classed, and colonized 'others,' whom Gustavo Gutiérrez calls the 'nonpersons.' "

23. E. Schüssler Fiorenza, "Text and Reality—Reality as Text," 19.

24. Ibid., 20.

25. E. Schüssler Fiorenza, *Bread Not Stone*, xiv.

26. On patriarchy in Japan, see below, pp. 15-21.

Feminists generally define it as a complex system of male dominance. This system involves religious, political, economic and other factors. It involves the intersection of age, race, religion, class, and gender. The rule of elite males means the subordination of non-elite males as well as that of females and children. It does not mean that women are only victims without any agency at all. Nor does it mean that sex/gender systems are all alike."[27]

I agree with Anderson in the sense that any definition of patriarchy reflects what one experiences as patriarchy in one's own historical context. Definitions given by Western white middle-class feminist theologians seem to me quite different from what we have experienced in our society. My own detailed definition of patriarchy is that it is the ideology of male supremacy that supports male dominance in every unit of society and engenders a hierarchical power structure of the society and monarchy. It is true that "the rule of elite males means the subordination of non-elite males," but non-elite males are superior to non-elite women and subjugate them. And it is true that elite women can subordinate non-elite men, but elite women, if there can be such, can never be equal or superior to elite men. The definition of "elite males" is not clear and I never want to use "elite" for describing patriarchy. Patriarchy is an ideology to legitimize male dominance in every unit of life. I must admit that because of this ideology there is the possibility and reality that even women can be dominant and segregational.

To critically study androcentrically-biased texts in the patriarchal society of first-century Palestine, it is essential to know how the social strata of individuals and social standings of groups were maintained. When we deal with biblical stories that include individuals of different social classes and genders without understanding such social systems, various patterns of speech called "literary forms" could be taken as apatriarchal or unhierarchical.[28] I will take the widely accepted feminist understanding that patriarchy pervades every sphere of a society and has power politically, economically, socially and culturally.

Patriarchy in first-century Palestine may well be described by using Bruce Malina's anthropological analysis, which is done in the frame of structuralism.

Ched Myers, introducing Bruce Malina's theory based on cultural anthropology, says that Judaism in first-century Palestine could be described as an "honor culture," a "highly formal system [that] determined to whom and how one could speak and interact, regulated social roles and transactions, and circumscribed mobility within the system."[29]

27. "Mapping Feminist Biblical Criticism: The American Scene, 1983-1990," *Critical Review of Books in Religion* (Atlanta: Scholars Press, 1991), 24.

28. Bruce Malina, *The New Testament World: Insights from Cultural Anthropology* (Atlanta: John Knox Press, 1981), 25-26.

29. Ched Myers, *Binding the Strong Man: A Political Reading of Mark's Story of Jesus* (New York: Orbis Books, 1988), 198.

According to Malina, in first-century Palestine three boundary markers functioned to situate persons in their rightful places. They are called (1) power, (2) sexual status and (3) religion, that is, respect for those above one, including one's God. And "where they come together, what they mark off, is something that is called *honor*."[30]

> Honor is the value of a person in his or her own eyes (that is, one's claim to worth) *plus* that person's value in the eyes of his or her social group. Honor is a claim to worth along with the social acknowledgment of worth. Society shares the sets of meanings and feelings bound up in the symbols of power, sexual status, and religion. Whom you can control is bound up with your male and female roles, which are also bound up with where you stand on the status ladder of your group. When you lay claim to a certain status as embodied by your power and in your sexual role, you are claiming honor.[31]

In the culture of honor, the sense of honor becomes the main clue to situating a person in her or his rightful place in society as well as on the status ladder of the community. It is very important to know that a person's claim to honor is effective only when the public grants the person social reputation. Honor becomes honor only when the claim from inside and the reputation from outside coincide. Therefore the person is required to keep a constant dialectic, "a thinking back and forth between the norms of society and how the person is to reproduce those norms in specific behavior,"[32] while maintaining his or her social boundaries at the intersection of power, sexual status, and respect for others, including God.[33] It is obvious that these boundaries entail hierarchical structure.

Power—collective honor. A power boundary indicates the point beyond which one violates a superior's honor. The boundary-crossing on the side of inferiors implies the intention of dishonor.[34] The power structure is never to be neglected. "The purpose of honor is to serve as a sort of social rating which entitles a person to interact in specific ways with his or her equals, superiors, and subordinates, according to the prescribed cultural cues of the society."[35]

The remarkable characteristic of such a society is found in the fact that "along with personal honor, an individual shares in a sort of collective or corporate honor. Included within the bounds of personal honor are all those worthies who control a person's existence, i.e., patron, king, and God—all whom one holds vertically sacred. Also included is one's family—the hor-

---

30. Malina, *The New Testament World*, 26.
31. Ibid., 27.
32. Ibid., 28.
33. Ibid., 34.
34. Ibid., 36.
35. Ibid., 47.

izontally sacred. The reason for this is that like individuals, social groups possess a collective honor."[36]

Individualism was not considered the pivotal value for the people in first-century Palestine as it is for Westerners today, but collective or corporate honor was a major focus. In such a society "I am who I am and with whom I associate."[37] The head of each group, ranging from individual and nuclear family, to kingdom or region, "is responsible for the honor of the group with reference to outsiders, and symbolizes the group's honor as well. Hence members of the group owe loyalty, respect, and obedience of a kind which commits their individual honor without limit and without compromise."[38]

The social precedence of the heads of groups is normally convertible into ethical honor or implicit goodness. Consequently, it also characterizes the person as sacred.[39]

Sexual status. The dynamics of the "female" and "male" roles are also important for the maintenance of the system. "The male role was concerned with the defense of status and entitlement; the female role preserved the consciousness of group boundaries, or 'shame.' "[40]

Women are required to maintain sexual exclusiveness or sexual "purity" in order for men related to them to gain honor. The honor of the male is thus based on the sexual purity of the women related to him (mother, wife, daughters, and sisters), not on his own sexual purity. This means that women are confined in inside spaces in the house or the village.[41]

36. Ibid., 38.

37. Ibid., 40.

38. Ibid., 40.

39. Ibid., 42: "Honor (social precedence) guarantees against dishonor (immoral or ignoble ethical bearing). Thus the king of the nation (or the father of the family) simply cannot be dishonored within the group; he is above criticism. What he is guarantees the evaluation of his actions. Any offense against him only stains the offender.

"Further, the king in his kingdom (like the father in his family) can do no wrong because he is the arbiter of right and wrong. Any criticism apart from conventional, usual ones is rated an act of disloyalty, a lack of commitment. No one has a right to question what the king decides to do, just as no individual in the group has any right to follow what he or she might personally think is right or wrong. The king (father) must be followed and obeyed; he is sufficient conscience for all concerned. This proper attitude is symboled in rituals of honor, and one must pay honor (worship originally meant worthiness, a recognition of worth) even if one does not feel inclined to. On the other hand, honor felt is honor paid, and honor paid indicates what ought be felt. In sum, honor causes a society to derive what ought be done from what in fact is done. That is, the social order as it should be is derived from the social order as it actually is. Paying honor to those to whom it is owed legitimates established power and further integrates societal members in their system of obligatory consent."

40. Myers, *Binding the Strong Man*, 198.

41. Malina, *The New Testament World*, 44, 45-46. "As mentioned previously, honor means a person's (or group's) feeling of self-worth and the public, social acknowledgment of that worth. Honor in this sense applies to both sexes. It is the basis of one's reputation, of one's social standing, regardless of sex. In this common context, where honor is both

Examples of virtuous characteristics expected from women are "submission to authority, unwillingness to risk, deference, passivity, timid[ness] and restraint."[42] As long as they live according to such selfless devotion for the sake of men, they are honored because of their sensitivity to shame. Malina calls it "positive sensitivity" to the good repute of individuals and groups.[43] If they dare to refuse such subjugated lives, they are said to become shameless and their honor can never be regained.

Respect for those above one — Dyadic personality. In such a society in which sensitivity to honor and shame are pivotal values, how others see a person and what reputation they give him or her become all-important. Individuals have to be very sensitive to the world outside and to their own response to it, so that they may live up to their concept of what the world expects of them. Malina characterizes this as the "nonindividualistic, dyadic self-awareness."[44]

In the biblical world, "a meaningful human existence depends upon an individual's full awareness of what others think and feel about him, and his living up to that awareness. Conscience is sensitivity to what others think about and expect of the individual; it is another word for shame in the positive sense. ... As a result, the person in question does not think of himself or herself as an individual who acts alone regardless of what others think and say. Rather, the person is ever aware of the expectations, of others, especially significant others, and strives to match these expectations. This is the dyadic personality, one who needs another simply to know who he or she is."[45]

In this case the measure of good and bad depends on whether a certain behavior brings honor or shame to others and to oneself. A person is always to be alert about what the outside world expects him or her to be, behave or say. So if women are expected to be subordinate and silent and to do menial work, they would not think of any other way of being. They are to

male and female, the word "shame" is a positive symbol, meaning sensitivity for one's own reputation, sensitivity to the opinion of others. To have shame in this sense is an eminently positive value."

"However, actual, everyday, concrete conduct that establishes one's reputation and redounds upon one's group is never independent of the sexual or moral division of labor. Actual conduct, daily concrete behavior, always depends upon one's sexual status. At this level of perception, when honor is viewed as an exclusive prerogative of one of the sexes, then honor is always male, and shame is always female. Thus in the area of individual, concrete behavior (and apart from considerations of the group), honor and shame are sex-specific ... Female shame ... covers a range running from the ethically neutral to the ethically valued: feelings of sensitivity or "shame" to reveal nakedness, shyness, blushing, timidity, restraint, sexual exclusiveness — all this is positive shame for the female and makes her honorable."

42. Ibid., 45.
43. Ibid., 48.
44. Ibid., 53.
45. Ibid., 67.

be fully embedded in group-oriented thinking and find their satisfaction and happiness in their given status.

Even though neither Myers or Malina mentions it, we may surely call such a society a patriarchal social system that excludes women from power, subjugates them, and confines the space of their activity to the domestic field. This results in the situation of unequal rights between male and female.

Feminist Hermeneutics: A Hermeneutics of Suspicion

Facing Mark's Gospel as a partial as well as biased record of the early Christian history, I need to apply a "hermeneutics of suspicion" to my investigation to "detect ideological deformations."[46]

> As androcentric texts, our early Christian sources are theological interpretations, argumentations, projections, and selections rooted in a patriarchal culture. Therefore they need to be read critically for their theoretical-theological androcentric tendencies and their polemical theological patriarchal functions. Such texts must be evaluated *historically* in terms of their own time and culture and assessed *theologically* in terms of a feminist scale of values.[47]

Since Mark's writing could be partial because it is the record of male-centered experience, and biased because Mark could not be free from the patriarchal-ideological perspective of his time, references to women could be "dimorphic": women could be seen as participants in history and objects of oppression at the same time.[48]

It is very possible that the more liberated and active the women became in the community of faith, the more prescriptive Mark's way of depicting women would get. I may expect, therefore, there might have been many more women like those who are recorded in the gospel as marginalized and subordinated and yet made whole and having recovered selfhood through interacting with Jesus. Thus I might get a glimpse of rhetorical clues and allusions indicating the reality.[49] And it is also possible that Mark did happen to record the oldest stratum of positive traditions about women, even if they only happened to serve his purposes for writing his Gospel. And if the women of Mark's faith community were no longer so deeply involved in the actual practice of discipleship and all that it entailed Mark might have felt at ease with composing positive descriptions of women in Jesus'

---

46. E. Schüssler Fiorenza, *Bread Not Stone,* 107-8, 148.

47. Ibid., 108.

48. Ibid., 109.

49. Elisabeth Schüssler Fiorenza, "The Will to Choose or to Reject: Continuing Our Critical Work," in Letty M. Russell, ed., *Feminist Interpretation of the Bible* (Philadelphia: Westminster Press, 1985), 134.

movement because they would have posed less of a threat. In any case, we must be aware that we cannot rely on biblical texts about women as only describing women.

In order to break the silence of the texts and to derive meaning from androcentric historiography, we must today be in a situation in which we can engender creative critical-historical interpretation. In fact, we can make use of the power of imagination based on our common experiences of being marginalized, our knowledge of comparison between the past and the present, and our existential commitment to dialogue with the people who lived and live in their particular political, social, cultural, and religious circumstances.

The perspective of feminist liberation theology helps us look at the texts "about" women and "without" women as the records of sufferings and struggles endured by women. The subversive power of the sympathy we feel toward the women hidden in the texts will help us reclaim the "remembered past" in the new framework of reference.[50] Thus we participate in recovering the reality of women who interacted with Jesus through a historical-critical reconstruction of biblical history from a feminist perspective.

PATRIARCHY IN JAPAN

Introducing Malina's anthropological analysis on first-century Palestinian society, Myers focuses his observation on the "formalities" of honor. He uses the case of indigenous people on a newly-independent Pacific island as an example to explain these formalities, but his case study seems to tend to look for phenomenal differences of expressions.[51] The point I get from Malina's analysis on the other hand, is the mentality or philosophy of life that motivates people's behavior in certain patterns and forms. Malina's contribution is that he succeeded in elucidating the human dynamics in the social structure of Palestine by applying interactional terms of honor and shame.

"Honor culture" may still predominate among many indigenous peoples,

---

50. E. Schüssler Fiorenza, *Bread Not Stone*, 141, "Because of the critical and future-oriented dimensions of biblical scholarship as 'interpretation for' the church of women, a critical feminist hermeneutics of liberation must have a fourfold dimension, as discussed in Chapter 1. It must be a hermeneutics of suspicion, critically entering the biblical worlds and the works of scholars in order to detect their ideological deformations; a hermeneutics of remembrance, facilitated by literary and historical critical reconstructions; a hermeneutics of proclamation critically evaluating what can be proclaimed and taught today as an inspired vision for a more human life and future; and finally a hermeneutics of actualization that celebrated its critical solidarity in story and song, in ritual and meditation, as a people of the 'God with us' who was the God of Judith as well as of Jesus (148)." See also "The Will To Choose or To Reject: Continuing Our Critical Work," ed. Letty M. Russell, *Feminist Interpretation of the Bible*.

51. Myers, *Binding the Strong Man*, 199-200.

as Myers says, but it is often seen in modernized cultures too. For example, the power dynamics of honor and shame have been the main socially shared norm controlling the behavior of individuals as well as groups in Japan, one of the most highly industrialized countries in the world. "Honor culture" is not the monopoly of indigenous people, I must say.[52]

For us Japanese, so-called Western individualism has been foreign, though we have learned its positive characteristics and even tried to assimilate it ourselves. We have been accustomed to the patriarchally-biased "culture of shame" (I do not use "culture of honor") for so long that we are influenced and controlled, consciously or unconsciously, by that mentality.

As a woman, I can feel closer to the women in the Bible, since our experiences as women have so much in common with theirs. Such common experiences of shame/honor with boundaries of power, sexual status, and respect for others, in a group-oriented society of dyadic personalities, provide me with a powerful methodological device for studying the women and their experiences in Mark's Gospel.

I will analyze patriarchy in our country applying Malina's anthropological structural analysis.

In the case of our country it seems that "shame" and not "honor" functions as the standard of norms. We may call it a culture of "shame/ honor" in comparison with the culture of "honor/shame." Honor may be claimed only negatively by avoiding shameful behavior, thoughts and language. Thus "honor" is rarely referred to. The individual is expected to restrain her- or himself from deeds and words that may bring disgrace on various groups to which one belongs on different occasions.[53]

52. Since the well-known study by Ruth Benedict was published, it has been unfortunately common among Westerners to think that honor/shame culture is found only among more primitive peoples.

53. Ruth Benedict, who in her book *The Chrysanthemum and the Sword* distinguished Japanese culture (which relies heavily on shame) from Western cultures (which rely heavily on guilt), describes "shame" as follows: "A failure to follow their explicit signposts of good behavior, a failure to balance obligations or to foresee contingencies is a shame (*haji*). Shame, they say, is the root of virtue. A man who is sensitive to it will carry out all the rules of good behavior. 'A man who knows shame' is sometimes translated 'virtuous man,' sometimes 'man of honor.' Shame has the same place of authority in Japanese ethics that 'a clear conscience,' 'being right with God,' and the avoidance of sin have in Western ethics" (p. 224). Though her analysis of "shame" has been criticized and deepened by others, and her observation is not complete, this paragraph is a good introduction to the concept and function of "shame" in our culture. She has been criticized in the following points:

1) When she says, "True shame cultures rely on external sanctions for good behavior, not, as true guilt cultures do, on an internalized conviction of sin" (p. 223), she clearly assumes the culture of guilt to be superior to the culture of shame.

2) When she says, "Shame is a reaction to other people's criticism. A man is shamed either by being openly ridiculed and rejected or by fantasizing to himself that he has been made ridiculous. In either case it is a potent sanction. But it requires an audience or at least a man's fantasy of an audience. Guilt does not. In a nation where honor

To keep up appearances becomes most important for one. For that purpose, one needs to discern what is the expected norm for living by watching what others do. This is the knack for being comfortable with others. To be nonindividualistic and inconspicuous are the required characteristics to be accepted by groups. It is shameful for anyone to stand out among one's contemporaries. Each member must be sensitive to well-adopted social norms. There is a saying to express this: "Don't do anything to get yourself talked about." To avoid disgrace brings honor. In other words, honor is expressed only in negative ways.

The negative expression "avoiding disgraceful conduct" was engendered by Confucian teachings: "Pay due reverence to anyone above" or "Precedence should always be given to anyone older than one." Though the expression takes negative forms, honor has always been attributed to men, if we pay attention to the social map of gender grid. In general, women have been trained to sacrifice themselves for men, not to lose face and to keep up appearances. In this sense, it may be plausible to say that women have been shouldered with the shame of the society as the women of first-century Palestine were.

Disgrace differs subtly depending on the group in which one is located at the moment, but on the largest scale it is regulated by the patriarchal mindset that was engendered by the emperor system spiritually supported by Shintoism and morally influenced by Confucianism. It had been most shameful to disgrace the name of the emperor. Needless to say, one is always expected to be careful not to disgrace the ones above and over one. And I wonder if patriarchy in Palestine might have been strengthened by their worshiping the one true God, Yahweh.

Patriarchy was institutionalized by the "emperor system" that was the politico-legal institution recognized by the Meiji constitution and supported spiritually by State Shintoism since 1890. The authoritative power of the emperor had its vicarious agents, who belonged to the nobility and ruled the country politically, socially and culturally. Since every policy was decided under the authoritative name of the emperor, no one was allowed to speak against it.

Japan was forced to abolish the "emperor system" in 1945 as a result of the defeat in the Second World War. However, patriarchy remained as a norm for living, influencing and forming the frame of reference for thinking, morals, and beliefs: in other words it shapes people's mentality.

A symbol of how the emperor system is still in effect in our society is

means living up to one's own picture of oneself, a man may suffer from guilt though no man knows of his misdeed and a man's feeling of guilt may actually be relieved by confessing his sin" (p. 223), she assumes that there is no relation between guilt and shame, which is not supported by other cultural anthropologists and psychiatrists.

3) Her description of "shame" lacks some other important phases of shame.

On the above, refer to Chuji Inoue, *'Sekentei' no Kozo* (Tokyo: NHK Books, 1977), 120ff., and Takeo Doi, *'Amae' no Kozo* (Tokyo: Kobundo, 1971), 48f.

the series of enthronement ceremonies of the new emperor held in November 1990. The new emperor went through a Shinto rite in which he was supposed to assume divine character and which stirred much discussion and objection among the people.

As a related issue, we may also refer to that of the era name (gengo). In 1979, a new law was promulgated requiring all institutions that serve the public to indicate dates not by means of the Christian era, but by means of the era name and year associated with a given name of the present emperor. The year 1993, for example, the fourth year of the reign of the new emperor, is known as "Heisei 5." Needless to say, most Christian institutions and groups are against the law and do not use the era name.

It has played a central role in creating the concept of ethnicity at the cost of the concept of individuality, and it has forged the mentality of submission to superiors. The people often feel more comfortable doing things as directed rather than doing them on their own responsibility.

The emperor had been the norm by which the individual chose her or his deeds and words. In order to avoid disgracing the emperor, a person needed to be sensitive to what the vicarious authority intended. The best way not to be against the authority was to be sensitive to the well-accepted social standards and behave within their boundaries. Even now, to maintain decency means not to be individualistic but to be well adapted to circumstances. And that brings honor and self-respect to the individual. Because of the tradition that one will be alienated and ostracized and considered dysfunctional if one is recognized as having brought shame on one's group, even now each member of a group tends to become overly sensitive to whatever is generally expected in each group. The mentality of group-oriented society is at work.

Patriarchy under the "emperor system" with the spiritual support of State Shintoism could not but be hierarchical. The emperor was the purest and the most high, and the people were divided into classes—four classes of samurais, farmers, craftsmen, and merchants for three hundred years until 1868 (in the Edo Era), and four classes of nobility down to the common from 1868 to 1945, as well as the outcast class. The impure, despised outcast class was artificially made so that the upper- and middle-class people might keep their self-respect and integrity as groups. That was all to keep honoring the power on high.

At the end of the Second World War, by the policy of the Allied Powers, the class system was also totally abolished. With the miraculous growth of the economy most Japanese have come to think of themselves as belonging to the middle class. The middle-class consciousness has also revived the traditional class consciousness, which reminds people of the upper- as well as lower-class strata. Descendents of "good" families with long genuine family lineages, of the once-nobility, or of entrepreneurs get special attention. On the other hand, low-paid workers or migrant workers are considered lower-class people and are exposed to the despising gaze of the people.

Patriarchy penetrated into family life as a small-scale model of the emperor system. The emperor was to be honored as the absolute authority of the one big family of Japan. In every household, the father was to be the authority and the rest of the members, including his wife were subjected to the head of the household. The system was strengthened by the Confucian teaching on family, according to which all the people should have felt moral indebtedness to the favor shown by the emperor; this was to be concretely expressed in daily life by the devotion of family members to their paterfamilias. Thus all the people were to pay full loyalty and filial piety to the emperor and the paterfamilias.

Thus the hierarchical structure as One Big Family State was well ordered in different kinds of groups concentrically piled up: from the family as the smallest unit to the nation as the largest. Collective honor was kept in each group: in Japan as a country, in the social classes, and in each family. Heads of groups were the norms and authorities for the rest of the group. Patriarchy had to become discriminatory and demand submission and obedience of the socially weaker groups. Patriarchy in Japan has become notorious for its racial exclusivism promoted for the purpose of maintaining ethnic purity. The mindset that prefers to be controlled rather than to raise questions and be creative is still alive in various aspects of social life.

To support the system of nationwide patriarchy, the family system was fully utilized. And as a matter of course sexual status was clearly defined. Fathers became absolute at home symbolizing the emperor domestically. Thus wives and children were made subordinate to fathers. The system lasted for eighty years, and the system itself was abolished forty-five years ago. But we have never been successful in shaking off the mentality. Women suffer from and struggle with its vestigial effects.

It engendered the gender-role system and legitimated the division of labor between woman and man. The family system negated the individual autonomy and personhood of both woman and man but demanded that each member learn how to give selfless devotion to one's superiors. There was no idea of affirming individual human dignity. Thus the concept of the family was distorted so much that a partnership between husband and wife could never function on an equal level.

While husbands functioned as patersfamilias, the ideal that women were asked to pursue was to become "good wives and wise mothers." Since the time education was first opened to women at the end of the nineteenth century, to raise "good wives and wise mothers" has long been the main purpose of women's schools. There were, of course, no coeducational schools till the end of the Second World War. The slogan is still alive in conservative women's schools.

Women's education based upon such an ideal was to prepare women for serving men who rendered their allegiance to their country and worked themselves to the bone. Needless to say, there was no way for a woman to get a college education. The only way women could contribute to their country was to stay at home, give birth to boys, maintain their household, and obey their paterfamilias. The idea confined their life to the space inside the home. As a result, they were spiritually isolated into closed circumstances. To be obedient, to keep silent, and to be invisible behind their husbands were considered women's most admired virtues. Most women endeavored to fit themselves to these ideals. What else could they be when they were distorted this way from their birth?

To our regret, the traditional male-centered orientation has powerfully affected our mentality. We, especially women, have been suffering from and struggling with our own subconscious enslavement to the traditional value system.

Under this kind of family system, marriage has been a matter not of two individuals but of two families. Marriage could never be contracted as a personal matter. Social classes and family lineages have been the two important elements to be considered when one decides one's partner. Quite often marriages were decided between parents without asking the consent of the individuals concerned. Because the authority of the paterfamilias was legitimated by law, men's tyrannical decisions became absolute. There were many brides who had never met their bridegrooms until their wedding day. Even now we often hear residual expressions: "Give a daughter to another family," "To dispose of a daughter," "Move a daughter from her family to another," "Take a bride," and "Receive a daughter-in-law from another family."

Despite the new constitution guaranteeing equal rights between wife and husband and abolishing the paterfamilias system — and the people welcomed it — the traditional manners and habitual customs have remained. The law cannot transform human mentality or consciousness so easily.

Here is a good example we have experienced. As recently as 1986, an Equal Employment Opportunity law took effect in our country. The law has not necessarily helped us women pursue equal rights with men. Even though it should reflect the government's will to eliminate all sorts of discrimination against women practiced in employment, discrimination is found in each phase of recruitment and appointment, placement and promotion, wages, and type of work. We find the law putting more emphasis on what employers should try to do than on what they are obliged to accomplish.

So that the law may be fully utilized, men have to change their worldview that has driven them to devote themselves to increasing the profits of their companies. Their worldview is firmly supported by the long preserved idea of division of labor: men work outside, while women guard homes. Based on the men's full devotion at the sacrifice of everything else, including their family lives, Japan has achieved its high economic growth. There are many men who find their work the only thing worthwhile in their lives.

If a man feels he should be a workaholic, an employee who devotes everything he has to his work, he must accept stringent working conditions that demand that he pay no attention to his family life. In fact he needs his wife to sustain his harsh life. Therefore unless Japan as a country seeks a new policy on working conditions, the true Equal Employment Opportunity Law will not be activated. As a matter of course, when a woman gets married, it has been almost impossible for her to keep the job she had before. It is always wives who are pressed to change their life patterns.[54]

The traditional male-oriented idea that men are to control and lead history is alive as an undercurrent of the law that declares "equal" rights between woman and man. Patriarchy helps the Japanese view the world in terms of a sexual division of labor and produce the gender-separate, non-individualistic norms of honor and shame.

Imperial theology sanctified the whole country as a special space based on sacred origin and the ideology of the family state with the divine emperor as its patriarch. It was based upon absolute imperatives given by those in authority and the total devotion of the people. It engendered hierarchical strata in the society supported by group-oriented human relations. It also generated the myth of ethnic superiority, which resulted in Ultranationalism.

As Malina says, in American society it seems much easier for individuals to maximize their self-development, because they need to pay less attention to other people.[55] But where "the people are rather 'dyadic' personalities," they depend very much upon the opinions and evaluations of others, and such daily "checking out" by others heightens awareness of irregularities whenever they occur.[56] Where social relations or kinship is very important, social integrity and community become main concerns. And to maintain their integrity, each member must keep their dyadic relations with the group so that the dynamics of the group may not be lost or distorted.

In such a society, holiness is defined in a way that cannot help but exclude those who cannot meet its conditions. People are expected to be heteronomous.

> Holiness requires that individuals shall conform to the class to which they belong. All holiness requires that different classes of things shall not be confused. . . . Holiness means keeping distinct the categories of creation. It therefore involves correct definition, discrimination and order.[57]

54. I must also refer to the fact that there have been various women's movements to encourage women looking for autonomous lives and to support them through networking and study groups.

55. Malina, *The New Testament World*, 54-55.

56. John J. Pilch, "Healing in Mark: A Social Science Analysis," *Biblical Theology Bulletin* 14 (1985), 142-50.

57. Mary Douglas, *Purity and Danger: An Analysis of Concepts of Pollution and Taboo* (London: Routledge and Kegan Paul, 1966), 53.

To remain in one's group, one needs to be careful about not deviating from the standards and norms of that group. One needs to be very careful about behaving very individualistically or creatively. It is very important to learn how to gain influence upon one's group. Thus women are so used to adapting themselves to the circumstances, behaving in group patterns, and being directed what to do that they may not even be conscious of their dyadic personalities.

Thus we notice many parallels and similarities between the modern Japanese and ancient Mediterranean cultures. We who share the social scenarios that shaped the perspectives of the people of the early Christian age have an advantage experientially in understanding them.

A SECOND APPROACH TO MARK: CRITICAL RHETORICAL STUDIES

Literary and historical-critical analyses of a text clarify how it constructs what it includes or silences. The search for various *Sitz im Leben* of the elements that have participated in creating or transforming biblical texts at different stages helps us to retrace traditions to their life-worlds and their sociopolitical and cultural-religious contexts. We see the texts not as data and evidence but as perspectival discourse reflecting their worlds and symbolic universes as affected by the "androcentric" mindset. Therefore we can never be free from the rhetorical strategies of the texts in the historical context of the patriarchal society of their origin. All these together function to silence and marginalize women, even though there were surely women who were participating in history. To restore the silenced to history so that we may restore history to women, we need to establish our own vantage point from which to read the texts, in order to investigate them with our own methodology and thereby reconstruct and construct a different socio-historical reality.

Patriarchy is the heuristic key over against which we construct our hermeneutical standpoint. As I have already stated, our particular experiences of patriarchy in traditional and contemporary Japan can be very close to those experiences of the women in first-century Palestine. Two common characteristics are (1) the "group-oriented" society that prevents any outbreak of individualism and seeks the honor of men at the sacrifice of women and (2) the "dyadic" personality that achieves more stability through adapting itself to social norms. Commonality of experiences will help us greatly when we trace how women in first-century Palestine lived and how they became conscious of being marginalized, empowered as being individuals, and activated as equal disciples. This constitutes a part of my methodology.

Elisabeth Schüssler Fiorenza uses a comprehensive term, "rhetorical," to explain such study of texts as acts of persuasion. I will now describe some aspects of my methodology of feminist socio-historical "rhetorical" reconstruction of the early Christian origin.

Elisabeth Schüssler Fiorenza argues "that we must reconceptualize biblical studies in terms of critical rhetorical studies as developed in social, political and historical studies."[58] She calls for a rhetorical-ethical paradigm to replace the literary-hermeneutical paradigm that has been pursued for the last two decades, defining "rhetorical" as "not linguistic manipulation but a communicative praxis that links knowledge with action and passion."[59] The rhetorical-ethical paradigm "relies on the analytical and practical tradition of rhetoric in order to insist on the public-political responsibility of biblical scholarship."[60] In contrast to the strong emphasis on value-free objectivism and scientific methodism of previous biblical scholarship, this paradigm includes interests, values, and visions as inevitable elements: It requires a critical reflection on the rhetorical theological practices of biblical studies in their sociopolitical contexts.[61] Therefore, "a rhetorical hermeneutics does not assume that the text is a window to historical reality, nor does it operate with a correspondence theory of truth."[62] Rather, it has the task to stand against such a hermeneutics that internalizes oppression through a literalist reading of the Bible.[63]

The feminist critical theory challenges the dualistic opposition between historical reality and text and engages in theological "detective" work for an imaginative reconstruction of the reality of the participants in the history.[64]

Antoinette Clark Wire explains "rhetorical" in more detail,

Today, rhetorical analysis takes as its province all persuasive discourse, recognizing that its major contribution is not in generating or dissecting proper speeches but in illuminating how words function to persuade. Once we focus on function it is clear that all argument—some say all speech—is shaped for an effect and works to persuade.[65]

Rhetorical criticism focuses on the persuasive power to motivate the audience to praxis and literary strategies of a text which has a communicative function in a concrete, specific historical-political situation.[66]

58. E. Schüssler Fiorenza, "Text and Reality—Reality as Text," 23. "I have chosen rhetorical criticism for such an analysis because it is one of the oldest forms of literary criticism that explores the particular historical uses of languages in specific social political situations" ("Rhetorical Situation and Historical Reconstruction in 1 Corinthians," *New Testament Studies* 33 [1987], 386).

59. E. Schüssler Fiorenza, "The Ethics of Biblical Interpretation: Decentering Biblical Scholarship," *Journal of Biblical Literature* 107/1 (1988), 10.

60. Ibid., 4.

61. Ibid., 12.

62. Ibid., 15.

63. Ibid., 16.

64. Idem, *Bread Not Stone*, 112.

65. Antoinette Clark Wire, *The Corinthian Women Prophets: A Reconstruction Through Paul's Rhetoric* (Minneapolis: Fortress Press, 1990), 2.

66. E. Schüssler Fiorenza, "Rhetorical Situation and Historical Reconstruction in 1 Corinthians," 387.

According to Elisabeth Schüssler Fiorenza, rhetorical practices have three moments: (1) "a referential moment about something," (2) "a moment of a self-implication by a speaker or actor," and (3) "a persuasive moment of directedness to involve the other."[67] Wire explains the same points in her historical analysis of rhetoric.[68] Both assume texts to be "communicative interaction"[69] between the writer of any text and the readers. So the text itself is expressing the dynamics of relationships held among various persons concerned with their settings. Therefore we may say the real author of the text is both the writer and the audience involved. Thus we are led to realize that "as historical, cultural, political and religious discursive practices biblical texts and their contemporary interpretations involve authorial aims and strategies as well as audience perceptions and constructions."[70]

By applying the three moments in interpreting Mark's Gospel, we may be able to disentangle the four-layered, webbed complex of the actual relationships held between Jesus and women, between tellers and hearers of oral and literary traditions, between those who transmitted sources orally and in writing and Mark, and between Mark and his contemporary community. If we can distinguish the tension that Mark experienced between the "history" before him and his contemporary community—which must have also been his motivation for writing his Gospel—we would have a better chance of delineating the women in their relation to Jesus. In other words, traditions, the Gospel, and our interpretation all view the past from the perspective of contemporary participants facing the future.

Wire, dealing with the issue of "reconstructing as accurate a picture as possible of the women prophets in the church of the first-century Corinth," points out the "argumentative situation" in which Paul found himself:[71]

67. E. Schüssler Fiorenza, "Biblical Interpretation and Critical Commitment," *Studia Theologica* 43 (1989), 9. "Rhetorical criticism must distinguish between the historical argumentative situation, the implied or inscribed rhetorical situation as well as the rhetorical situation of contemporary interpretations which works with the canonical collection and reception of Paul's letters" ("Rhetorical Situation and Historical Reconstruction in 1 Corinthians," 388).

68. Wire, *The Corinthian Women Prophets*, 2: "I look to the modern revival of classical rhetoric for my primary analytical tools in this task, the movement called in Chaim Perelman and L. Olbrechts-Tyteca's comprehensive description 'The New Rhetoric.' The major distinctions made in the ancient discipline are retained. For example, the writer's self-presentation (ethos) is expected to dominate the introductory part of a speech, the rational argument (logos)—often including a narration of the case—is anticipated in the body of the discourse, and direct appeals to the audience (pathos) are looked for in conclusions."

69. E. Schüssler Fiorenza, "Text and Reality—Reality as Text: The Problem of a Feminist Historical and Social Reconstruction Based on Texts," *Studia Theologica* 43, 19.

70. E. Schüssler Fiorenza, "Biblical Interpretation and Critical Commitment," 10. See also "The Ethics of Biblical Interpretation," 4.

71. Wire, *The Corinthian Women Prophets*, 1.

Here rhetoricians are suggesting that an argumentative text does not give only one side of an argument—unless the speaker is completely incompetent—because to argue is to gauge your audience as accurately as you can at every point, to use their language, to work from where they are in order to move them toward where you want them to be. So what we have is not just one individual's viewpoint but a window into a volatile situation, volatile yet not amorphous because certain points of agreement are clear in premises taken and authorities cited; certain points of conflict vanish by one argument while others congeal into Gordian knots.[72]

In such a critical analysis, we will also be required to pay closer attention to the existence, viewpoint and reaction of the audience on whom the writer's rhetoric works its effect. We cannot ignore the fact that Mark, as he planned his Gospel, was always conscious of his audience, their circumstances, and their needs. It is possible that Mark was seeing or portraying the members of his faith community in his Gospel. Therefore we must assume that many things were presupposed or left out and many things directed or proscribed. We must become involved with the dynamics of relationships at work.

To get into the dynamics, we first need to discover the horizons of knowledge and the expectation of both Mark and his audience. These two horizons of knowledge and expectation are intertwined, and they are engendered through experiences of life in various environments. The horizons create diverse conceptual frameworks in which the writer produces her or his text and the recipients try to understand what the text means. So the recipients play an important part in the process of the writer's persuasive rhetoric.[73] We should be able to detect the dynamics of the same quality at each level of transmission of the traditions. By tracing those dynamics of communication and persuasion backward, we reach the earliest stage.

We need to engage in the critical evaluation and rhetorical interpretation of texts from the feminist perspective of liberation theology, because this audience-oriented approach reveals how heavily texts are concerned with male interests. "The convention of addressing the male section of a community encourages promotion of the male perspective on the part of those who prefer to ignore the female element of the audience."[74]

Schüssler Fiorenza writes

A rhetorical paradigm-shift situates biblical scholarship in such a way that its public character and political responsibility become an integral

72. Ibid., 3.
73. Francis Schüssler Fiorenza, "The Crisis of Scriptural Authority," *Interpretation* 44/4 (1990), 48-51 (Japanese edition).
74. Lilian Portefaix, "Women and Mission in the New Testament: Some Remarks on the Perspective of Audience. A Research Report," *Studia Theologica* 43 (1989), 143.

part of its literary readings and historical reconstructions of the biblical world. In distinction to formalist literary criticism, a critical theory of rhetoric insists that context is as important as text. What we
see, depends on where we stand.[75]

The rhetorical paradigm-shift seems to urge our commitment to and
involvement with contemporary issues so that we may be more able to
discern the situations that marginalize women. The urge comes from the
fact that the Gospel was written in its particular political, social, cultural
and religious context with its particular issues in mind. It also arises from
our need to distance ourselves from the text, its writer, and its community,
to relativize them and us in reading the texts, and to encounter the texts
dialogically and existentially. We are expected to be self-critical in this way
as well as to know the texts as fully contextual.[76] Therefore,

One's social location or rhetorical context is decisive of how one sees
the world, constructs reality, or interprets biblical texts. Therefore,
competing interpretations of texts are not simply either right or wrong.
They constitute different ways of reading and constructing historical
meaning. Not detached value-neutrality but an explicit interrogation
of one's commitments, theoretical perspective, ethical criteria, inter-
pretative strategies, and socio-political location are appropriate in
such a rhetorical paradigm of biblical studies.[77]

It is not possible to fix the text's meaning as one objective, detached
truth.[78] It is never possible to fix its meaning by silencing or excluding
"others."
So Elisabeth Schüssler Fiorenza calls for a *double ethics*; an ethics of
historical reading and an ethics of accountability.[79]

An ethics of historical reading changes the task of interpretation from
establishing historical facts and finding out "what the text meant" to
the question of what kind of readings can do justice to the text and
can elaborate the rhetorical strategies of the text in its historical contexts. It investigates how the text constructs what it includes or
"silences." Such a focus on the ideological scripts of a biblical text
and its interpretations does not replace historical text-oriented readings but presupposes them. As literary and historical critical exegesis
attends to the text in its historical contexts, so rhetorical criticism

75. Elisabeth Schüssler Fiorenza, "Biblical Interpretation and Critical Commitment,"
10. See also "The Ethics of Biblical Interpretation," 5.
76. E. Schüssler Fiorenza, *Bread Not Stone*, 130.
77. E. Schüssler Fiorenza, "Biblical Interpretation and Critical Commitment," 10.
78. E. Schüssler Fiorenza, "The Ethics of Biblical Interpretation," 11.
79. Ibid., 14.

seeks to make conscious how the text 'works' in its complex historical as well as contemporary cultural, social, religious or theological contexts.[80]

Historical reading thus allows us to evaluate texts critically and to put into their proper perspective the one-sided or biased yet, at their time, authoritative-sounding claims. To encounter God and activate our faith in our contemporary situation, "biblical texts must be understood as embedded in the religious-cultural-political life-world of their authors and communities,"[81] because God works through people in specific places and times.

The reality of women of the age of Jesus is now claimed to be refracted through triple-focused lenses; one lens is that of the original-source carriers, another is the author's and the last is that of contemporary male scholars. All have their own life-worlds. And the reality of women also had their own life-world. That means that when we examine the biblical texts, we need to go through three different life-worlds critically and carefully until we meet women in their contextual circumstances. Therefore we are not aiming at finding anything absolute or authoritative that may directly control us. Rather, we are committing ourselves to distinguishing historical layers of experiences, interacting with Jesus in each occasion through triple-focused lenses and aided by historical-critical and feminist-theological methods of analysis. Each layer of experiences is supported by interaction between deliverers and receivers. I would like to remove each layer carefully, one by one and finally reach the stage where we may see how Jesus interacted with women and vice versa. For this perspective, it is surely true to say that "a new critical hermeneutics does not center on the text but on the people whose story with God is remembered in the texts of the Bible."[82]

So we must cultivate a theoretical self-reflexivity that can explore the experiences and interests that generate and determine biblical interpretation and its rhetorical-historical situation today.[83]

Our vantage point must be keenly sharpened. The texts we have are not just processions of letters but records of a three-dimensional life-world, "the religious-cultural-political life-world of their authors and communities."[84] The fact also demands that our scope be three-dimensional. Just as historical-critical analysis presupposes the social, political, cultural, and religious engagements of the author and the people or the community concerned, so are we also called to engagement in our social, political, or religious issues. Unless we are actually aware of the contradiction between

---

80. E. Schüssler Fiorenza, "Biblical Interpretation and Critical Commitment," 11.
81. Ibid., 16.
82. E. Schüssler Fiorenza, *Bread Not Stone*, 147.
83. E. Schüssler Fiorenza, "Biblical Interpretation and Critical Commitment," 16.
84. Ibid.

our experiences and our self-understanding, we will not be able to reach the women who were participants in history and yet outsiders to their society. Unless we feel the common power-structure of both their and our societies that marginalize and oppress women, we will not be able to undermine the male rhetorical strategies. The rhetorical-critical analysis comes out of our commitment to any form of the enterprise that emancipates the oppressed. Otherwise we will get into an impasse, because the biblical texts cannot be free from "presuppositions, commitments, beliefs, or cultural and institutional structures."[85] The dynamic, organic relation of questioning and responding must be reciprocally realized between the past and the present. And that relation engenders our ethics of accountability, as Elisabeth Schüssler Fiorenza says.

I look for the liberation of the silenced and the marginalized through this process of focusing on the interaction between women and Jesus. If liberation is an important part of salvation, this alternative vision of the new birth and creation cannot but urge us to work for the transformation and restructuring of our socially, politically, and ideologically biased circumstances in the church as well as in society. Such an existential response that aims to eliminate dominance-submission patterns from our contemporary situation and that hopes for the full realization of the partnership of equals in our churches and society will be the foundation of our eschatology. "We cannot split a spiritual, antisocial redemption from the human self as a social being in socio-political and ecological systems."[86]

85. Elisabeth Schüssler Fiorenza, *In Memory of Her: A Feminist Theological Reconstruction of Christian Origins*, xxii.

86. Rosemary Radford Ruether, *Sexism and God-Talk: Toward a Feminist Theology* (Boston: Beacon, 1984), 215-16.

2

THE HEMORRHAGING WOMAN

(5:25-34)

PATRIARCHAL DISCRIMINATION AGAINST WOMEN
REINFORCED BY RELIGION: THE POLLUTED

As I pointed out in the previous chapter, the patriarchy that we Japanese women have experienced in our history has much in common with that experienced by women in first-century Palestine. Both societies may be characterized as having a culture of honor/shame, with its strong sense of group-oriented consciousness, of dyadic personality, and of gender-role difference. Women have been subordinated to bear all the shame of society so that men can seek honor.

Just as patriarchy in first-century Palestine was reinforced by faith in Yahweh God, so has that in Japan also been reinforced by the worship of the emperor as divine. Moreover, the religious teachings of Shintoism, Confucianism, Buddhism, and Christianity, of which all except the last have histories of more than 1,500 years, have helped to perpetuate patriarchy. They are unanimous in segregating women, though expressions may differ. They have evolved the concept of the polluted, which was engendered out of the fear of death and the awe of life. Fear and awe are caused by childbirth, menstruation, and death.

Buddhism

In Buddhism, the theory of "five obstacles" which is applied only to women excludes them from attaining nirvana or salvation. The five obstacles are impurity, dishonesty, jealousy, anger, and caprice. In Gokuraku (paradise) only the purely male can be found. They are completely separated from the defiling influence of the female. The only way for women to attain Gokuraku is to seclude themselves from all earthly bondages, practice asceticism, and renounce their womanhood until they metamorphose into men.

Then they are called "metaphorically male." Womanhood is not only worthless to begin with, but also substantially negated and despised as impure.[1]

Women find themselves placed in subservient worthlessness and may only expect their vicarious salvation through giving birth to boys who would devote themselves to the teachings of Buddhism. Thus, women have been hopelessly segregated by Buddhism in Japan.

Confucianism

In Confucianism, there is a teaching of "three obediences," again for women. Women are defined as being men's property all through their lives. Women are to obey their fathers while they are unmarried, to obey their husbands when married, and to be under the protection of their sons in old age.[2] Even today, the Family Registration Law requires every citizen to register as a member of a certain family.

Shintoism

In Shintoism, a woman is not considered polluted as a person, but menstruation and childbirth have been considered unclean. For certain periods, she must be secluded so that she may not defile others, and only after she is purified may she resume her ordinary life.[3]

In Japan, women's bleeding has long been considered polluting. Women used to isolate themselves in special lodges during their periods, during pregnancy, and after giving birth. It is not difficult to find places where this custom was practiced until recently, especially in rural areas. Women stayed in lodges apart from their families so that they might not contaminate food by cooking. They remained there longer—three weeks or more—after giving birth. Even when they returned to their homes, they stayed in detached rooms for a while until their pollution might be cleansed. Even those women who did not practice such cultic customs were taught, or thought themselves, that their bleeding was abhorred by society as unclean.[4]

Thus in our society, just as in first-century Palestine, religious purity codes have contributed to the establishment of cultural identity and to the support of the power structure and various kinds of segregation. It should be noted that the authority needs to expel the unclean in order to keep its

1. Aiko Okoshi, Junko Minamoto and Akiko Yamashita, *Seisabetu suru Bukkyo* (Sexism in Buddhism) (Kyoto: Hozokan, 1990), 29. Since 1986, Buddhist and Christian feminists have met together regularly in order to investigate the elements of sexism neglected by these mainstream religions.

2. *Passionate Journey: The Spiritual Autobiography of Satomi Myodo,* transl. and ed. Sallie B. King (Boston and London: Shambhala, 1987), 171.

3. Okoshi et al., *Sexism in Buddhism,* 98, 134.

4. Emiko Namihira, *Kurasi no naka no Bunka Jinruigaku* (Cultural Anthropology of Our Daily Life) (Tokyo: Hukutake Shoten, 1986), 134-6. Yukio Monma, " 'Kegare' to Buraku Sabetu," in *Shukyo to Buraku Mondai* (Osaka: Kaiho Shuppansha, 1990), 238.

hierarchical order unthreatened. In this sense, we may say that women have been "labeled" polluted.[5] What is different from first-century Palestine is that Japan has been a multireligious country, but the several religions have only helped each other in discriminating against women as unclean based on various premises, to be explained in a later chapter.

Institutionally or legally, these teachings about discrimination against women have not been enforced for the last fifty years. Yet the prejudice against women has not disappeared and has been reflected in our daily life in the form of long-established social conventions.

For example, in 1989, the woman representative of the government was refused the right to step up on the Sumo ring for the prize-giving ceremony, because she was a woman. Sumo has long been said to be the national sport practiced only by men, and the Sumo ring has been considered to be a holy place from which women have been excluded. Even nowadays, Shinto priests are invited to exorcise the ring of evil spirits prior to the beginning of every seasonal tournament.

Women have also been dismissed from tunnel construction teams because they are defiled and might invite disasters. When a tunnel was built between Honshu and Hokkaido in 1988, a congresswoman who tried to visit the construction site to inspect the working conditions was not permitted to go inside. The reason given by the public office was that laborers at the site did not want a woman to come into the tunnel, because they were afraid she might make the mountain goddesses furious. It is believed that mountain goddesses get jealous if a woman comes into the tunnel and gets men laborers into danger. In both cases, the implication is that women are unclean.

It has also been said that women invoke the wrath of the gods if they pass under *torii* (divine gates in front of Shinto shrines) during their periods, because it is believed that gods cannot tolerate women who come to the precincts and worship in their polluted condition. During the festival seasons, there are still shrines and temples that put up a huge sign to announce that no unclean person is permitted to participate. This includes those who are in mourning and women who have recently given birth, have their periods, or are pregnant. After the Second World War, most shrines removed the conspicuous signs saying "No Admittance to Women."[6]

Nowadays most people are not even conscious that these conventionally accepted customs originate in religious purity codes, but they live their actual lives following those codes. This is one of the main reasons that Buddhism, Shintoism, and Confucianism have established themselves firmly in the minds of the common people. Even now, cleanliness has much impact upon peoples' minds. Always taking off shoes at entrances of houses, clean-

5. Mary Douglas, *Purity and Danger* (London: Routledge and Kegan Paul, 1966), 7-28.

6. *Passionate Journey*, 208. Namihira, *Kurasi no naka no Bunta Jiuruigaku*, 130-32.

ing dishes very carefully, not using individual utensils for serving food, and not sitting on the place where we walk with shoes are noticeable differences from the conduct we experience while staying in America. According to studies done by anthropologists, we Japanese form behavior patterns and hygiene customs by our sensitivity to the concept of pure/impure.[7]

To keep ourselves clean implies preventing ourselves from being defiled. Because we are accustomed to such ways of life, we do not feel them to be troublesome. But because we have lived in a purity-oriented culture[8] and practice these subconsciously suppressed restrictions, we can feel vividly how brave the hemorrhaging woman was and how revolutionary and liberated Jesus was, all the more so in first-century Palestine where the purity codes were openly enforced and the restrictions were considered to be norms of personal and social integrity.

Thus we Japanese women have a long history in which we have been alienated as unclean and culturally despised, and have endured nonperson status for centuries. This experience is very close to that of the hemorrhaging woman. I identify myself with her in this sense.

Only in the last fifty years in Japan have women been affirmed as legally equal with men, and of course this is not yet realized in fact. The Equal Employment Opportunity Law that took effect in 1986 in our country has not necessarily helped us women pursue equal rights with men. The Law is full of recommendations without obligation. If even the social legitimation is poorly executed as stated above, it is not difficult to imagine how conservative the mentality of both men and women could be. Even though they say that special monthly holidays for women, maternity and nursing leave have been promoted in big companies in big cities, women rarely take advantage of them.

MY PERSPECTIVE

Our struggle to liberate women and men from this patriarchal "mentality" and my striving, from a theological perspective, to be liberated from patriarchal "labelings" gives me a new perspective for rereading biblical texts and the story of the hemorrhaging woman.

So I view the story not from the traditional viewpoint of Jesus, the miracle worker, but from the relational viewpoint of the interaction between the woman and Jesus. In addition, this perspective makes clear the social context of the oppression that the woman suffers, which in turn exposes another side of the significance of the miracle.

The social stigma of her pollution is not due to her volition, nor is it caused by her birth, but by the "labeling," as I have already pointed out.

7. Monma, " 'Kegare' to Buraku Sabetu," 250-53.
8. Ibid., 156-62.

"Labeling" is done by those in authority. The powers-that-be need that kind of social structure for keeping their status quo as well as their integrity. The woman's hemorrhage threatens the community's integrity and its holiness, just as women's bleeding and childbirth have threatened the holiness and integrity of the male-dominant structure of our society. What she earnestly seeks is the recovery of her "wholeness and holiness" so that she may be accepted as a person within the circle of the society.[9] In the patriarchal society where hierarchical class strata are strictly maintained, the boundary between the pure and the impure becomes very important. To make it hard to cross barriers, socially banned persons are given another label of being contagious and are abhorred. It is necessary for the authority to keep her invisible. In order for her to come out of the closed world, the boundary between her and the rest of the society must be broken down. So the miracle that cures her disease symbolizes her challenge to the society to be transformed. Later I will introduce another incident in our country that is parallel to hers and occurs in what is said to be the least-known of the minority groups in the world.

I view the woman in three categories: (1) as an outcast, (2) as a volitional agent, and (3) as a challenger to the establishment.

THE HEMORRHAGING WOMAN AS OUTCAST

Her Twelve Years

The story of the hemorrhaging woman begins by describing her with a surprisingly large number of participles (seven) until the woman's action is finally expressed by a verb — that is, "she touched his cloak." This expression is used because her active motion of touching Jesus' cloak is the peak of her life story and the beginning of the miracle. So far she has been miserable in many senses, "suffering from hemorrhage for twelve years, enduring much under many physicians, spending all that she had, and being no better but rather growing worse."

It is interesting to notice that Matthew's Gospel has no reference to her case history and makes the whole story briefer, while Luke abbreviates the reference and moderates the disparaging allusion to the physicians. Both Matthew (9:20-22) and Luke (8:43-48) lessen the particular impact of the Markan story here. The Markan story may sound rough and crude, but it is true to life. Mark has the story speak aloud what the parties concerned deal with in silence.

In comparison to the detailed description of her sickness, we never hear the woman's name. She is an anonymous, poverty-stricken woman with a

9. Elisabeth Schüssler Fiorenza, *In Memory of Her: A Feminist Theological Reconstruction of Christian Origins* (New York: Crossroad, 1985), 121.

desperate sickness. The situation identifies her with no class or authority. In another healing story of the daughter of Jairus (5:21-24 and 35-43), into which the story of the hemorrhaging woman is interpolated, Jairus, one of the rare named persons in Mark's Gospel, is contrasted with her in terms of economic status and honor. As the head of both his family and his social group, "one of the leaders of the synagogue," he occupies a position of power and is entitled to speak for his daughter.[10]

The ordeal of the hemorrhaging woman is described in three ways. First, she is sick with hemorrhage, the most dismal kind of disease that makes women gloomy as well as unhealthy. Second, she has suffered from her disease for so long. Twelve years of bleeding coincides with the age of the daughter of Jairus. At twelve it is said that girls reach the official age of puberty and marriageability. While the girl is getting ready for becoming a female, the woman suffers from her femaleness.[11] The woman's twelve years describe the long period of gloomy affliction she has had to bear physically, emotionally, and mentally. Moreover, she is also socially oppressed because she has to "suffer many things" under the inefficacious treatments of the physicians. The woman must have felt ashamed to visit physicians (probably all male) one after another and expose her body with such a disease. Marla J. Selvidge points out that the expression "suffer many things" is only used of Jesus and the woman (8:31; 9:12).[12] In addition to this expression, in Mark blood is only used of Jesus' new covenant (14:24) and of this woman (5: 25; 29). Body (5:29; 14:8, 22; 15:43) and plague (5:29; 10:34) are also words only used of Jesus and this woman.[13] Selvidge concludes plausibly that "Mark recognizes the suffering of this woman in society as similar to that which Jesus experienced before his death."[14] It is interesting to see that both Matthew and Luke omit these, for Mark, seemingly key terms, except "blood." This may confirm that Mark's intention was so clear that Matthew and Luke omitted them. Mark dared to identify the woman's suffering with that of Jesus. The implication becomes clear later in this chapter.

She had spent all that she had for her physical treatment. We can imagine how seriously ill she was as well as how badly she wanted to get well. She could be a target of money-seeking physicians just as widows' houses were devoured by the religious authorities (12:38-39). Thus she was financially victimized, since the story suggests that she had some amount of

10. Ched Myers, *Binding the Strong Man,* 200. Fernando Belo, *A Materialist Reading of the Gospel of Mark* (New York: Orbis Books, 1981), 22. Eduard Schweizer, *Das Evangelium Nach Markus,* Japanese edition (Tokyo: NTD, 1976), 156.

11. Rita Nakashima Brock, *Journey by Heart: A Christology of Erotic Power* (New York: Crossroad, 1988), 83. Vincent Taylor, *The Gospel According to St. Mark* (London: Macmillan, 1953), 291.

12. Marla J. Selvidge, *Woman, Cult, & Miracle Recital: A Redactional Critical Investigation of Mark 5:24-34* (Lewisburg, Penn.: Bucknell Univ. Press, 1990), 105.

13. Ibid., 105.

14. Ibid., 105.

property, even though no husband or family is mentioned.

Although she was victimized physically and financially and wounded in self-esteem, she persisted in seeking her health. And her suffering life reached its peak in her volitional act of touching Jesus' cloak. Before we proceed, we should be aware that Mark intended to communicate something important to his readers by describing her ordeal in minute detail. Her solid constitution, shown in her tenacity in the face of constant disappointment and deteriorating health, must be paid attention to in two ways.

First, her persistence, paralleled by that of the Syrophoenician woman,[15] is one of her characteristics that Mark wants to communicate. Second, her unusually strong desire for recovery points up for us the religious and therefore inevitably social oppression she has to face because of the purity laws. It appears that the second is more serious for her.

The Purity Laws

The purity laws are found in Leviticus, which was written down in the post-exilic period. (Chapters 12, 15, and 20 deal with these laws, among other health and dietary laws.) The laws render women impure and restrict women's behavior at home as well as in the social and religious spheres of life.[16] There are two main causes of uncleanness in women, one related to menstruation and the other to childbirth. Women are unclean not only during their menstrual periods, but they also must be secluded for a week thereafter. If her cycle is irregular, or a lengthy gynecological problem exists, the woman remains "infectious" until the problem is cured. Anyone that she touches, or that touches her, or touches anything she has touched "will be unclean until evening." If a man sleeps with her, he will be unclean for seven days also and his contagious condition can be spread to others (15:19-28). Not only does she feel degraded herself, but she must feel responsible for not contaminating others. However, a man who has a seminal discharge is considered unclean only until evening. If a menstruating woman touches anyone, or anyone touches her, that person is banished until evening (15:19, 21).

Women are considered unclean after childbirth as well. They are unclean for seven days after giving birth to a boy and fourteen days after giving birth to a girl (12:2, 5). They are subjected to a further "purification period" of thirty-three days for the birth of a boy and sixty-six days for the birth of a girl, during which they are not allowed to enter the worship area (12:4). Thus the birth of a daughter is such bad news, because the baby is unwelcome and her mother is subjected to eighty days of restrictions.

15. Ibid., 107-8. See also the next chapter.
16. Marla J. Selvidge, "Mark 5:25-34 and Leviticus 15:19-20: A Reaction to Restrictive Purity Regulations," *Journal of Biblical Literature* 103:4 (1984), 619.

The ultimate humiliation is the sin offering required both after menstruation and after childbirth (12:6-8; 15:29-30). "The priest shall make
for her before the Lord the expiation required by her unclean discharge"
(15:30).

In all these cases, the woman becomes untouchable during the period
of impurity; that is to say, she is separated from the pure in the spaces of
the house and of everyday life.[17] Death is the expected penalty if these laws
are not observed (15:31). Such actions are actually thought to defile God's
"tabernacle which is set among them" (15:31). The temple is the cultic and
social center for the Israelites. Meticulous purity laws serve to organize
every area of life, even her sexuality. If she attempts to keep the command
given to Noah to reproduce (Gen. 9:1), she would be secluded at least
eighty days out of every year if she was pregnant, and up to ninety-one days
if she was not pregnant.[18]

It is difficult to imagine the effect of this stigma of sin and uncleanness
on the women of Jesus' days and the early Christian age. Of course we
must assume that the Levitical writers have portrayed an androcentric view
of the Israelites' life, and so we may expect that daily life was less restrictive
than what the law says.

We may summarize the restrictions imposed on women but not on men
as follows:

1) Biologically healthy but different functions are treated differently.

2) Uncleanness is treated more harshly in the case of women.

3) A woman contaminates and defiles a man, but not vice versa.

4) A woman herself is declared to be impure, while a man is never called
unclean except if his discharge is unclean.

5) The sphere of activity is more limited for a woman than for a man.

In Leviticus the lower estimation of women seems general (cf. 27:2-7).
Selvidge reports that Jewish writings all through the history of Israel deal
with purity laws very severely. According to Josephus, the ancient purity
laws were strictly practiced even during the first century C.E. All of the
Pseudo-Philonic literature, the Mishna and Talmuds, and the Dead Sea
Scrolls are in accordance with Josephus in supporting menstrual purity
laws.[19]

It is not easy to define how much these restrictions were actually at work
and how this stigma of impurity influenced the women of Jesus' time and
the early Christian age. Even though "the formal canons of codified patriarchal law are generally more restrictive than the actual interaction and
relationship of women and men and the social reality which they govern,"[20]
it is also true that laws, orally spread by people and distorted in transmission, generally exert a superstitious binding power among ordinary people.

17. Belo, *A Materialist Reading of the Gospel of Mark,* 41f.
18. Selvidge, *Woman, Cult, and Miracle Recital,* 55.
19. Selvidge, "Mark 5:25-34 and Leviticus 15:19-20," 621-22.
20. Elisabeth Schüssler Fiorenza, *In Memory of Her,* 108-9.

At this stage, laws tend to get more serious and strict. If we accept that women were considered untouchable during the period of impurity and were separated from the pure in the house, from society, and from the cult,[21] we must wonder how a woman's normal biological rhythm becomes something abnormal and abhorred. It is very interesting to read that a woman's menstrual cycle was considered a time of cleansing (*katharos*) to the Greeks, while the Jews added a negative prefix and called it unclean (*akathartos, akatharsia*).[22]

Selvidge draws our attention to the similarities in vocabulary between Leviticus and the story of the hemorrhaging woman. After closely comparing the key words used by both she concludes that the story clearly preserves a tradition that suggests an attitude of dissention toward the purity laws in Leviticus.[23]

Taking all these circumstances into account, we now know that the woman is discriminated against, degraded, and dehumanized. She is taboo to all, because of her physical otherness. She is labeled as unclean and consequently secluded from the society she belongs to, from the temple, and herself. Bleeding symbolizes death for women because it signifies total isolation from all the common routines of life, breaks down her dignity as human, and labels her religiously impure. From our investigation thus far we cannot agree that "menstrual blood is a positive symbol of woman in the domestic domain, but taboo in the public domain."[24] The story is apparently concerned with purity laws and their negative effects by depicting in detail how much she has to suffer. The woman's problem is not just the physical ailment—it is more complicated because of both the religious and the social implications of her physical ailment. It is here that we must see the decisive reason for Mark's identification of her suffering with that of Jesus.

The Sickness She Suffered

John J. Pilch, referring to a social science grid, warns against posing biomedical questions about this story from the Western understanding of human health problems.[25] Introducing the anthropological terms "etic and emic" used by Bruce Malina, he explains:

Etic describes "an outsider perspective" on reality, while emic describes "an insider perspective." . . . In other words, the New Testa-

---

21. Selvidge, *Woman, Cult, and Miracle Recital,* 83. Belo, *A Materialist Reading of the Gospel of Mark,* 41-42.

22. Selvidge, *Woman, Cult and Miracle Recital,* 55.

23. Ibid., 47-51.

24. Emiko Ohnuki-Tierney, *Illness and Healing among the Sakhlin Ainu: A Symbolic Interpretation* (Cambridge: University Press, 1981), 129-30.

25. John J. Pilch, "Healing in Mark: A Social Science Analysis," *Biblical Theology Bulletin* 14 (1985), 142.

ment documents are emic documents. Outside interpreters create etic models to understand that reality.[26]

If we use a biomedical perspective (which is distinctively Western), it concentrates on seeing abnormalities in the structure and/or function of the organ system. This is called "disease," designating a pathological state independent of whether or not it is culturally recognized. Disease affects individuals, and only individuals are treated. On the other hand, within the culture "illness" may be used to reflect a sociocultural perspective that is concerned with personal perception and experience of certain socially disvalued states including, but not limited to, disease. Illness inevitably affects others: the family, the community, and the religious circle.[27] And "sickness" can be taken not just as a blanket term for disease or illness as sometimes interpreted, but as "a process for socializing disease and illness."[28] Following his theory, the condition of the "disease" described as "a flow of blood" from a biomedical perspective is taken to threaten the community's integrity and holiness, and a sociocultural perspective indicates that the person with the "illness" must be secluded from her or his social, cultural, and religious networks.[29] Thus the life problems created by sickness demand the healing of illness for the total recovery of the person as a whole. She needs to regain her life's true purpose and meaning in her community. The curing of disease is absolutely necessary but not sufficient. The words "illness" and "disease" seem to be used interchangeably in the biblical texts, but it is important to understand the emic reality behind the use of the terms. We can probably say that Jesus and all the people around him dealt with sickness as illness and not as disease. Illness concerns the sociocultural dimension of a sickness experience. Therefore symptoms that are very essential to disease are almost disregarded in Jesus' healing. That does not mean that he is not interested in healing disease. He tries to cure the disease and provide a social solution to the life problems resulting from the illness.

Mark 5:26 tells us that the woman was visiting physicians to find a cure for her disease, but we must know that the curing of disease is not the goal she was seeking. What she was earnestly seeking was the recovery of her "wholeness and holiness,"[30] which of course involves the cure of the disease, and acceptance by her community as their legitimate member. Mark's story indeed underscores the failure of physicians who belong to the high class

26. Ibid., 142-43.

27. Ibid., 142.

28. Allan Young, "The Anthropologies of Illness and Sickness," *Annual Review of Anthropology* 11 (1982), 257-85.

29. John J. Pilch, "Biblical Leprosy and Body Symbolism," *Biblical Theology Bulletin* 11 (1981), 108-113.

30. E. Schüssler Fiorenza, *In Memory of Her,* 124.

of the social ladder. Some see here Mark's class consciousness.[31] In contrast, Luke says only that "no one" was able to heal her.

In a society in which kinship and social relations speak powerfully and group-oriented thinking is the principle of integrity, the sick become of great concern to the entire community. Concern for community integrity declares certain uncontagious diseases contagious and dictates that the sick people be quarantined. Thus group identity and its security had priority over public health care, a situation of which this woman was a victim.

THE POLLUTED: SOCIETY'S LABEL

As I have already explained, the woman's state of pollution is not due to her own volition, nor was she born that way, rather, it is caused by the "labeling" by society. The woman's experiences within her social system correspond with what the "outcast" people in Japan have experienced. In both societies the status of the high and the low is distinguished by the religious concept of the pure and the polluted. By the time Buddhism came into Japan in the sixth century c.e. and was accepted by the aristocracy to keep their power and to guard the nation, this religious concept began to reinforce the social status.

One of the ten commandments in Buddhism, "Do not kill a living creature," became the main reason for targeting certain people as outcast in society.[32] Those who dealt with the dead, flayed animals, and did tanning were labeled unclean. By the middle of the modern age, they were called hopelessly polluted, and so they were secluded in certain areas (the Hisabetu-buraku). Some other lowly people, such as wandering entertainers, beggars, ferrymen, and dyers, whose working places were often around the shores of rivers, were also classed as outcasts.

Their residence area was extremely restricted. When they left their segregated villages, they were required to wear certain uniforms that clearly showed who they were. They could never marry persons other than offspring of outcasts. They did not have any family registration, which was required of all the other people in the country.[33]

The pain caused by their alienation and segregation is beyond descrip-

31. Myers, *Binding the Strong Man,* 200. Belo, *A Materialist Reading of the Gospel of Mark,* 131.

32. Hiroshi Noma and Kazumitu Okiura, *Ajia no Sei to Sen: Hisabetumin no Rekishi to Bunka (Purity and Impurity in Asia: History and Culture of the Discriminated)* (Kyoto: Jinbunshoin, 1983), 223. Other commandments are: Do not steal, do not indulge in adultery and fornication, do not lie, do not take liquor, do not embalm one's body, do not become interested in cultural amusement, do not sleep on a luxurious bed, do not satiate oneself, and do not decorate oneself with luxuries.

33. Concerning *Hisabetu-buraku,* I consulted the following books: Buraku Kaiho Kenkyusho, ed., *Shukyo To Buraku Mondai* (Osaka: Kaiho Shuppan, 1990); and Teruo Kuribayashi, *Keikan no Shingaku* (Tokyo: Shinkyo Shuppan, 1991).

tion. Just because they are born in the outcast villages they are labeled polluted at their birth and have to endure nonperson status for their whole lives. If an outcast woman becomes pregnant, she agonizes until her baby is due over whether she should have an abortion. She cannot stand to see her baby suffer various hardships that she has suffered. She knows for certain that there is no way out of that life.

When a person passes away in a village of the outcast, people who come to visit the dead say to console them, "Now you are liberated from all the agony. Congratulations." Generally, when a baby arrives, people wish the best, and when a person passes away, people lament. But in segregated villages of the outcast, the birth of a new life cannot be a blessing, and only death brings peace.

Because the outcast villages are completely segregated socially and geographically, most people do not even know that such villages still exist. Those who leave their villages and come to other places can never admit that they come from the segregated villages. For a long time, the government has not wanted to touch the problem. Therefore, a World Council of Churches report has said that segregated villages of outcasts are the least-known instance of minority groups in the world.[34] There are about six thousand segregated villages with three million outcast people in Japan. Women in the villages are, needless to say, doubly segregated.

Both the hemorrhaging woman and women (and men) in the outcast villages are "labeled" polluted by the authorities for the purpose of maintaining the status of the powers-that-be and the integrity of the societies. The people who can claim purity willingly accept the distinction and behave accordingly. The polluted become the minority in the society and are easily dehumanized. They are victims of the social structures which have made use of the religious concept of pollution. There are no intrinsic reasons for claiming that these people are polluted; rather the label has been given to them from outside. Therefore there is a need to break down the barriers between the pure and the polluted, or, rather, it should be said that the possibility and hope exist for us to remove this label that has no justification.

THE HEMORRHAGING WOMAN AS VOLITIONAL AGENT

She Triggers a Miracle

It is not until the end of verse 27 that the main verb of this long sentence appears after seven participial modifiers: at last we get to know that "she

34. Barbara Rogers, *Race: No Peace without Justice* (Geneva: World Council of Churches, 1980), 29. "Perhaps the least-known case of group oppression is that against the Buraku in Japan, which shows only too vividly that once an identifiable group has been marked out for oppression at some point in history, it is extremely hard to eliminate the stigma."

touched his cloak." It was the crucial moment for her in many ways. It is never permissible for socially banned persons to come into the crowd and touch anyone, because they contaminate others and break down the integrity of the holy community.

"If I but touch his clothes . . ."

She must be thoroughly aware of the ban. The restriction itself explains why she is so intent on getting out of her miserable situation. Two instances point to her intentness. The first is her thinking, "If I may touch even his garments, I will be made well" (v. 28). This expresses considerable assurance that the statement will be realized in the near future.[35] It explains the intensity of her desire, which is directly connected with her healing.[36] It should be noted that "be made well" is to be literally translated "be saved." The word implies not only physical cure, but also recovery of social and religious wholeness. It is also remarkable that the woman is not going to ask Jesus to touch her and help her; rather, she, the polluted "sinner," is going to gain her healing by her will and action.

Her attitude is in striking contrast with Jairus, who falls at Jesus' feet and beseeches him to lay his hands on his daughter. Jairus seems to be very polite and honors Jesus as his superior. He is actually supported by the esteem given him by the culture of honor, which allows him to do honor to Jesus. The woman, of course, is not in such a position. Rather, she must know that the social structure of her time and place prevents Jesus from helping her, even if she were to come out in front of Jesus.[37] Jesus is a member of a society in which men should not be shamed in such a way. She must remain invisible.

Thus she has somewhere developed the strong conviction that the "touching" will surely bring her salvation, which in turn, is based upon the healing of her disease. So her touching is not a simple trial to find out whether he can do it or not, even though her experiences with physicians must have made her doubtful every time she visited a new one. She is determined this time. Her conviction is supported by the verb "kept saying." Not only once, but repeatedly, she has made it clear that Jesus is the one to save her. She has decided to stake her whole life on Jesus. What has given her such a firm conviction is "hearing about Jesus."

Mark uses "hearing" as a vehicle whereby people come to belief (e.g., 4:23; 6:11),[38] while both Matthew and Luke omit it in this story. Evidently the rumors and reports of his healing ministry have reached her and formed her conviction. We cannot be clear if "kept saying" is added by Mark or has been in the tradition.

35. Tateo Kanda, *New Testament Greek* (Tokyo: Iwanami Zensho, 1956), 117.
36. Taylor, *The Gospel According to St. Mark,* 290.
37. Brock, *Journey by Heart,* 83.
38. Selvidge, *Woman, Cult, and Miracle Recital,* 84.

It is recorded that in the early Christian church even handkerchiefs and aprons carried from the healer were held to possess healing virtue (e.g., Acts 19:12), as also did healers' shadows (e.g., Acts 5:15). The garments and shadows of healers were looked upon as extensions of their personality.[39] Mark's story clearly points out that the woman touched Jesus' clothes (v. 27, 28, 30, and 31). Though Matthew and Luke both emphasize that it is only the fringe of Jesus' clothes that made contact with her (Matt. 9:20; Luke 8:44; cf. Num. 15:38), the fact of "her touching" cannot be erased. Under the Levitical purity laws, she definitely defiles Jesus.

Overcoming the Barriers

The second evidence of her seriousness is found in the fact that she dares to take the risk of overcoming the barriers that have been set in front of her by the purity law and the patriarchy. In the patriarchal society with its "honor and shame" structure, a woman is naturally supposed to be "embedded" in a man.[40] A woman is most usually part of the property of her father, husband, or son. Therefore it is normal to see Jairus pleading for his daughter. But it is out of the ordinary for a woman to plead her own case. Even though the hemorrhaging woman only intended to touch his clothes in secret, she still dared to deal with her own trouble by touching Jesus.[41] She summons up the courage to violate the patriarchal social taboo.[42] And on her own volition and initiative she comes out in public, even though she is fully conscious of being labeled unclean and considered quarantined, and would convey this uncleanness to those whom she touches. Thus she consciously defies the established system of holiness.

She wants her disease to be cured so that her sickness may be healed; she wants to be culticly saved and to be restored to wholeness in her society. The social implication of her disease is so pitiable and serious that she dares to come out in public. Yet she touches Jesus' clothes from behind. She reaches out from the cover of the crowd. Because she is a woman and because she is labeled contagiously unclean, she has become doubly poor and is doubly discriminated against. Such circumstances have made her move in a concealed way.

Although she is thoroughly aware that her touching will not only contaminate Jesus but also bring him shame, because she is bleeding and female, she must also have gained an insight that Jesus will share the shame with her. In her most devastated situation, I say, she has perceived who Jesus really is. Thus she is challenging the arbitrary boundaries set by the authorities in order to maintain the status quo.

39. Taylor, *The Gospel According to St. Mark*, 290.
40. Bruce Malina, *The New Testament World: Insights from Cultural Anthropology* (Atlanta: John Knox Press, 1981), 100.
41. Pilch, "Biblical Leprosy and Body Symbolism," 147.
42. Brock, *Journey by Heart*, 84.

The Disease Is Healed

"Immediately her hemorrhage stopped . . ."

Verse 29—"Immediately her hemorrhage stopped; and she felt in her body that she was healed of her disease"—has several delicately related points that we cannot overlook. First, the cure was immediate. The bleeding stopped when she touched Jesus. And second, Mark or the tradition uses two aorist tense verbs ("was dried up" and "knew"), which indicate definite past happenings, and then a perfect tense verb ("is cured"), which shows an abiding consequence. The verb stresses the durability of her cured condition.[43]

Yet what the woman has expressed is not what she had been saying: not "will be saved" but "am cured." In Greek thought, *iaomai* has the idea of restoration, making good and release from physical suffering. The verb here explains the alleviation of her physical-emotional suffering.[44] Here the restoration of the bodily wholeness is stressed.[45] Mark or the tradition reserves her salvation for later. And finally, although she is cured, she is cured from the plague, not just from her disease. "Plague" is used only twice in Mark (3:10 and here) and seems to imply suffering caused by social ostracism and pain because of the disease.[46] We can see here the depth of her social dilemma caused by her physical ailment. Moreover, Matthew completely omits the verse and Luke changes "hemorrhage" to "flow" with a different verb. While the Markan story uses natural, metaphoric terms and gives us a vivid image of the change in the body, Luke describes it physiologically but flatly. Matthew avoids having her as the center of the story. Her character, illness, and actions are abbreviated and Jesus' response to her becomes more important.[47]

"Immediately aware that power had gone forth from him . . ."

"Immediately aware that power had gone forth from him, Jesus turned about in the crowd and said, 'Who touched my clothes?'" (v. 30). This time, Jesus "immediately knew" what had happened in himself. We see several levels at work in her healing process. Myers draws our attention to "the double realization of physical sensation by both the woman and Jesus."[48] Thus the story carefully depicts the miracle as reciprocal, not unilateral. Now she is involved in a live relationship with Jesus.

43. Taylor, *The Gospel According to St. Mark,* 291.
44. Albrecht Oepke, "ιαομαι" *Theological Dictionary of the New Testament* 3 (1965), 198-99.
45. Myers, *Binding the Strong Man,* 201.
46. Selvidge, "Mark 5:25-34 and Leviticus," 622.
47. Ibid., 622.
48. Myers, *Binding the Strong Man,* 201.

According to the purity laws, Jesus should be contracting the contamination, but the story reports instead that she is cured and that Jesus perceives his power going out of him. Through this physical contact her disease is cured. From the vantage point of this story the contact symbolizes that the cultic order described in the purity laws is overturned. The woman violates the law and the violation evidences Jesus' power reversing the contamination into a cure. They both subvert the myth of contamination attached to female bleeding and prove by her direct contact with him that the myth of its being contagious is not true. Thus they have broken down the barrier that has distinguished the clean and the unclean. Myers, disagreeing with this point, says rather unconvincingly:

> I would contend that the primary level of signification in this episode, however, lies in the fact that Jesus accepts the priority of the ("highly inappropriate") importunity of this woman over the ("correct") request of the synagogue leader.[49]

Jesus asks, "Who touched my clothes?" because Jesus knew that the power had gone out of him. The power, in this context, is the personal power that resides in Jesus and is available for healing.[50] The woman touched Jesus and not Jesus her. And now he looks for her in the crowd and not she for him. She would rather have kept quiet and been ignored.

JAPAN: THE OUTCASTS WHO TOUCHED CHURCHES

Just like the woman who touched Jesus on her own volition, the outcast people in the segregated villages of Japan took the initiative to break through the solid boundary that was set all around them and to set their liberation in motion in 1922. They wrote their own declaration of human rights based on the Christian faith, even though they were not Christians. Their black flag had a red crown of thorns in its center. They identified their suffering and martyrdom with that of Jesus. They identified their liberation process with that of the exodus. They were convinced that they would eventually be liberated if they kept up their struggle, just as the despised Israelites were freed from their fetters in Egypt and led into "a land flowing with milk and honey." They declared that they had once been abandoned but then were elected by God's special call. They perceived that the core message of the gospel is in the liberation of the oppressed. Their indescribably miserable experiences of oppression gave them an insight into who God is and led them to "touch" God and challenge the churches in Japan. Their move was just like that of the woman.

49. Myers, *Binding the Strong Man,* 201.
50. Taylor, *The Gospel According to St. Mark,* 291.

THE HEMORRHAGING WOMAN AS CHALLENGER OF AUTHORITY

"How can you say, 'Who touched me?'"

Jesus and the woman are each aware of the moment of their definite personal contact, but the disciples do not recognize it at all. Jesus is in the center of circles of people. The disciples are expected to form an inner circle for Jesus, surrounded by a bigger circle of the unknown crowd. The woman, who could belong to the crowd, yet has been outcast, who has no name or status, and who does not have anyone to defend her as the daughter of Jairus has her father, has edged her way deep into the center of Jesus' circle and, as a result, unintentionally creates the space and opportunity for her to encounter Jesus.[51]

Even when Jesus tries to have personal contact with her, the disciples become irritated and try to hinder him. Their answer implies that it is foolish to ask who touched him. This could be an example of Mark's criticism of the disciples, which is characteristic of Mark. The fact that the curt remonstrance of the disciples is omitted by Matthew and softened by Luke suggests that such criticism reflects the primitive character of the Markan account.[52] Matthew especially is consistent throughout the story in omitting all the references to her positive attitude toward Jesus and Jesus' concern for her. Matthew's intention seems to be found in his emphasis on depicting Jesus as the miracle worker.

Jesus is determined to single out the woman

"Jesus looked all around to see who had done it" (v. 32). Previously she was determined to touch Jesus despite all obstacles, and now Jesus is determined to single out the person. "But the woman, knowing what had happened to her, came in fear and trembling, fell down before him, and told him the whole truth" (v. 33). She is in fear and trembling because she dared to touch a person whom she was never supposed to touch. She was soiled, unclean, and contagious. She caused him to be unclean. She has contaminated Jesus. He will have to observe certain cleansing rituals. Not only that, but she has taken some of his healing power.

She could not help but think of the condemnation of society and religion, both of which were androcentrically organized. She was also trained, as a result of living long in a patriarchal society, to despise herself without being conscious of it, because of her disease and its implications. The long period of ostracism by society has made it impossible for her to develop that self-

51. Belo, *A Materialist Reading of the Gospel of Mark*, 30-32.
52. Sasagu Arai, *Iesu Kirisuto* (Tokyo: Kodansha, 1979), 252, 414f. Taylor, *The Gospel According to St. Mark*, 292.

esteem which must have been restored through the miracle experience.

She is very conscious of the tradition that "women were not only to be seen as little as possible, they were also to be heard and spoken to as little as possible."[53] But she exposes herself in front of Jesus so that she may become visible instead of invisible. Actual interactional relationship between Jesus and the woman begins at this moment. The story does not stress the publicity of her action, which Luke does, but affirms that she told him everything. Luke who tends to emphasize sinful existence, also thinks that her motivation to reveal herself is her consciousness that she had already been found out. Matthew omits any reference to her action, in accordance with his intention to stress Jesus as the miracle worker.[54] Mark might want to describe her as being trustworthy, "She told him the whole truth." She engages herself in life-communion with Jesus.

 She is trembling with fear and yet not paralyzed by the emotion. Her faith is the kind that overcomes such obstacles. All three stories, in Mark, Matthew, and Luke, agree that her faith took the initiative in her healing miracle. Overcoming the obstacles and the impossible is one of the main characteristics seen in this kind of miracle story.[55]

"Your faith has made you well"

He said to her, "Daughter, your faith has made you well; go in peace, and be healed of your disease" (v. 34). The expectation of the woman, the disciples, the crowd, and ourselves is that Jesus would reprimand her for being in the middle of the crowd or for touching and defiling him. Rather than condemning her, Jesus tells her that her faith has saved her and made her whole.[56]

To begin with, it is unusual for a religious leader to talk to a woman in public.[57] According to the Mishnah, "He that talks much with womankind brings evil upon himself and neglects the study of the Law and at the last will inherit Gehenna."[58] Moreover, it is unexpected for Jesus to admire her faith that has triggered the miracle. Jesus' affirmation of her and her faith means that he has also overcome the ritual border that separates the clean from the unclean. Even though he does not attack the purity laws directly, he negates them by ignoring them. Jesus must see her as a person dehumanized by the laws that have been used only to satisfy the honor of men with power. It should be noted, however, that the woman sets the stage,

53. Leonard Swidler, *Women in Judaism* (Metuchen, NJ: Scarecrow Press, 1976), 123.

54. Taylor, *The Gospel According to St. Mark,* 292.

55. Antoinette Clark Wire, "The Structure of the Gospel Miracle Stories and Their Tellers," *Semeia* 11 (1978), 107.

56. Jeremy Moiser, " 'She Was Twelve Years Old' (Mk 5, 42): A Note on Jewish-Gentile Controversy in Mark's Gospel," *Irish Biblical Studies* 3 (1981), 183.

57. Irene Brennan, "Women in the Gospels," *New Blackfriars* 52 (1971), 294.

58. *The Mishnah: Aboth* 1:5, tr. Herbert Danby (Oxford: Clarendon, 1933), 446.

and Jesus responds by becoming a "boundary breaker." The woman is the one who takes the initiative. She challenges the boundary and makes Jesus become truly a savior.

Jesus calls her "daughter." The nameless, statusless, destitute, and defiled woman is now one of Jesus' family members. Of whom does the family consist? Jesus does not explain it here, but earlier (Mark 3:33-34) Jesus has defined his family as those who do God's will. The hemorrhaging woman is declared to be "doing God's will."

Why is she declared to be doing God's will? She breaks through the barrier between the unclean and the pure, through the act of touching Jesus, asks that he restore her life, and engages in relationship with Jesus. We may say that Jesus affirms her volitional act of breaking through her impasse as "doing God's will."

She is called from the very fringe of the society to its center. Thus she is not only cured of her incurable disease but also healed of her permanent uncleanness. Only when both her physical health and her identity with the community of faith have been restored, is she saved. Jesus has brought her into the center of the community of faith by admiring her faith. Jesus has given her thorough affirmation and accepts her as she is. Such a strong affirmation is given by Jesus only to one other healed person in the Gospel of Mark, the blind beggar Bartimaeus (10:52).

What a shame it is for a man to affirm the most marginalized in public. It is all the more so for the Son of God. By accepting the same defilement that she has suffered from, Jesus breaks through the ritual barrier that separates the pure and the polluted. He who shares shame with her stands with her. Thus her liberation is completed.

Nevertheless, it should be repeated that the stage for this epoch-making event is set for Jesus by the woman, and he responds, by becoming a "boundary breaker." This interaction implies that Jesus accepts her challenge to authority as valuable and effective. Thus she becomes a paradigm of discipleship.

Jesus affirms her faith directly and the meaninglessness of the purity laws indirectly. Mark might have been disturbed that his community of faith was following the purity code and practicing discrimination. Apparently Mark contrasts the woman's faith with the disciples' lack of faith. Her salvation has come to her in a way that she never anticipated. Her first and last desire was to be "saved" without knowing definitely how the salvation would come about. In her case, faith is the perception that Jesus is the life-giving Christ. According to Fernando Belo, faith is "the reading of the power of the practice-seed of J[esus] as the good news of the eschatological power."[59] "Faith, as a reading of the power of J[esus], has released the energy that passes in a powerful body-to-body contact,"[60] and Jesus' "read-

59. Fernando Belo, *A Materialist Reading of the Gospel of Mark*, 257.
60. Ibid., 257.

ing of the 'truth' . . . links *faith* with the effect of the work of the power that has gone out of J[esus'] body."[61]

"Go in peace"

Jesus says to her, "Go in peace, and be healed of your disease" (v. 34). Peacefulness and wholeness fill her now as she is cured and saved. Her healing is completed by Jesus and, thus, her perception confirmed that Jesus brings good news. The expression "Go in peace" corresponds to the Hebrew *Shalom* and is often used idiomatically in the Old and New Testaments as an expression of greeting (cf. Judg. 18:6; 1 Sam. 1:17; 2 Sam. 15:9; 1 Kings 22:17; Luke 7:50; Acts 16:36 and James 2:16). Here it may be more plausible to say that Jesus uses the expression to confirm the miracle, as he does in the stories of the leper and the Gerasene demoniac (1:44 and 5:19).[62] It signifies a state of rest that implies prosperity, lack of suffering, or an alternative to war. It can also be applied to the state of the soul, connoting the relationship with God as well as the eschatological salvation of the whole person.[63] The expression must have touched the depth of her heart and also conveyed the state of her soul and body most appropriately and powerfully after her dehumanizing agony. She no longer needs to worry about the degradation and suffering that are the social consequences of her physical condition. She can be whole because she is cured of her disease.

But it is more accurate to say that she can be whole because she is accepted as a member of the community as she is. Mark very carefully chooses the terms that express key themes in the story. What the woman desires is "to be saved." And what she desires to be freed from is plague. She wants to be whole so that she may be free from being rejected, segregated, and dehumanized. She cries out to become human. She needs to be cured of her disease, but that is not her ultimate goal. She wants her life back; she needs the resurrection of life. For her the crowd was the obstacle to be overcome, as Wire points out,[64] but, it seems to me, the real obstacle was concealed in the purity law.

61. Ibid., 133.

62. Arai, *Iesu Kirisuto,* p. 252.

63. Werner Foerster, "ειρηνη," *Theological Dictionary of the New Testament* 2 (1964), 411-12.

64. Wire, "The Structure of the Gospel Miracle Stories," 83-110. She categorizes all gospel miracle stories according to their organizing interactions between and among characters into four groups: the exorcism, the exposé, the provision, and the demand. They have a common function, that is, "the structure of the miracle story as such is the juxtaposition of an oppressive context and an extraordinary breaking out of it." Both the story of the hemorrhaging woman and that of Jairus's daughter belong to the fourth category: the demand. The demand stories are "built out of the struggle for and the realization and telling of a demand addressed to the miracle worker," and they are intensified in one of three ways, either by a rebuke for expecting too little, by life's common obstructions, or by direct opposition from the miracle worker. The hemorrhaging woman, in a story belonging to the second type of intensification, faces the crowd's obstruction, while she herself becomes the obstruction in the story of Jairus's daughter.

CONCLUSION

By interacting with the woman, Jesus shows that he does not at all mind being touched by the one who is forbidden to touch anyone else for the sake of the integrity of the community. Thus he has broken down the barrier that defines the elect and cuts off the unclean. Furthermore, he does not mind sharing his power with the untouchable. This way he has opened up the community of faith to all, so that all may be accepted as they are. He rejects the dehumanizing situation that binds the community from being free and whole. Jesus' action shocks and undermines the counterfeit community of faith. I agree with Elisabeth Schüssler Fiorenza, who says, "Not the holiness of the elect but the wholeness *of all* is the central vision of Jesus."[65] Moreover:

> The *basileia* of God is experientially available in the healing activity of Jesus. . . . The *basileia* vision of Jesus makes people whole, healthy, cleansed, and strong. It restores people's humanity and life. The salvation of the *basileia* is not confined to the soul but spells wholeness for the total person in her/his social relations.[66]

But I would go so far as to say that the hemorrhaging woman symbolizes the bleeding borne even by healthy women on various occasions. She symbolizes the burden put on us women because of our femaleness. By being touched by her, Jesus is led to make clear that the cultic barrier established between women and men by the purity laws is broken down. Also by talking to her personally in public he has broken down the social barrier of "honor" that is restricted to men. From these two points, we may conclude that the custom of shunning blood is definitely related to the patriarchal structure of the society. At her demand, Jesus breaks through the barrier of male privilege and status that separates him from the woman. Otherwise, one half of the human race is continually kept far from their wholeness. Then what Jesus really must defend is his accepting the woman as she is, even if she is bleeding. Only then can her action result in "Kenosis of patriarchy."[67] Only then can her miracle experience witness both to this kenosis and to the senseless, dehumanizing situation that women have had to tolerate. I take her challenge in this sense. She challenges the authorities and witnesses to the change that can liberate the outcast. That may be called the true miracle of barrier breakdown: that is, to accept any person as she or he is. Yet Jesus knew that this simplest thing—to accept her as she

65. E. Schüssler Fiorenza, *In Memory of Her,* 121.
66. Ibid., 123.
67. Rosemary Radford Ruether, *Sexism and God-Talk,* 1-11. Brock, *Journey by Heart,* 84.

was—was desperately difficult for the people to do. Therefore the miracle of healing her disease had to occur.

The mainstream churches in Japan have kept their focus on the individual issues of middle-class intellectuals and have been indifferent to the social and political issues of the destitute. Even though the outcast people in the segregated villages "touched" churches in Japan, their cries echoed in the void and were barely heard. Churches have failed to discern the outcasts' thirst for liberation as a challenge to their faith. Churches have been numb, even though they have been "touched." We are seriously challenged by the "untouchable" to become touchable and to become sensitive enough to discern which "touching" is most needed.

I, a woman of Japan, as one of the oppressed in a patriarchal society, keep touching Jesus and disturbing the churches as the hemorrhaging woman does, and at the same time I identify myself with those labeled "defiled" as Jesus does, so that I will be one of those who stand with the oppressed to gain liberation and realize miracles in our lives in solidarity.

In the following chapters, I will go on to interpret other Markan stories of interactions between women and Jesus from the same perspective as that in this chapter. It is a perspective I have formulated through experiences of us Japanese women and by awareness of the missions that confront us as women.

3

THE SYROPHOENICIAN WOMAN

(7:24-30)

CULTIC PURITY

The story of the Syrophoenician woman begins with a plea for healing and ends with the success of the healing, but it is clear that the miracle is not reported for its own sake. The discourse between the woman and Jesus centers around eating bread, granted that "eating bread" is a metaphor.

The story is preceded by long discourses with the Pharisees and some scribes concerning the fact that Jesus' disciples eat with unclean hands, purity in dietary activities (7:1-13), and a discourse with the disciples on personal defilement by things from within (7:17-23). Jesus openly undermined the purity laws and the traditions built up around them by citing phrases from Isaiah (29:13) and showing that recent traditions were making void God's commandment. Then Jesus gave his disciples additional teachings on internal and external sources of defilement.[1]

Restrictions on food and eating, which played a very important role in cultic purity and integrity of the holy (Lev. 11) could also be the major barrier between the Israelites and Gentiles. Not only the length of the discourse,[2] but the emphatic pursuit of its main idea through different examples signify the importance of the theme in Mark's Gospel and suggest how deeply the Israelites were bound by their concept of purity, which was the cause of their exclusive attitude toward outsiders.

1. Gail R. O'Day, "Surprised by Faith: Jesus and the Canaanite Woman," *Listening: A Journal of Religion and Culture* 24 (Fall, 1989), 291. Ben Witherington III, *Women in the Ministry of Jesus: A Study of Jesus' Attitudes to Women and Their Roles as Reflected in His Earthly Life* (Cambridge: University Press, 1984), 65. T. A. Burkill, "Mark 6:31– 8:26: The Context of the Story of the Syrophoenician Woman," *The Classical Tradition: Literary and Historical Studies in Honor of H.Caplin,* ed. L. Wallach (New York: Cornell Univ. Press, 1966), 331-32.

2. Karen A. Barta, *The Gospel of Mark* (Delaware: Michael Glazier, Inc., 1988), 100-101.

Jesus here again challenges the barrier-building between the pure and the unclean and negates an artificially-warranted cultic purity. He has executed another boundary-breaking feat. Achtemeier points out that Mark's schematic intention is apparent here.[3] His perspective toward the mission to the Gentiles may already be implicitly suggested in this section.

If the main obstacle to integrating the Jews and Gentiles is removed, the concrete practice of accepting Gentiles will follow.[4] So the next story may be a practical illustration of the liberation from the prejudice engendered by the purity laws. If Jesus leaves the land and the people who claim to be "clean" and enters into an "unclean" land, the definition of defilement will be put to the test and the tradition made void by Jesus himself. This is what Mark may have intended.[5] Apparently the story has absorbed Markan insights motivated by his redactional intentions for the community of faith of his time.

MARK'S CROSS-RACIAL COMMUNITY

The issue, however, has become intense for Mark, because he is writing his Gospel when Gentiles already belong to the community of faith.[6] Mark has to be concerned about social separation and attitudes that would be very unbecoming for the new community.[7] Thus Mark's Gospel reflects the struggles being undergone in his community.

But we do not dare say that all these pericopes are the evangelist's inventive creations. The story of the Syrophoenician woman, which follows the record of these discourses, could have been detrimental to Mark's purpose, given his current situation. Yet he did not adjust his story accordingly. Therefore by depicting Jesus' interaction with the woman and his healing of a pagan Gentile—the only example of this in Mark's Gospel[8]—the story may reflect much of Jesus' own attitude toward Gentiles. We will see this later in detail. According to Taylor, the linguistic characteristics in the story suggest Aramaic tradition and Mark has adapted the story in the interests of Gentile readers.[9]

By putting the story after Jesus' long discourse with the Pharisees and the scribes and then with his disciples over the purity laws, Mark lets Jesus withdraw from Jewish territory to Gentile territory (7:24). "From there he set out and went away to the region of Tyre." Thus, Mark opens up the

3. Paul J. Achtemeier, "Toward the Isolation of Pre-Markan Miracle Catenae," *Journal of Biblical Literature* 89 (1970), 288. Howard C. Kee, *Community of the New Age: Studies In Mark's Gospel* (Philadelphia: Westminster Press, 1977), 92.

4. Myers, *Binding the Strong Man*, 440-41.

5. O'Day, "Surprised by Faith," 291.

6. Witherington, *Women in the Ministry of Jesus*, 63.

7. Selvidge, *Woman, Cult, and Miracle Recital*, 89.

8. Witherington, *Women in the Ministry of Jesus*, 63.

9. Taylor, *The Gospel According to St. Mark*, 349.

opportunity of Jesus' Gentile itinerary and allows Jesus to avoid possible danger after he has dismissed the most important part of the traditional Jewish laws.[10]

There is much discussion among scholars about whether or not Jesus really crossed the border. There should have been nothing hindering Jesus from going any place, but it is another question whether Jesus actually intended a mission to the Gentiles. We can see Jesus' perceptive and receptive attitude toward Gentiles only from his interaction with the woman. Possibly the attitude shown in his words and deeds might have prepared the way for a Gentile mission in the days to come.

> [Mark] wishes to illustrate the Lord's freedom from the purity regulations and to demonstrate that the apostolic mission to the Gentiles was prefigured in the earthly ministry; and he infers from the tradition's reference to the woman's Syrophoenician connections that the journey beyond Palestine was an excursion into the region of Tyre and Sidon—totally disregarding the possibility that she may have been thought of by the tradents as an *emigree* resident in Galilee.[11]

In an age and culture that made a clear distinction between the holy land and the rest, the journey covering the entire Gentile region surrounding Galilee from "the region of Tyre" (7:24) to "the region of Decapolis through Sidon" (7:31) is very symbolic. Tyre may be mentioned because the woman is a Syrophoenician, but since in the Old Testament Tyre is said to be proud and a threat to the Israelites and is always recorded with Sidon[12] (Isa. 23; Jer. 47:4; Ezek. 27, 28; Joel 3:4-8; Zech. 9:2) as polluted by materialism,[13] it is again very symbolic that Jesus dares to cross the border and go into the most despised, unclean territory.

All the places have already been mentioned (3:8; 5:20) in the Gospel. Some, including Bultmann, reject the idea that the journey to the Gentile territory could have been historical. It may be that in order to edit the healing miracles in the Gentile cycle,[14] Mark added the two verses to "provide a topological framework and connecting links, to show that Jesus' fame had spread beyond the border of Palestine, and to give a missionary coloring."[15] Elisabeth Schüssler Fiorenza, too, finds the original location of

10. Witherington, *Women in the Ministry of Jesus*, 63-4.

11. T.A. Burkill, "The Syrophoenician Woman: The Congruence of Mark 7:24-31," *Zeitschrift für die neutestamentliche Wissenschaft* 57 (1966), 35.

12. Some important manuscripts such as Sinaiticus, Alexandrinus, Vaticanus, and others add "and Sidon" after "Tyre" in verse 24.

13. O'Day, "Surprised by Faith," 291. J. Duncan M. Derrett, "Law in the New Testament: The Syro-Phoenician Woman and the Centurion of Capernaum," *Novum Testamentum* 15 (1973), 163-64.

14. Myers, *Binding the Strong Man*, 204.

15. T.A. Burkill, "The Historical Development of the Story of the Syrophoenician Woman (Mark 7:24-31): New Light on the Earliest Gospel," *Novum Testamentum* 9 (1967), 177.

the story in Galilee.[16] It should be said for certain that the horizon of Mark's worldview is expanded from that of Jesus' earthly mission as Mark tries to respond to the needs of Gentile readers.

Many have also assigned the "first" of verse 27 to Markan editorial work, because the "first" weakens the impact and the comparison on which Jesus' rejection relies, but the remainder is assigned to the unitary composition.[17]

JESUS TRIES TO HIDE FROM THE CROWD: THE WOMAN'S UNEXPECTED BEHAVIOR

"And from there he set out and went away to the region of Tyre" (v. 24). Jesus seems to be seeking privacy. After a lengthy dispute with the Pharisees and the scribes that included a bold denunciation of their tradition on purity, his life may be in danger. Also, perhaps he is withdrawing to reflect upon his ministry.[18] He may be filled with sorrow for the hardness of people's hearts that makes their faith exclusive, and for his lack of success at proclaiming the good news in the heart of the temple-centered religion.

Seclusion from the crowd is repeatedly recorded in Mark's Gospel (1:35-39; 2:1; 3:20; 6:31, 45-46; 7:24; 9:30-31). In this particular case Jesus enters into a house, in line with the pattern in this Gospel that he never enters a synagogue to teach after his visit to Nazareth.[19] As usual, the seclusion is not successful. Somehow his fame has reached a Gentile woman who comes to interrupt him.

As investigated so far, the story of the woman's encounter with Jesus is probably complete in verses 25-30, with verse 24 added by Mark. So the story begins with verse 25: "But a woman whose little daughter had an unclean spirit immediately heard about him, and she came and bowed down at his feet."

"Immediately" after the woman has heard of Jesus, she comes to him. What she has heard is not written, but probably she has heard something about Jesus as a popular healer, because she has a daughter with an unclean spirit. Though "bowing down at his feet" may show one's inferior position in the social relationships in the patriarchal society, it is an action only accepted among men. Her bowing down is not considered to honor the status of Jesus as a male teacher.[20] On the contrary, it is a serious misdeed which brings disgrace on him. Women of the time are not expected to come out of their homes where they have their role, much less to make a plea in

16. E. Schüssler Fiorenza, *In Memory of Her*, 137.

17. Rudolf K. Bultmann, *The History of the Synoptic Tradition*, transl. John Marsh (Oxford: Basil Blackwell, 1972), 36. Achtemeier, "Toward the Isolation," 287. E. Schüssler Fiorenza, *In Memory of Her*, 137. Burkill, "The Historical Development," 177.

18. Belo, *A Materialist Reading of the Gospel of Mark*, 145.

19. Brock, *Journey by Heart*, 86-87.

20. Myers, *Binding the Strong Man*, 203; also chapter 1.

a public setting. There is some evidence that the contacts with Hellenism and Roman society may have given some impetus to an improved status for women.[21] But, generally speaking, her invasive solicitation would make a man lose his face in the culture of honor/shame. It is something very unusual for an anonymous woman, unknown and unrelated to the Jews, to dare to break his privacy. Nevertheless, she does.

She is introduced as "a Gentile, of Syrophoenician origin." "Syrophoenician" is used to distinguish "Syrian-" from "Carthaginian-" and "Libyan-" Phoenicians. These designations reflect the nations of Jesus' own day. Matthew changes this to "Canaanite," which was traditionally used to characterize local people hostile to the Jews. So racially she is Syrophoenician, but politically and socioculturally she is described as a Gentile. Thus she is introduced not only as a non-Jew but also as a pagan by upbringing.[22]

Myers, who assumes that Jesus journeyed to the north beyond the border, sees here "another Markan archetype, representative of the hellenized populations of the area."[23] Others argue that such a detailed description of the woman should not occur in a place where almost everyone is Gentile; it would be more suitable if the story were set in Galilee, a foreign place to her. Or it may be a way of letting the listeners to whom the miracle story is addressed know that she is not a Hellenistic Jew but a foreigner. She is presented as a Gentile whom the traditions of the Jews have excluded and whom the community of Mark is to accept.[24]

It becomes clear that she is "unclean" by birth, a foreigner and a female, and "untouchable" because of her daughter who is possessed by an unclean spirit. She must know well as a woman of that culture and that time that she would defile Jesus and would be accused by his disciples. From the very fact that she dares cross her Rubicon, we can infer that she is on the verge of being desperate in her great need of help for her daughter. Daughters' issues are mothers' issues. They are both thus triply polluted: foreign, female, and demon-possessed. She tries to be as polite as possible, but she is already far beyond the reserve she is expected to show. She is determined to encounter Jesus. "She begged him to cast the demon out of her daughter" (v. 26).

JESUS' RESPONSE TO THE WOMAN

The phrase that follows her begging—"And he said to her"—is very important in this story. It is naturally expected that a man put off by aggres-

---

21. Frederick H. Borsch, "Jesus and Women Exemplars," *Anglican Theological Review.* Suppl. no. 11 (1990), 29-30. E. Schüssler Fiorenza, *In Memory of Her,* 106-110.

22. Burkill, "The Syrophoenician Woman," 23. O'Day, "Surprised by Faith," 291. E. Schüssler Fiorenza, *In Memory of Her,* 137. Taylor, *The Gospel According to St. Mark,* 349.

23. Myers, *Binding the Strong Man,* 203.

24. Theissen, *The Miracle Stories,* 126. Burkill, "The Historical Development," 172. Achtemeier, "Toward the Isolation," 287.

sive cries for help will turn away with anger in that patriarchal society. In addition, rabbis are prohibited contact with women. Matthew has Jesus giving her the silent treatment, as expected.

According to Mark, Jesus answers in two sentences: "Let the children be fed first," and "for it is not fair to take the children's food and throw it to the dogs." Most scholars have investigated the meanings and implications of the words "first" and "dogs" in his answer. Both words function to support Jewish superiority and define Gentiles as second-class citizens, though "first" may soften this tension by suggesting the possible existence of a "second."

In any case, Jesus' rebuff of her is understandable only if we pay attention to the social context of the culture of honor/shame. Jesus was expected to defend the collective honor of his people. And from the structural viewpoint we can see that the difficulty to be overcome in the story is increasing, since the miracle worker himself becomes the obstacle. In this case another tension between different cultures is perceptible.[25]

Scholars suggest that "first" is an editorial insertion by Mark, who had Gentile readers in mind (cf. "to the Jew first, and also to the Greek," Romans 1:16). [26] Bultmann adds that the word "weakens the comparison on which the argument of Jesus is based" and that the whole first sentence may be a later addition to Mark's text.[27] Burkill sees here the influence of Pauline teaching in Romans 1:16 and 11:11.[28] On the other hand, Taylor supports verse 27a as original, with the reason that it is what provokes the woman's witty reply in verse 28.[29] Belo asserts more positively that the first stage of Jesus' strategy aims at satisfying the Jews and the second at satisfying Gentiles.[30]

There is no question that Jesus, as a Jew, started his ministry among the Jews. And his movement then became a sect of Judaism. Mark seems to think that the Jews have priority over the Gentiles in hearing the gospel, the Gentiles hearing the gospel only after Jesus' crucifixion (15:38-39 and 13:10). Yet, he wants to make clear that the mission to the Gentiles is prefigured during Jesus' earthly ministry. He adds "first" in 27a in light of the new second wave in the community of faith.[31] Therefore I conclude that Jesus' original answer lacked the "first" and sounded very blunt to the woman.

The harshness continues in the latter half of Jesus' answer. The word

25. Theissen, *The Miracle Stories*, 254.
26. Bultmann, *The History of the Synoptic Tradition,* 38. Taylor, *The Gospel According to St. Mark,* 350. Burkill, "The Historical Development," 109. Myers, *Binding the Strong Man,* 203.
27. Bultmann, *The History of the Synoptic Tradition,* 38.
28. Burkill, "The Historical Development," 109.
29. Taylor, *The Gospel According to St. Mark,* 360.
30. Belo, *A Materialist Reading of the Gospel of Mark,* 145.
31. Burkill, "The Historical Development," 97-99, 114.

used for "dogs" is a diminutive indicating "little dogs" or "puppies." There is evidence of Jewish writers describing Gentiles as "dogs," though not as "puppies," when they refer to their vices.[32] In the Bible the word is applied to "unclean" persons such as Gentiles and Sodomites (Deut. 23:18; Rev. 22:15). Taylor thinks that the use of "puppies" rather than "dogs" softens the apparent harshness of Jesus' answer by giving a gentler tone to his speech and showing that Jesus is speaking of household dogs. He suggests that this testifies to "a tension in the mind of Jesus concerning the scope of his ministry, and that, in a sense, he is speaking to himself as well as to the woman. Her reply shows that she is quick to perceive this."[33] Taylor goes beyond the text into analyzing the psyche of both Jesus and the woman.

Myers, in contrast claims that Mark uses "puppies" to express a traditional insult for the purpose of giving dramatic effect. He also quotes Theissen to say that the story both assumes and reflects the ethnic, cultural, and sociopolitical hostility between the Jews and their Gentile neighbors.[34]

Others claim that "puppy" is taken from a maxim, a proverb, or an epithet popular among the Jews.[35] Burkill, using form-critical analysis to trace back four evolutionary phases of the story, states that the oldest phase of the story reflects a time when the Jews were still enjoying the first prerogative. He sees no hint that "there is some uncertainty in Jesus' own mind about the character of the divine purpose."[36] Opposing Taylor's attempt to soften the harshness, he says: "To call a woman 'a little bitch' is no less abusive than to call a woman 'a bitch' without qualification."[37] According to his analysis, there was no need to soften any harshness until the Gentiles began flowing into Mark's community of faith. His form-critical analysis gives some clues about how the story underwent crucial changes.

Nevertheless, says Burkill, the woman "was able to indicate the shape of things to come. Her insight was foresight; she discerned in advance the Lord of the Gentile churches, and duly received a miraculous award."[38] Yet to go this far may well be speculation. For the moment, I will not try to clarify what "puppy" means, but simply to take Jesus' phrase as the same kind of harsh expression in the woman's face as in the first half with "first" being added later.

But other important words seem to have been overlooked by the scholars quoted above. Why does Jesus use "allow" (in the second person singular

32. E.g., Rabbi Eliezer: "He who eats with an idolator is like unto one who eats with a dog," etc. Quoted in Taylor, *The Gospel According to St. Mark,* 350. Also O'Day, "Surprised by Faith," 297.

33. Taylor, *The Gospel According to St. Mark,* 350.

34. Myers, *Binding the Strong Man,* 204.

35. O'Day, "Surprised by Faith," 297. Derrett, "Law in the New Testament," 172. Burkill, "The Historical Development," 118. Witherington, *Women in the Ministry of Jesus,* 170.

36. Burkill, "The Historical Development," 112-13.

37. Ibid., 113-14.

38. Ibid., 98.

imperative) and command her directly, instead of using "let them be fed"? Why does he use the rather rough word "throw" instead of "give"? His language sounds defensive.

THE WOMAN'S PERSISTENCE

If any woman in a contemporary, individually oriented society were to hear such a response, she would become too angry even to remain there, preferring to endure her daughter's suffering rather than swallow such an affront. But this woman has been accustomed since birth to being subjugated and looked down upon; she has shouldered all sorts of grief and sacrificed herself for the honor of men. Having been taught to remain silent, hidden, and obedient all through her life, she only hears from Jesus what she is used to hearing. His response would not upset her. On the contrary, she must be well aware that merely her appearing there is defiling and goes against the accepted custom.

But she is also determined. That is why she can take him on and respond very actively. She is caught between life and death and she has to be aggressive if she and her daughter are to live. So she uses the same word that Jesus uses but in her own way. For her, to be a dog does not mean to be servile. She answers, "Sir, even the dogs under the table eat the children's crumbs" (v. 28). For her, dogs are domestic animals. The way she uses the word shows that she thinks of them as cherished parts of the family. If the Jews had also used the word in this sense, the negative connotation would not have existed and the Jews would not have identified the Gentiles with animals that they loved. The woman's response to Jesus indicates cultural difference in attitudes toward dogs. In any case, she is unexpectedly defending the right of her people.

Witherington is uncertain that the Jews in this period had domesticated dogs, although he finds examples of the Jews playing with puppies.[39] Francis Dufton has drawn our attention to the different cultural backgrounds of the Jews and the Gentiles:

> The Jews were not pet-lovers. To them dogs were the dirty, unpleasant and savage animals which roamed the streets in packs, scavenging for food.[40]

If this is the case, it would have been quite natural for the Jews to use the word to abuse Gentiles, infidels, and, later, Christians. Dufton even

39. Witherington, *Women in the Ministry of Jesus,* 63, 70. See also Hermann L. Strack and Paul Billerbeck, *Kommentar zum Neuen Testament aus Talmud und Midrasch* (München: C.H. Beck'sche Verlagbuch handlung, 1956), vol. 2, 726.

40. Francis Dufton, "The Syrophoenician Woman and Her Dogs," *Expository Times* 100 (Aug. 1989), 417.

adds that "the word was appropriate not only because these people were despised, but also because they were outside the house of Israel."[41]

On the other hand, the woman is talking about dogs *inside*. If the Gentiles have a special fondness for dogs, children would enjoy giving them tidbits from their tables. Thus we can also understand why Jesus uses "throw," which refers to bread for the dogs running outside. The Jews need to "throw" the bread from the window if they wish to feed dogs.

It is clever of the woman to affirm Jesus' saying at first[42] and then make full use of it to strike right back. She is intent on opening up the impasse she is facing. All we know about her daughter is that she has an unclean spirit and is very sick. In a society in which women are men's property from birth to death and are valued by giving birth to boys, girls are often regarded as a troublesome burden to their families until they can be safely married off to a suitable husband.[43] To accomplish this, fathers have to protect their virginity and to prepare a large dowry. But this daughter cannot count on following this process since she is sick and unclean, secluded and ostracized. Apparently she has been left with her mother, or the woman has been left with her daughter. In any case, it is the mother who has to face adverse circumstances and carve a way out. The woman who expected to be invisible becomes visible and acts; suppressing any feelings of fear and hesitation that she might have, she knows they have little to lose and they must gain life.

Though many scholars, including women scholars, admire her wit or uppityness, I do not think these qualities are the issue here. Rather, a woman who is oppressed and held to be worthless, living in such a patriarchal society and caring for her suffering daughter, is driven into an impossible situation and cannot find any other solution than to forget tradition, neglect social custom, and rush ahead recklessly to Jesus. She can no longer turn back. She risks everything on Jesus. This is her last resort. If she should be admired for anything, it is for her self-commitment in trust.

INTERACTION BETWEEN THE WOMAN AND JESUS

We are now ready to deal with the question of why Jesus' answer to the woman is extremely offensive. Metaphor or not, proverb or not, Jesus in fact compares her and her people to dogs and directly expresses his people's hatred toward them. Sharon H. Ringe correctly observes that there is no

---

41. Ibid., 417.

42. David Rhoades and Donald Michie, *Mark as Story: An Introduction to the Narrative of the Gospel* (Philadelphia: Fortress Press, 1982), 131.

43. Sharon H. Ringe, "A Gentile Woman's Story," in *Feminist Interpretation of the Bible*, ed. Letty M. Russell (Philadelphia: Westminster Press, 1985), 70. See also the chapter on Sexuality.

scene of domestic coziness here, with family and pets happily coexisting under one roof.[44]

Jesus, rejecting her plea point-blank, elbows her aside and tries to shake her off. "Allow" at least indicates that Jesus is personally facing her. As Ringe says, he might "be tired" or expressing "the racism and sexism that characterized his society."[45] We cannot tell why he answers so bluntly, but we do know that the Gentile woman hangs on tenaciously and refuses to be shaken off.

Mark places the story after the long debate with Jesus' opponents and the long didactic conversation with his disciples. Jesus may wish to be left alone for meditation. He may be filled with sorrow and exasperation because he has to face the reality that the heart of the gospel has not reached his people. Why would he accept a Gentile woman when he is so concerned about his compatriots? Or he might be wondering how this Gentile woman could understand and accept him while his own circle is so obtuse. In the latter case, then, he paradoxically affirms her. And furthermore, the phrase "Allow the children to be fed *first*" could mean that Jesus has in fact been open to the Gentiles. He could be taking out his feelings on this Gentile woman, using harsh words not because of her but because of his compatriots. Seen the other way around, Jesus could be attacking the lack of understanding and faith of his fellow Jews.

Jesus said to her, "For saying that, you may go. The demon has left your daughter" (v. 29). His attitude seems to have changed from rejection to affirmation. She has made it clear to Jesus that Jesus should become Jesus and challenged him to cross another "holy" barrier between Jews and Gentiles: the racial barrier. As a Jew, Jesus is embedded in the social and cultural circumstances that may have made him hesitate to cross the border. In this context, she frees Jesus to be fully himself. Jesus, "the boundary-breaker," may not have needed the encounter with her to cross the racial barrier, but certainly it is the woman that has created the opportunity for him to cross it and step over to her side. She has set the stage for him to act out his mission. She has enabled Jesus to see the situation in a different way and freed him to act in a way apparently blocked to him before.[46] Thus, the barrier between the Jews and Gentiles has been opened.[47]

Scholars have made a variety of comments about this woman. (1) The intelligent retort of her argument prevails over that of Jesus. She "wins" the contest.[48] (2) Her bold, assertive faith wins Jesus' favor and he grants her request.[49] This is woman's wit and persistence.[50] (3) Jesus interprets

---

44. Ibid., 69.
45. Ibid., 71.
46. Ibid., 71.
47. Belo, *A Materialist Reading of the Gospel of Mark,* 145.
48. E. Schüssler Fiorenza, *In Memory of Her,* 137.
49. Burkill, "The Historical Development," 91.
50. Taylor, *The Gospel According to St. Mark,* 351.

her persistence as "faith" and tells her it has been effective.[51] (4) Her verbal riposte gives the twist to this story.[52] (5) Jesus endorses the woman's indomitable spirit.[53]

These are not appropriate when we read the story from the viewpoint of interactional relationship without which this story cannot be understood. Her intuition about who Jesus should be and Jesus' sensitivity to the marginalized are drawn into one vortex and create a mutual transformation.

Thus Jesus, crossing the boundary, allows himself to be "defiled" and to become least in order to break through the exclusively group-oriented faith of his fellow Jews and redefine the community of faith in its radically new sense. The woman, along with her daughter, has been resurrected from death. The event clearly sets forth who Jesus is to be as the life-giving Christ. Jesus is motivated to act, inviting the Gentile, the socially outcast, the materially poor, the sick, the oppressed, and the rejected into God's community, which has been occupied by the privileged people protected by their purity laws.

PARALLELS WITH JAPAN

I would like to point out some parallels between first-century Palestine and Japan on the issue of ethnic exclusivism and human rights claims.

The Israelites kept their ethnic identity and national integrity through holding to the laws and cultic traditions. It was very important, especially for men, to keep their family lineages pure. So they excluded foreigners from their ethnic borders in order to retain their purity of blood. Given their history, it might have been inevitable for them to live this way; geographically they were defenseless against foreign invasions and were invaded by one foreign power after another. Thus it also seems natural for Jesus as a Jew to defend his people and not to want to dilute their ethnic integrity.

Japan's Ethnic Exclusivism

Japan as a country is also known for its ethnic exclusivism, though the causes are different from those affecting the Israelites. Geographically the land of Japan, consisting of four main islands surrounded by almost four thousand small islands, is separated from any other country by the oceans. Even the nearest country, Korea, is at least ninety-three miles across the Japan Sea, which is very rough with storms and seasonal typhoons. Because of these geographical advantages, Japan has never been exposed to the

51. Belo, *A Materialist Reading of the Gospel of Mark,* 145.
52. Myers, *Binding the Strong Man,* 204.
53. Rachel Conrad Wahlberg, *Jesus According to a Woman* (New York: Paulist Press, 1986), 16.

threat of being conquered by other countries. In addition, the country is favored by mild climate.

Ethnically, there has been a myth, which is actually an illusion, that the Japanese people are a homogeneous race. This myth has given rise to the belief that it is important to maintain the purity of Japanese blood. It has also cultivated a spirit of homogeneous "harmony" that functions only centripetally and goes hand-in-hand with the characteristics of the culture of shame: group-orientedness, dyadic personality, and gender-role difference. The result has been difficulty in accepting and respecting other people as they are, and in the colonized people and aborigines being deprived of their human rights. Ethnic homogeneity has been identified with superiority, connected with the religious concept of purity, and used by the authorities to exploit other peoples.

The "Koreans Living in Japan"

The racial exclusivism of the Japanese has persecuted the seven hundred thousand "Koreans living in Japan"—Ainus, Okinawans, and the outcast village people—as "inside others."[54] These people have been discriminated against and deprived of their right to live with their distinct cultures. They have been dealt with as if they were objects and treated as if they never existed. Ainus and Okinawans are aborigines who have been victimized throughout the course of history as a minority. "Koreans living in Japan" and "Chinese living in Japan" have a different history. They are the victims of the colonial invasions carried out by the Japanese military government between 1910 and 1945. They are those who were forced to leave their home countries and come to Japan as a cheap labor force, and their children who were born during and after the Second World War. During the war, it was claimed that they were all Japanese, and they were thus made to participate in the war in many degrading ways, one of the worst being the case of young girls who were taken to the battlefields to comfort Japanese soldiers.

These things were all done by the Japanese military government under the name of imperial commands. All kinds of exploitation of human rights were thus carried out by the divine will of the emperor. The power of this word, when directly connected with the divine power, wielded dictatorship. With the defeat of Japan, the Koreans, the Chinese, and all people in colonized Asian countries who had been claimed to be Japanese were liberated from the dictatorship of the Japanese military government. In 1910, only 780 Koreans lived in Japan, but in 1945 the Korean residents swelled to between 2,400,000 and 2,600,000. (So far about 300,000 Koreans have chosen to be naturalized as Japanese citizens.) Many Koreans and Chinese

54. Sanjung Kan, "Japanese Orientalism—Distortion Lurked in Internationalization of Japan," *Sekai* (Dec. 1988), 133.

who were in Japan at the end of the war returned to their home countries, while many others remained in Japan because of the unsettled circumstances and for economic reasons. The new Japanese government unilaterally deprived these people of their Japanese citizenship. In addition, a last imperial edict was issued just a day before the new Constitution came into force. This edict has bound all the remaining Koreans and Chinese until today, drastically changing their destiny. Actually it took the form of an immigration control act, but it apparently aimed at maintaining public order by exercising strict control over the remaining Koreans, the number of whom reached more than 700,000. They were classified as "inside others" without citizenship, voting rights, or social security.[55]

At present there are about 687,000 Koreans and 68,000 Chinese living in Japan, 90 percent of whom belong to the second or later generations without speaking Korean and knowing traditional Korean life. Since they speak, think, and behave just like Japanese, it is hard to tell from their appearance whether or not any given individual is a Korean living in Japan.

Despite this fact, under the Alien Registration Law they have been required as foreigners to carry their registration cards with their fingerprints. Criminals are the only ones required by Japanese law to be fingerprinted. Therefore when "Koreans living in Japan" become sixteen years old and get their fingers printed on the registration cards they must always carry, they are made to feel like criminals. There have been many grassroots movements against the fingerprinting policy, among both foreigners and Japanese.[56]

Worst of all, exclusivism based on the myth of a single-race nation with pure blood had fermented among the Japanese people an idea that the Koreans represented an undeveloped, retrogressive, stagnant, and uncivilized society.[57] Thus they have been subjugated, dehumanized, and despised in every imaginable way. We Japanese people have failed to ask ourselves how we should relate to those who have a different and distinctive culture. Besides the poor legal supports, these people have had to suffer social discrimination as well as degrading treatment by Japanese citizens. It is a tragedy for both sides to live with such prejudice.

Like the people in the outcast villages, they had to conceal their identity by using Japanese names for a long time.[58] Recently more Koreans have dared to claim their identities as Koreans, but even in primary schools, children need a good deal of courage to claim their Korean names. Children, despised by their classmates, feel ashamed of themselves and afraid

55. Eunja Lee, "Together with Our Neighbors," *Kyokai Hujin Rengo Tayori* 50 (May 26, 1992), 1-3.

56. The fingerprinting was abolished in 1993, but they are still asked to register their family names.

57. Kan, "Japanese Orientalism," 137.

58. Aiko Utumi, "To Live with Asian People," *Laborers from Asian Countries,* ed. Aiko Utumi and Yayori Matui (Tokyo: Akasi Shoten, 1988), 50-56.

of being assaulted, isolated, and made "inside others."

The deep-rooted Japanese prejudice has caused most Koreans to hide themselves as if they were "guilty." Koreans themselves tend to accept negative self-images created without foundation. From an early age they have had it drummed into them that they are inferior humans. Eunja Lee claims that Koreans' distorted self-esteem must be recovered and reclaimed.[59] Although they speak, think, and behave like Japanese, the decisive difference lies in their experiences of all kinds of oppression and discrimination. Originally they did not come to Japan of their own free will but were forced to be Japanese, mercilessly exploited, and in the end granted no legal rights or support. Naturalization was also very difficult. Of course, it was natural for the Koreans to claim to be Korean, but they were also deprived of being able to identify themselves with their home country Korea after having lived in Japan for so many years.[60]

Where To Go from Here

Feminist theologians of Korea and Japan started an Annual Study Forum in 1988. Since the second Forum, Korean women living in Japan have also taken part in the group. Listening to stories shared by Korean women who have suffered from the hatred felt toward the Japanese that was long harbored deep in their hearts, and hearing stories shared by "Korean women living in Japan" who have suffered from discrimination and exploitation, we Japanese women also suffer from the guilt of what the Japanese have done. Through sharing our pain and extending our apologies, the relations of hatred have turned into relations of forgiveness and reconciliation. From there, we began anew to reconstruct the parts of the history of exploitation that had been kept secret, so that we may do justice to those who have been victimized and forgotten. Through this process, we have been challenged to overcome the boundaries between us and built a new community of faith. "Community" designates our living together in diversity. Here we have experienced a healing of our pain and guilt. A Korean woman theologian living in Japan claims, "For Koreans living in Japan it is most important and urgent to be liberated from their distorted, negative self-images. For that purpose, we need to learn how to love ourselves in order that we may renew our alienated selves. In other words, asking who we are, we need to regain affirmative self-respect in ourselves. This identity construction process is not an easy one. It demands much struggle inside and outside of oneself."[61]

Only when we Japanese learn the truth about what has happened to the colonized and the victimized people in history, and how deeply ethnic exclu-

---

59. Lee, "Together with Our Neighbors," 1-3.
60. Ibid.
61. Ibid., 1.

sivism based on the religious concept of purity of blood has affected our mentality, can we attain a basis for regaining a right relationship with our neighbors of different cultures. On the basis of affirming and accepting each other as neighbors created in the image of God, we will be in the circle of Jesus' community of faith. Our struggle toward this goal has just started, and we realize that it will take a long time to overcome prejudice. Yet we are already walking in solidarity and in diversity toward building one true church. As Jesus dared to break down barriers by responding to the challenge by the Syrophoenician woman, churches in Japan are challenged to participate in breaking down barriers built around people's hearts.

4

THE POOR WIDOW

(12:41-44)

In the Gospel of Mark, there are two women who are usually forgotten but who in fact play important roles. Both of them must be faithful Jewish women, and seemingly have had no direct contact or personal relationship with Jesus. This latter fact may be the reason why little attention has been paid to them.

One of these women is the servant-girl of the high priest, who in the courtyard observes that Peter has been with the Nazarene, Jesus. The other woman, who will concern us here, is the poor widow who offers her whole living to the temple.

Just before the passion narrative, Jesus enters Jerusalem (11:11), where he finally clashes with Jewish as well as Roman political power (11:27-12:17) and the Jewish religious authorities (12:18-34). This is followed by the eschatological discourse (13:3-37).

The story of the poor widow with her two coins is located at the end of Jesus' confrontation with the authorities in Jerusalem. He begins by rejecting Davidic messianism (12:35-37) and ends with his harsh attack on the political economy of the temple (12:38-44). A sharp contrast between "rich" scribes and "poor" widows (12:40) leads into the final episode of the poor widow (12:41-44), which tells how the temple-centered spirituality has become the facade for exploitation.

Mark's framework of reference is Jesus' harsh opposition to the temple-state. The narrative keeps reminding us of the importance of Jesus' final confrontation with all sectors of the ruling class, including the chief priests, elders, scribes (11:18, 27; 12:12, 28), and even the Sadducees (12:18). These authorities, who usually are engaged in strife with one another, now conspire to oppose Jesus, for Jesus is a threat to their power.

THE SOCIAL BACKGROUND

In order to locate widows in the social context of patriarchy in first-century Palestine, we need to refer to the discourse on divorce in Mark

10:2-12. Elisabeth Schüssler Fiorenza regards this discourse and the question on the resurrection (12:18-27) as "the pre-Markan controversy stories in which Jesus challenges patriarchal marriage structures."[1] As we have already seen, it is normally acceptable for husbands to dismiss their wives at will, something possible only in the androcentric mindset of a patriarchally organized society: as Schüssler Fiorenza says, "divorce is necessary because of the males' "hardness of heart,"[2] that is, "because of men's patriarchal mind-set and reality." Divorce is a completely one-sided system; it deprives wives of being equal partners with their husbands and reduces them to being their husbands' commodities.

The question on the resurrection, involving the woman with seven husbands (12:18-27), is sometimes used as evidence of the protection of widows through the social institution of Levirate marriage (Deut. 25:5-10). But this system serves above all the interest of the Sadducees, who belong to the upper class and are rich landowners, in keeping their family lines safe so that they may secure their property, wealth, and inheritance as their own. The system also serves the patriarchal structure of the house in which the family line is passed on through the male. Here Mark deals with "the crude materialism of the powerful, who are concerned solely with class succession."[3]

The Old Testament usually depicts widows as poor and suffering much hardship. The anonymous widow in 2 Kings 4:1-7 is a typical representative Israelite widow. She has nothing in the house but a cruse of oil and the debt left by her husband and for which the creditors claim her two sons. Widows are associated with orphans (Isa. 1:23; Job 22:9; 24:3), the poor (Isa. 10:2; Zech. 7:10), the day-laborer (Mal. 3:5), and aliens (Exod. 22:22; Deut. 10:18; 24:7). They are regularly the objects of injustice (Isa. 10:2; Ezek. 22:7; Job 24:3). They are not to marry the high priest (Lev. 21:14) or even ordinary priests unless they are the widows of priests (Ezek. 44:22). They are not ensured of their rights (Isa. 1:23). Pointing out that the Hebrew word for "widow" closely resembles the word for "unable to speak," Bonnie Bowman Thurston notes that the widows are, symbolically at least, those without legal power of speech in the Hebrew tradition. Therefore warnings against injustice done to widows are frequent (Exod. 22:22; Deut. 24:17; 27:19; Jer. 22:3; Zech. 7:10). The Deuteronomic admonitions to treat widows benevolently are further evidence that it is difficult for them to secure their rights and that they are often deprived of them. The fact that Isaiah found it necessary to speak up for widows' rights (1:18) is revealing.[4]

The cause of the perilous legal and social status of widows is found in the structure of the patriarchal society in which men esteem them lowly,

1. E. Schüssler Fiorenza, *In Memory of Her,* 143.
2. Ibid., 143.
3. Myers, *Binding the Strong Man,* 316.
4. Gustav Sthählin, "χηρα," *TDNT* 9:440. Bonnie Bowman Thurston, *The Widows: A Women's Ministry in the Early Church* (Minneapolis: Fortress Press, 1989), 12-15.

throw them away as worthless, and despise them as useless: note such expressions as the "shame of widowhood" (Isa. 54:4) and "I shall not sit as a widow, neither shall I become childless" (Isa. 47:8).

In Mark's Gospel, the discourse on divorce and the question on the resurrection assume both women to be the property of men, houses, or families with important names. This implies that to be a widow means to be liberated from the patriarchal bond of marriage and Levirate marriage. It seems at first glance that a widow is at least free from being treated as a man's property, but it does not mean that she can pursue an independent way of life as we would think of it today. She may suffer from the poverty caused by the patriarchal structure of society and the shame caused by barrenness in patriarchal marriage. Thus one misfortune follows close on the heels of another. As is generally said, in patriarchal societies the worst and most tragic thing for a woman is to become a widow. When she is left alone because of her husband's death and still has to remain in her husband's family, she may be completely dehumanized and dealt with as nothing more than labor power for the family. Thus many widows prefer death at the burial of their husbands to living without them.[5]

JESUS' REPROACH TO THE SCRIBES (12:40)

J. Duncan M. Derrett, surveying the exegetical history on the passage, records a few interpretations of the passage, "Beware of the scribes ... They devour widows' houses and for the sake of appearance say long prayers."

Roughly speaking, there are two kinds of interpretations:

1. There are scribes who take large sums from credulous old widows as a reward for the prolonged prayer that they profess to make on their behalf.

2. Religious leaders make undue use of their influence over wealthy widows in the cause of religious institutions, through ostentatious and hypocritical exhibitions of piety.[6]

In the first interpretation, scribes' prayers seem to be serious while in the second, their hypocrisy is obvious. In both interpretations, scribes look down upon widows.

Derrett himself suggests that "for the sake of appearance" does not mean "excuse," or "pretext," and that the motive for their long prayers is to "eat up" the widow's estate. He takes the word in the meaning of "a true reason or occasion."[7] Therefore he rejects the notion that they make

5. Sthählin, "$\chi\eta\rho\alpha$," *TDNT*, vol. 9, 441-42. In Japan, a most common word signifying widows means "a woman who has not yet died." Originally the word implied that a wife, once her husband died, has lost any meaning for her life and only waits for her death. Widows might have thought they should have died along with their husbands.

6. J. Duncan M. Derrett, " 'Eating up the Houses of Widows': Jesus' Comment on Lawyers?" *Novum Testamentum* 14 (1972), 1-2.

7. Ibid., 7.

long prayers in order to persuade widows to make gifts to them. His translation reads: "those that 'eat away' the estates of widows, and, with such
an end in view, indulge in lengthy prayers."[8] He focuses on the abuse of
the Jewish inheritance law, because the law provides that the estate can be
administered by a trustee. Of course the scribes' public reputation for piety
is helpful.

Harry Fleddermann, on the other hand, sees something more specific
than the general accusation of exploitation.[9] From the two parts of v. 40
(1) who devour widows' houses and (2) for a pretense make long prayers,
he concludes, "Not only do the scribes drain the widows' resources but they
do this on the religious pretext of saying long prayers."[10]

Economic exploitation itself is bad enough, but if greed is satisfied
deceitfully in the name of religious piety, the result is more offensive. In
addition to the fact that widows' properties are all taken away, their faithfulness is also exploited, and they may even not be conscious of the deceit.
Blind to what is happening, they are "devoured" socially, economically, and
spiritually. It is more plausible that this is why Jesus accused the scribes.

We notice that: (1) since entering Jerusalem (11:12), Jesus often goes
into the temple (three times); (2) Mark often records Jesus' references to
the destruction of the temple (13:2; 14:58; 15:29-30; 15:38); (3) Jesus starts
his anti-temple action by expelling the buyers and sellers from the temple
(11:15-16). For Jesus the temple should "be called a house of prayer for
all the nations," but "you have made it a den of robbers" (11:17). "You"
indicates those who are buying and selling, and the activity of "the buying
and selling" itself is called robbery. They sell and buy in order to provide
the offerings and sacrifices necessary for the temple cult. The cult has
replaced prayer as the center of their faith, the logic being that the greater
your offering, the greater the blessings you receive. Thus someone thinking
themselves to be seriously in need of blessings might well jeopardize themselves economically. Conversely, the more destitute one becomes, the more
one feels impelled to invoke God's blessings through sacrifice. Widows are
typical victims of the temple-centered religion.

It may seem that Jesus' criticism of temple-centered religion ends with
the warning on the scribes (12:38-40). But Mark adds the story of a poor
widow (12:41-44), although this is not explicitly a criticism of temple-wor-
ship. References to widows occur only twice in Mark (12:40, 41-44), and
not at all in other sources of the synoptic tradition, except for the parallel
story in Luke (21:1-4) and Luke's special materials (2:36-38; 7:11-17; 4:25f;
18:2-5).

8. Ibid., 8.
9. Harry Fleddermann, "A Warning about the Scribes (Mark 12:37b-40)," *The Catholic Biblical Quarterly* 44 (1982), 61.
10. Ibid., 65.

THE POOR WIDOW

The story of the poor widow who put two coins, or lepta, into the treasury is located at the end of Jesus' harsh criticism of and teachings in the temple (11:11-12:44). Here again Jesus talks to his disciples.

Located at the beginning of the introduction of the passion narrative, the story must be read in the atmosphere of the increasing tension between Jesus and his opponents. We cannot simply see the episode as "a beautiful story" or as "a beautiful act in the desert of official devotion," as commentaries commonly say,[11] nor, given its context, as merely showing a "genuine piety" either.[12] The story is also located just before Jesus' eschatological warnings (13:1-37), which predict that the temple — the political and social symbol of the religious state — will be completely thrown down ("Not one stone will be left here upon another" [13:2]). If we take into account the fact that at the time Mark wrote his Gospel the gorgeous temple had been threatened or recently destroyed by the Herodians and Romans, Mark's rhetorical intention gives a stronger impact to Jesus' words (13:1-2).

According to Ched Myers and Addison G. Wright, the story has been given little attention or rather mishandled as a quaint vignette.[13] Their analyses are quite original, compared with many by other scholars that seem to miss the point. However, neither of these authors is on the side of the widow.

The Story

"Jesus sat down opposite the treasury, and watched the crowd putting money into the treasury" (v. 41). Thus he intentionally takes a position from which he can see clearly what is happening. Together with the similar sentence in 13:3 ("When he was sitting on the Mount of Olives opposite the temple"), this position suggests his intense concentration on the whole issue.

Some commentators say that Jesus must have been "facing thirteen trumpet shaped chests placed round the walls of the Court of Women in which the people threw their offerings."[14] Or according to Billerbeck (ii, 37-45), the reference is to "the treasury itself, where donors have to declare

---

11. Schweizer, *Das Evangelium nach Markus,* 358. Herman C. Waetjen, *A Reordering of Power: A Socio-Political Reading of Mark's Gospel* (Minneapolis: Fortress Press, 1989), 256.

12. Myers, *Binding the Strong Man,* 320.

13. Addison G. Wright, S.S., "The Widow's Mites: Praise or Lament? — A Matter of Context," *The Catholic Biblical Quarterly* 44 (1982), 256. Myers, *Binding the Strong Man,* 321.

14. Taylor, *The Gospel According to St. Mark,* 496.

the amount of their gift and the purpose for which it was intended to the priest in charge, everything being visible and audible to the onlooker through the open door."[15] If Billerbeck is right, which seems to me more probable, then Mark's description takes on more meaning. If the amount of one's offering is declared in public, this is surely a means of pressuring a donor to give more than he or she can afford. These are shrewd tactics. Many rich persons gave much (from their abundance), and one poor widow gave two coins, or lepta. How shameful she would feel if the amount of her offering was loudly announced to be heard by all.

"Lepton" is a term used in late Greek for the smallest coin in circulation, and Mark explains that the two lepta equals one kodranth, which is Roman coinage. Kodranth is a transliteration of the Latin *quadrans*.[16]

At the conclusion of the story Jesus addresses his disciples. The phrase "Truly I tell you" indicates that he is about to give an important teaching.[17] Again he speaks in strongly contrasting terms: "This poor widow has put in more than all those who are contributing to the treasury. For all of them contributed out of their abundance; but she out of her poverty has put in everything she had, all she had to live on" (v. 44). Myers puts the verse as follows: "They all gave from their affluence. She in her destitution gave everything she had—her whole life."[18]

There is one question we need to ask. That is, for what is she offering her whole life? What is motivating her to this particular action?

Offering in the Old Testament

The Israelites had long kept the tradition of helping the needy in the nation (Deut. 14:28-29; 15:4, 11). Though they never institutionalized a social security system as such, they redistributed a part of the tithe to the needy and helped them in various practical ways. The temple acted as the center for storing the tithe products and distributing them to ensure enough for everyone in Israel. However, this temple-based economy of distribution was obviously corrupt and failed to live up to its purpose. The products, money or property seemed to accumulate only in the hands of the ruling class. Under the pressure of Roman state power, the already privileged ruling class made use of their privilege and exploited the society as they wanted.[19]

In addition, the voluntary or freewill offering custom had long been kept by the Israelites (Exod. 35:29; 36:3; Lev. 7:16; Num. 15:3; Deut. 12:17; 16:10;

15. Strack and Billerbeck, *Kommentar zum Neuen Testament aus Talmud und Midrash,* vol. 2, 37-45.

16. Schweizer, *Das Evangelium nach Markus,* 497.

17. Taylor, *The Gospel According to St. Mark,* 497. Myers, *Binding the Strong Man,* 321.

18. Myers, *Binding the Strong Man,* 321.

19. Ibid., 48-50, 432-34, 442f. Halvor Moxnes, *The Economy of the Kingdom* (Philadelphia: Fortress, 1988), 170.

31:14; 35:8; Ezek. 46:12, etc.). The offerings to the temple treasury were meant for redistribution among the poor.[20] Although there was no statutory regulation controlling it, it is easy to imagine that everyday offerings that were not legally required may have been encouraged by the authorities in order to get as much money as possible from the poor.

The Focus of the Story

Survey of Exegesis

Wright classifies exegetical comments found in the commentary literature into five categories:[21]

1) The *true measure of gifts* is the point of Jesus' commendation. How much remains behind, the percentage of one's means or the degree of self-denial are most important in this concern (used by nineteen exegetes).

2) The *spirit* in which the gift is given does matter. Self-offering, self-forgetfulness, unquestioning surrender, total commitment, loyalty and devotion to God's call, gratitude, generosity, humility and unobtrusiveness, trust in God to provide for one's needs, and detachment from possessions are the central themes (used by forty exegetes).

3) The true gift is to *give everything* one has (one exegete).

4) Alms and other pious gifts should *correspond with one's means* (one exegete).

5) The *duty of almsgiving* is to be indicated (one exegete).

Among interpretations written after Wright's article, Waetjen says that "they [the poor—as represented by the widow] demonstrate in deed that they love God out of their whole heart, soul, mind and strength, even, like the widow, to the extent of giving all they have."[22] So I classify his exegesis into category 3. In contrast, Fernando Belo, who emphasizes the economy of the Christian circle in which people share all the means of life, speaks of "the center of the Jewish symbolic space that will be replaced by the practice of giving what one has."[23] He comes under category 5. Luke T. Johnson sees the "piety of the poor."[24] He stands in category 2.

Wright says, "Presumably the point of the story is to be found in Jesus' saying."[25] So all the categories above have emerged as the result of concentrating on Jesus' saying and its lesson, while ignoring the situation of the poor widow, the relationship of Jesus to the widow, and the visible but unspoken relationship of the widow to God. This particular woman has

20. Moxnes, *Economy of the Kingdom,* 71-73.
21. Wright, "The Widow's Mites," 259.
22. Waetjen, *A Reordering of Power,* 196.
23. Belo, *A Materialist Reading of the Gospel of Mark,* 195.
24. Luke T. Johnson, *Sharing Possessions: Mandate and Symbol of Faith* (Philadelphia: Fortress, 1981), 174.
25. Wright, "The Widow's Mites," 258.

faded away and just Jesus' saying is taken as giving a universal teaching: the value of the gifts of the poor, a revelatory announcement that the smallest gift of the poor has value before God, whereas human beings judge by quantity.[26] Wright evaluates only category 1 and claims that other categories are not valid. If we thus pursue category 1 we are left with a teaching on comforting the poor so that they should feel dignity in their small gifts. But for this woman, there is little meaning in such comfort and encouragement or in the comparison with others.

If the teaching is generalized as an observation on life, then we can easily find parallel teachings in Jewish tradition, Rabbinic literature, Indian and Buddhist literature, and Greek literature.

Although Wright assumes that Jesus at this time is not at all interested in the economic or social aspect of the temple-state and -religion, it is the case that Mark places Jesus' teaching in this particular context.

Bultmann's Apothegms

It may be plausible to say that the saying-centered interpretations are influenced by the idea of Bultmann's apothegms. Bultmann explains that the stories are added later as secondary frames around Jesus' sayings. In many stories in the Gospel this is right. The exegetes recorded above seem influenced by his theory and separate the saying from the context. But Bultmann also states that there are some instances in which the sayings and the stories inseparably go together from the beginning and are so transmitted.[27]

According to Bultmann, in Mark 12:41-44 the saying and the scene express the point together, and therefore the saying is intelligible only in relation to the situation.[28] But he does not take the interpretation further. And Sasagu Arai, even though he, too, admits that this story and the saying are inseparable, says that the story pictures an "ideal scene" for the paradigm of almsgiving.[29] His interpretation, which may be classified as belonging to category 2, appears unsatisfactory. I will read the story according to Bultmann's classification, but from my feminist interactional perspective.

The Context of the Story

Wright also tries to reread the story in the context of the Gospel of Mark. Finding the widow's action painful, he refers to Jesus' Corban statement (Mark 7:11-12), the point of which is, according to him, that "human needs take precedence over religious values when they conflict." From that point of view he questions whether Jesus would be enthusiastic over the

26. Ibid., 159.
27. Arai, *Iesu Kirisuto*, 174.
28. Bultmann, *History of the Synoptic Tradition*, 32f., 56.
29. Arai, *Iesu Kirisuto*, 218.

widow's contribution if it were done in negligence of her personal needs.
If so, Jesus contradicts himself.[30] So we may conclude, from Wright's point
of view, that Jesus is not praising the behavior of the widow. We may just
add here that the interpretations classified into category 2 express the opposite position and praise her spirituality. Even then, "the tragedy of her
destitute situation remains."[31] To support this view, if we read 11:15-18
and 13:1-2, we know that Jesus clearly attacks the structure and system of
the temple-religion and state altogether.

Then Wright, unlike most of the other commentators, proceeds to the
immediate context of the story. As we have already seen, Jesus' warning
about scribes who devour widows' houses is closely connected with the
story. The widow was "accomplishing the very thing that the scribes were
accused of doing." Therefore Jesus could never be pleased with what he
was seeing here. Thus Wright concludes:

> The story does not provide a pious contrast to the conduct of the
> scribes in the preceding section (as is the customary view); rather it
> provides a further illustration of the ills of official devotion. Jesus'
> saying is not a penetrating insight on the measuring of gifts; it is a
> lament. . . . She had been taught and encouraged by religious leaders
> to donate as she does, and Jesus condemns the value system that
> motivates her action, and he condemns the people who conditioned
> her to do it.[32]

Jesus' condemnation of the value system and the people who support it
and gain from it is a criticism of the religion that encourages the people to
give their whole living to religious institutions. Jesus' intensely challenging
attitude toward power can rightly be termed "indignation."

Halvor Moxnes says in his exegesis on the Gospel of Luke:

> The authority that Jesus challenges in these narratives [Luke 19:45-
> 46; 20:20-26; 21:1-4] is the power to control the collection and redis-
> tribution of resources belonging to the Jewish people.[33]

And Myers supports Wright's view, though he seems to put emphasis on
the exploitation by the scribal class as well as by the temple.[34]

A Feminist Perspective

Elisabeth Schüssler Fiorenza introduces this widow as typical of the
destitute poor who are one of the three distinct groups in Jesus' community

30. Wright, "The Widow's Mites," 261.
31. Fleddermann, "A Warning about the Scribes," 67.
32. Wright, "The Widow's Mites," 262.
33. Moxnes, *Economy of the Kingdom,* 70.
34. Myers, *Binding the Strong Man,* 322.

of faith. The story of the widow explains how dire the poverty of women is.[35] She does not go any further into this story. In other places, she insists that poverty and patriarchal structures are two sides of the same coin, in contrast to Luise Schottroff's thinking that liberation from patriarchal structures was not of primary interest to the Palestinian Jesus movement.[36] For Schottroff, equal discipleship realized in the common impoverished situation and supported by the hope for the Kingdom of God was decisive.[37] So Schüssler Fiorenza concludes that "therefore the common interpretation and 'feminist-historical' interpretation needed to be clarified further."[38] For Schüssler Fiorenza, economic exploitation and patriarchal oppression cannot be two different socio-economic systems. She sees widows and orphans as the prime paradigms of the poor and exploited, especially the widows who lost "male agencies that might have enabled them to share in the wealth of the patriarchal system."[39]

CONCLUSION

Following the method of Elisabeth Schüssler Fiorenza's feminist-historical and rhetorical interpretation I press my interpretation beyond the "indignation" of Jesus.

If we now interpret the entire story as Jesus' expression of indignation against the exploiting structure of power, for which purpose Jesus uses the poor widow as an example, the widow is simply objectified by him. And that may explain why Jesus refers to a woman whom he observes but with whom he apparently never interacts.

I have already explained how women are subjugated and oppressed in the passages of 10:1-12 and 12:18-27 and I have also noted Jesus' egalitarian attitude toward marraige as shown by his responses to the issues. And I have also noted his harsh criticism of scribes who devour widows' houses. From this evidence, it is difficult to conclude that Jesus simply makes use of the woman as an object for his teaching.

Conversely, from his saying, "Truly, I tell you, this poor widow has put in more than all those who are contributing to the treasury," one may suppose that Jesus is praising her behavior. Since it is customary for the people in first-century Judaism to offer to the treasury, it may be natural for the disciples to hear from Jesus that the more they give, the more praise they get. If we try to find any meaning in this interpretation, we should see Jesus' observation and comment on the widow as an ironical twist of rhetoric that overturns the usual value system.

35. E. Schüssler Fiorenza, *In Memory of Her,* 122.
36. Willy Schottroff and Wolfgang Stegemann, eds., *Frauen in der Bibel* (Munich: Chr. Kaiser, 1980), Japanese edition, 68. E. Schüssler Fiorenza, *In Memory of Her,* 140.
37. Schottroff, *Frauen in der Bibel,* 72.
38. E. Schüssler Fiorenza, *In Memory of Her,* 140.
39. Ibid., 141.

Jesus' criticism, then, is that the whole system is supported by those who are actually supposed to be supported by it. Therefore we must say that Jesus is not dealing with the issue of the quantity or the measure of true gifts; and of course the widow is not a model to be imitated. This interpretation is reinforced by his saying in 13:2 that the temple will be completely destroyed. He rejects the temple-religion itself; therefore there is no meaning in offering at all. So what irritates Jesus is the whole system of the hierarchically and patriarchally structured society.

I ask what influence if any, this woman has on Jesus. The story stands at the end of the series of discourses with the authorities of the temple-religion: the Pharisees, the Sadducees, the priests, the elders, and the scribes. And the story is located at the beginning of the final stage of his life, which is prefaced by the eschatological warnings (13:1-37), followed by the memorable story of the anointing woman (14:3-9).

From this context, Jesus, seeing her full devotion, may be challenged by the presence of the widow. In providing him with a model by silently bearing her own unjust situation—even neglecting her own needs—she may provoke him to make up his own mind to commit his whole life as she is devoting her whole life. She has spoken to him boldly, though she probably never knows Jesus is watching her.

Although Jesus expresses his indignation toward the whole system of temple-centered religion, he cannot do anything for the widow at the moment. Her presence may lead Jesus to accept his final collision with power which determines his fate. She inspires Jesus to be truly Jesus.

As supporting evidence, we may refer to Jesus' "Truly (Amen) I tell you" phrase, while Luke has "Truly (Aletho) I tell you." "Amen" phrases elsewhere in the Gospel of Mark are all used to refer to things in future time frames (3:28; 8:12; 9:1, 41; 10:15, 29; 11:23; 13:30; 14:9, 18, 25, 30). Only here does Jesus refer to a past action, but in doing so he could actually be pointing to his destiny in the near future. Only when we can feel Jesus' empathy with the widow's personal history as represented in this particular event can we accept the bitterness caused by the unfathomable distance between the woman and Jesus. Yet she is left alone.

She is left alone for sure, but Jesus, directly facing the treasury, watches her very carefully. His intense indignation cannot occur unless he stands on her side. Therefore we may infer that in Jesus' mind she is one of the first to be invited to the community of God. She is already a member of the community of faith, even though she does not know it. From her behavior, which can objectively be said to be meaningless, and from Jesus' reaction to it, we can only acknowledge the inclusive scope of the community of faith Jesus proclaims. For such a person as she who is victimized by the corrupt society in which she lives, Jesus confronts authority and endures pressure, hostility, and rejection. He also gives everything, his entire life.

Yet the widow is still left alone. We must ask what has led her to such behavior. First, she is the victim of the exploiting power of the society. She is taught and encouraged to offer until she loses her whole living. She is guided to seek her reward from God, although she is one of those who should be helped through the redistribution system of the Israelites. She is led into misguided piety by the deceitful piety of the institutional religion. Second, this deceitful piety has deprived her of her whole living until she feels that the only way of expressing her devotion to God is by offering everything even in her poverty. She lives in the blind faith that drives her to offer even her last two lepta. But, on the other hand, this is the only way she knows to call upon her God. She no longer cares about herself and her personal need. Therefore she pours out everything to God. For her it must now be God that acts.

The widow is just like Hagar in the wilderness calling for God's help (Genesis 21) and numerous women in the world who are oppressed by suffering and poverty with no means of alleviating their situations. There is no hope to get any help or support from the human side; therefore they put all their remaining energy into addressing God directly.

Why, if so, does Jesus only watch her?

Why does he not release her from the chains that bind her and pull her into a "we" relationship with him?

Who is Jesus for the widow, after all?

Mark may have not been interested in asking such questions, or he may have intentionally left these questions unanswered in order to hold them out as a challenge to the members of his faith community and to us. Mark may be asking: Who are the first to be included in the community of faith?

Jesus has not necessarily settled all the issues he has faced; therefore we see his indignation and probably his sorrow. Mark invites us to be implicated in Jesus' movement through identifying ourselves with the suffering and the exploited. Then it will be a matter of course for us to be involved in the political and social conflicts that may lead us to the "crucifixion." The widow's posture, pouring everything out to God from her side but being seemingly untouched by God's hand, will continue to trouble the community of faith with the question of whether her situation is just. She will keep throwing out the question until she is touched and involved in the circle of Jesus' movement. Until then, must she remain alone?

5

THE ANOINTING WOMAN

(14:3-9)

The story of the anointing woman has unique characteristics in each of the four gospels (Matt. 26:6-13; Luke 7:36-50; John 12:1-8), though each writer apparently makes use of an original tradition for his own theological purpose. Because each writer adapts and manipulates the original tradition to make it more applicable to his concerns and the issues that his community is facing, the variations found in the four gospel stories, if we could unravel the seemingly tangled threads, would illustrate the developmental history of the tradition. Comparative observations reveal certain characteristics of Mark, which, we expect, are affected by his male-oriented worldview.

FORM-CRITICAL OBSERVATIONS

Roughly speaking, the Markan and Matthean incidents are close to each other, but John and Luke are dissimilar from each other and from the Markan story. In all four stories, however, the basic event is the same: A woman anoints Jesus with perfumed ointment, people object, and Jesus defends her. This is the kernel of the story as all four writers report it. And except in Matthew, the event takes place at a meal in a house. In three of the stories (Mark, Matthew, and John) the event occurs in Bethany, while Luke only says "in the town" (probably in Galilee). And the woman is nameless, except in John, in which she is named Mary. It is a form-critical axiom that names are additions to stories. The unnamed objectors in Mark also become disciples in Matthew, the host Simon the Pharisee in Luke, and Judas in John.[1]

1. Robert Holst, "The One Anointing of Jesus: Another Application of the Form-Critical Method," *Journal of Biblical Literature* 95/3 (1976), 438. J.K. Elliot, "The Anointing of Jesus," *The Expository Times* 85 (1974), 105. Burton L. Mack and Vernon K. Robbins, *Patterns of Persuasion in the Gospels* (Sonoma, CA: Polebridge Press, 1988), 85.

The woman anoints Jesus' head in Mark and Matthew, but in Luke and John she anoints Jesus' feet. If the original tradition had reported that she anointed Jesus' feet, the tradition might not have been transmitted, because the anointing of feet was a common social practice in the first-century Mediterranean world. The peculiarity of the story must have been found in the anointing of Jesus' *head* and the anointing *by a woman.*

Bultmann classifies the Markan story as a biographical apothegm in his form-critical analysis of the literary forms in the Gospel. In a biographical apothegm, Jesus' saying generally comes at the end of the story to throw light on Jesus' personal character or a particular situation.[2] The main characteristic of biographical apophthegms is that the saying becomes clear only in relation to a particular situation.[3] Bultmann takes the point of the story to be Jesus' statement about the poor and "she did what she could" (7-8a), and considers the reference to Jesus' burial and the woman's memory to be a later explanatory addition (8b-9). The opening (3-7) is taken as a unitary composition about Jesus' life.[4]

Taylor also sees the story as almost a pronouncement story[5] and Tannehill calls it one of the pronouncement stories. According to Tannehill, "A pronouncement story is a brief narrative in which the climactic (and often final) element is a pronouncement which is presented as a particular person's response to something said or observed on a particular occasion of the past."[6]

MARK AS EDITOR

If we accept the anointing of Jesus' head by a woman as part of the historical kernel of the story, it can definitely be said that her behavior is a symbolic act of acknowledging a king's consecration (1 Sam. 10:1; 2 Sam. 2:4; 1 Kings 1:38-40; 19:15-16; 2 Kings 9:1-13; Ps. 133:2). The coronation story of the Messiah-king would have had political meaning.[7] If so, the story was probably connected with the story of Jesus' triumphal entry into Jerusalem, in which Jesus is hailed as the Messiah-king. It would then be a dangerous story.[8]

However, Mark seems to elaborate the story in a different way with his own purpose in mind. In writing his Gospel, Mark seems to be looking at other historical events concerning the women not being able to anoint Jesus'

2. Bultmann, *The History of the Synoptic Tradition,* 13, 36-37.

3. Ibid., 55-56.

4. Ibid., 36.

5. Taylor, *The Gospel According to St. Mark,* 529.

6. Robert C. Tannehill, "Introduction: The Pronouncement Story and Its Types," *Semeia* 20 (1981), 1.

7. J.K. Elliott, "The Anointing of Jesus," 105.

8. E. Schüssler Fiorenza, *In Memory of Her,* xiii.

body either at the burial (15:46-47) or at the tomb (16:1-6), which seems to motivate him to turn this story into a story of a prophetic anticipation of Jesus' burial. Elliot says that the Markan elaboration is to "remove the embarrassment felt by the early church at the neglected rites." But he may be more accurate when he suggests that the so-called "messianic secret" theme throughout Mark's Gospel leads him to avoid any overt messianic acts or words around Jesus.[9]

Jesus appreciates the woman's behavior in contrast to the objectors' worldly common sense. Thus, the earlier messianic anointing theme is diluted by Mark's twofold purpose.

Mark makes further use of the story by locating it in the passion story (14:1 — 15:47) and inserting it between the report about the chief priests' and scribes' anxiety to find a way to Jesus before the feast (14:1-2) and the solution that Judas offers to them (14:10). Because the story is fit into the midst of the treacherous plots against Jesus, the caring behavior of the woman is dramatically contrasted with the devious murder plot.[10]

Also, the story, sandwiched between the plot to arrest Jesus and the plot to betray him for money, serves to depoliticize the story of Jesus' passion. And Jesus is claimed to be the Messiah, but a Messiah who suffers and dies.[11]

In considering that Mark has placed the story within the context of the passion, we may assume that verses 8b and 9 have been added. And verses 6 and 7, called the saying of Jesus in the biographical apothegm, may also have been added to the core story at some stage to answer the objection raised by the people. If this is the case, the story ends with Jesus' words vindicating her in 8a: "She has done what she could."

If it was Mark who inserted the story between 14:1f and 14:10f in his process of editing, the story may earlier have been located just before the triumphal entry into Jerusalem: "six days before the Passover" (12:1), as John retains its place in the sequence.[12] But John also softens the political overtones of the act by changing the anointing of Jesus' head to that of his feet[13] and by emphasizing the loving devotion of the woman to Jesus rather than to the poor, and turning the polemic against the greed shown by Judas.

Matthew, on the whole, follows Mark's story, except that he has his own redactional intentions. His emphasis on Jesus as the Savior stands out, and

9. Elliot, "The Anointing of Jesus," 106.

10. C.J. Maunder, "A Sitz im Leben for Mark 14:9," *The Expository Times* 99 (Dec. 1987), 78. Burton L. Mack, *A Myth of Innocence* (Philadelphia: Fortress Press, 1988), 309-10. Elliot, "The Anointing of Jesus," 106. Bultmann, *The History of the Synoptic Tradition,* 203.

11. Elliot, "The Anointing of Jesus," 106. E. Schüssler Fiorenza, *In Memory of Her,* 330.

12. E. Schüssler Fiorenza, *In Memory of Her,* p. 350. Ben Witherington, *Women in the Earliest Churches* (New York: Cambridge University Press, 1988), 111. Maunder, "A Sitz im Leben," 78.

13. Maunder, "A Sitz im Leben," 79. Elliot, "The Anointing of Jesus," 107.

he omits references to Jesus praising or defending the woman's deed ("Let her alone" and "She has done what she could" [Mark 14:6-8]). The admonition given to the objectors is also cut off ("You can show kindness to them whenever you wish." [14:7]).

The Lukan story has become the most complicated and its development is unclear. Luke drastically alters the story to suit his own theological purpose. First, he does not locate the story at the beginning of Jesus' passion as the rest do. Second, the story is expanded by the parable of the two debtors. And third, the emphasis of the story changes when the sinfulness of the anointer and Jesus' forgiveness become Luke's essential themes. The strong contrast then falls between the Pharisee and the woman.[14]

Because of the similarities and dissimilarities among the four stories, the tradition history is not clear and the scholars' analyses are divided. Many seem to think that from one incident various stories arose during transmission and redaction. John and Luke have the most developed traditions. On the other hand, Eduard Schweizer claims that Luke preserves a completely different story from the oldest Markan account, and that what appears in John's Gospel is probably a combination of the two stories.[15]

Robert Holst holds the unique but unpersuasive opinion that the stories of John and Luke are not dependent on Mark but are themselves the more primitive versions of the story. He concludes that, "Although it is assumed that Luke read the gospel of Mark, Luke knew and used a more primitive version of the story."[16] Such a variety of observations means that a final conclusion about the history of the tradition cannot now be reached and is also beyond our task.

THE STORY

The House of Simon the Leper

At first our attention is drawn to "Simon the leper" in whose house the anointing occurred. In either case, people would have known which house Jesus was in if they heard the name "Simon the leper." The diagnosis of leprosy must have been a great shock for the patient and important news for the people in the community. If Simon still suffered from leprosy, he would have to be secluded from the community. If he could openly host a dinner in his house, he probably had been cured of leprosy.[17] If he were still leprous and did host a dinner, we see the fearlessness of Jesus the

14. Witherington, *Women in the Earliest Churches,* 110. Elliot, "The Anointing of Jesus," 105, 107. E. Schüssler Fiorenza, *In Memory of Her,* 128.

15. Eduard Schweizer, *Das Evangelium nach Markus,* 389.

16. Holst, "The One Anointing of Jesus," 436-46.

17. Schweizer, *Das Evangelium nach Markus,* 390. Elizabeth E. Platt, "The Ministry of Mary of Bethany," *Theology Today* 34 (1977), 34.

boundary breaker to accept an invitation to fellowship.

Modern medicine has made it clear that what is called leprosy in the Bible is not necessarily coterminous with the sickness called leprosy by modern medicine (technically "Hansen's Disease"), but encompassed a wider group of skin diseases identifiable by modern medicine.[18] Definitions of leprous skin diseases and explanations of various symptoms and their treatments are minutely recorded in Leviticus 13 and 14.

Now Jesus is said to be in the house of a man who has suffered from this dreaded skin disease. According to Leviticus, any person who is suspected of having a leprous disease must visit a priest so that he may examine and diagnose whether the case is indeed "leprosy" or not (Lev. 13:2-3). The priest does not offer any help or medical therapy, but determines whether or not the person has a leprous disease and pronounces the person clean or unclean in a cultic sense. The person declared unclean must be excluded from the worship assembly, and beyond that from community life in general (Lev. 13:3, 45-46; Num. 12; 2 Kings 5:1; 15:5; Deut. 24:8). The ancient Oriental mind considered skin diseases to be particularly serious because of their visible manifestations. Many appear to have suffered from such skin diseases in the New Testament period.[19]

People with skin diseases are considered to violate the purity code that protects the exclusive integrity and self-identification of the people of God; therefore they must be secluded from the community for endangering the integrity and holiness of the community, not simply for hygienic considerations involving the danger of infection. In addition, the diseases are feared because they are considered communicable. The diseased person is abhorred and set apart from any human relationships. According to Josephus, the person was almost dead:

> Four are considered the equal of the dead person: the poor, the leprous, the blind, and the childless.[20]

According to Waetjen, lepers, together with beggars, vagrants, thieves, outlaws, and others, belong to the very bottom of the social ladder and are called the "expendable" who are most deprived and dehumanized.[21] So, if a leper is healed, it means a recovery from the domain of the dead.

Yet the person has to go through the legal procedure again. After a priest examines and declares the person clean, the person must make reparation through sacrifices, from which the marketers profit (Lev. 14:10-32). Only then is the person ready to resume his or her normal position and activity in the community. We can easily imagine that the person will have

18. Klaus Seybold and Ulrich B. Mueller, *Sickness and Healing,* transl. Douglas W. Scott (Nashville, TN: Abingdon Press, 1981), 69.

19. Ibid., 38.

20. Josephus, *Jewish Antiquities,* III II 3.

21. Waetjen, *A Reordering of Power,* 11.

had a hard time being fully accepted and treated as a person in that culture of honor and shame. To restore the social wholeness once denied by the purity law would be difficult, because the purity code acted as the watershed between clean and unclean, inside and outside.

Jesus, entering the house of a "leper" and showing solidarity with him or his family by table fellowship, denies the order that segregates those who cannot fulfil the conditions demanded by the purity law and challenges the prevailing religious and social barriers.[22] It is very revealing that Jesus chooses to associate with those who cannot enjoy their social wholeness, perhaps even after they have recovered from their bodily disease. House gatherings, especially meals, are often used for the occasions of Jesus' teaching activity in Mark's Gospel (2:15-17, 18-22; 7:1-23; 14:3-9), making this a most appropriate stage for social inclusion to occur.

The Woman's Unusual Encounter with Jesus

Now a woman whose name is not given, and who is not invited to the closed, male gathering, makes her way directly to Jesus who is reclining for the meal. She "came with an alabaster jar of very costly ointment of nard, and she broke open the jar and poured the ointment on his head." It is obvious that she interrupts the table fellowship. The ointment she uses is of superior quality, for alabaster is used for preserving the best ointment.[23] Since ointment is regarded as a luxury,[24] her behavior seems "unorthodox."[25] The expression "breaking open the jar," may be influenced by "the common Hellenistic practice of placing the broken flask used for anointing in the grave with the corpse."[26] She does things namelessly and voicelessly. She is determined. Her behavior is eloquent enough so that she is not hindered in doing this. Apparently she does not mind at all breaking with traditional customs and the propriety required of women.[27]

Maunder proposes a threefold significance for the anointing in this story: (1) expression of hospitality, (2) preparation of a corpse for burial, and (3) a sign of messianic status.[28]

As prophets in the Old Testament anointed the heads of the Jewish kings, the woman's anointing of Jesus' head is to be identified with a prophetic recognition of Jesus as the anointed one. The "anointed one" reads "Messiah" in Hebrew and "Christ" in Greek. Anointing means the granting of divine power to the anointed.[29] Elisabeth Schüssler Fiorenza calls her

22. Myers, *Binding the Strong Man*, 142, 358.

23. Waetjen, *A Reordering of Power*, 110.

24. Ibid., 96.

25. Brock, *Journey by Heart*, 96.

26. Elliot, "The Anointing of Jesus," 106.

27. Elisabeth Moltmann-Wendel, *The Women Around Jesus: Reflection on Authentic Personhood* (New York: Crossroad, 1982), 98.

28. Maunder, "A Sitz im Leben," 79.

29. E. Schüssler Fiorenza, *In Memory of Her*, xiii. Brock, *Journey by Heart*, 96. Holst, "The One Anointing of Jesus," 442.

act a prophetic "sign-action."[30] Thus she as a woman breaks with the Israelite tradition and assumes the role of the "men of Judah" (2 Sam. 2:4). A
nameless woman consecrates Jesus and equips him for his kingly task.[31] The
politically "least" woman is assuming the position of "greatest."[32] She is
serving Jesus.

Anointing with ointment also carries healing connotations. Mark records
that the disciples "cast out many demons, and anointed with oil many who
were sick and cured them" (6:13). In their mission they used oil as part of
the healing arts. She has placed her hand upon Jesus' head with healing
ointment. Thus she comforts Jesus.[33] We should add the healing function
to the threefold significance of anointing proposed by Maunder. Probably
from this function the anointing came to be connected to burial, and the
women were all the more responsible for anointing bodies for burial.

Thus the woman plays a role as a prophet and a healer. For Mark, she
is the one that truly understands who Jesus is, recognizes what Jesus is to
be, and holds Jesus to whom he is to be. There is an unfathomable contrast
between her and Peter, who confesses, "You are the anointed one," without
understanding what it means. She clearly recognizes that Jesus' messiahship
means suffering and will end in death, so differently from kingship in the
patriarchal tradition.[34] The woman, subjugated, silenced, and denied a full
share in the community of the pure, understands how he will be denied by
society. Apparently she can sense Jesus' imminent death.[35] It is likely that
she cannot suppress herself from expressing her compassionate solidarity
with Jesus. She acts out her empathy with him. As a healer she comforts
Jesus, as a prophet she declares Jesus' kingship, and as a silenced woman
she shows Jesus his way to the cross. Her perception reflects "the paradigm
for the true disciple."[36]

The Reaction of Those Present

The woman's action, intrusive and unexplained, is absolutely embarrassing. To make matters worse, it takes place at a meal with guests. Social
codes of first-century Palestine can never accept it.[37] It cannot help but
cause a great stir among all those present. Though they are not so desig-

30. E. Schüssler Fiorenza, *In Memory of Her,* xiv.

31. Moltmann-Wendel, *The Women Around Jesus,* 98. E. Schüssler Fiorenza, *In Memory of Her,* xiv.

32. Myers, *Binding the Strong Man,* 359.

33. Seybold, *Sickness and Healing,* 155-56. Moltmann-Wendel, *The Women Around
Jesus,* 99. Brock, *Journey by Heart,* 96-97.

34. E. Schüssler Fiorenza, *In Memory of Her,* xiv. Moltmann-Wendel, *The Women
Around Jesus,* 98. Waetjen, *A Reordering of Power,* 94.

35. Jane Kopas, "Jesus and Women in Mark's Gospel," *Review for Religious* 44 (1985),
919.

36. E. Schüssler Fiorenza, *In Memory of Her,* xiv.

37. Mack, *Patterns of Persuasion,* 200.

nated, the other guests could also be the marginalized in society, if we infer from the situation that they let themselves attend a meal in the house of Simon the leper. But even then they cannot grasp the meaning of her action. They get angry (v. 4) and indignant with her (v. 5). Both verbs have a very strong connotation. "Be indignant with" is originally used when a horse snorts in anger. Taylor explains the word as "strong disapproval expressed in gesture and sound."[38]

To our surprise, however, their reproach does not focus on what she did to Jesus, but only on the economic aspect. She was accused of wasting money in light of the need of the poor.[39] "Why was the ointment wasted in this way? For this ointment could have been sold for more than three hundred denarii, and the money given to the poor" (v. 5). We see that the attention is shifted from asking what has happened between the woman and Jesus to trying to control the situation according to their common sense. The horizon of their knowledge forms the framework of reaction when they deal with such a seemingly emotive act. So it is easiest to become concerned with the value of the most precious ointment for the poor. Three hundred denarii amount to one year's wages of a day-laborer,[40] or more commonly, those of several growing seasons.[41] Her extravagance is simply blamed. She is not asked at all what has motivated her to do this in such an impolite way. Her existence is ignored by the men as usual. And they are not aware that they are also ignoring Jesus by reproaching her lack of economic sense. If they really cared about the poor, they would care about Jesus who is about to be killed for his solidarity with the poor. They fail to see the matter of vital importance underlying her behavior.

Here we see their captivity to the typical male-oriented thinking that tries to deal with any problem by objectifying and rationalizing the situation.

Jesus Responds

The woman's extravagant, unacceptable act is symbolic of Jesus' destiny and the imminence of his death. This is beyond the comprehension of the objectors. If she is the only one that really understands who Jesus is, Jesus would appreciate her action above anything else. Jesus has already shown his response by fully accepting her behavior. Such interaction cannot come into existence without heart-to-heart communication. We may infer that Jesus must treasure that kind of communication. His superb sensitivity has encouraged her to carry out her action. Thus he answers, "Let her alone; why do you trouble her? She has performed a good service for me." Jesus

38. Taylor, *The Gospel According to St. Mark,* 532.
39. Myers, *Binding the Strong Man,* 359. Elliot, "The Anointing of Jesus," 106. Mack, *Patterns of Persuasion,* 20.
40. Taylor, *The Gospel According to St. Mark,* 532.
41. Platt, "The Ministry of Mary of Bethany," 32.

considers the woman, while the objectors consider the money, which is not even theirs.

Since they do not understand the significance of her action and Jesus' impending destiny, Jesus answers them so as to persuade them. Thus Jesus also shifts the point of discussion to concern about the poor. But we may miss the key point of the whole story if we concentrate on justifying Jesus' saying, "For you always have the poor with you, and you can show kindness to them whenever you wish; but you will not always have me."

This pronouncement of Jesus could be very secondary to the story itself. Recognizing this, we should still deal with the issue of the poor, because Jesus is the very one that breaks down social class barriers and is on the side of the poor. Scholars try very hard to explain the saying. Taylor, with others, emphasizes "not always" in comparison with "always." Jesus was trying to indicate the urgency and temporariness of his presence and the ordinary presence of the poor.[42] Schweizer, referring to Deuteronomy 15:11 ("Since there will never cease to be some in need on the earth"), explains that the objection is right in the ordinary setting, but this case is exceptional and the objection becomes a wrong proposition.[43]

Another approach is to spiritualize the saying claiming that Jesus is speaking of the poverty that cannot be satisfied by money. Some distinguish between an occasional need and a general need. Or the specific case of anointing for burial takes precedence over the general issue of sharing the money with the poor.[44] Some evaluate her personal devotion to Jesus.[45] Belo distinguishes her action from the practice of the disciples, which will be carried on among the dominated, impoverished classes.[46] Many scholars carefully point out that Jesus is not legitimizing the continual existence of the poor.[47] Some go back to Deuteronomy 15:11 and remind the reader that Jesus is alluding to a written text.

R. S. Sugirtharajah suggests, from the third-world point of view, that Jesus has Deuteronomy 15:11 in mind. The chapter institutionalizes the nationwide "release" at the end of every seven years: "Every creditor shall remit the claim that is held against a neighbor" (Deut. 15:1-2). This is the socio-economic restructuring of a society in which the gap between rich and poor is widening. Because landlordism, money lending, and slavery inevitably result in maldistribution of resources, Jesus is pressing for a revolutionary and collective conversion that calls for new social relation-

---

42. Taylor, *The Gospel According to St. Mark*, 532.

43. Schweizer, *Das Evangelium nach Markus*, 392-93.

44. Mack, *Patterns of Persuasion*, 202. Myers, *Binding the Strong Man*, 359. Platt, "The Ministry of Mary of Bethany," 32.

45. Belo, *A Materialist Reading of the Gospel of Mark*, 206.

46. Ibid., 206, 327.

47. R.S. Sugirtharajah, " 'For You Always Have the Poor with You': An Example of Hermeneutics of Suspicion," *Asia Journal of Theology* 4 (January 1990), 103. Belo, *A Materialist Reading of the Gospel of Mark*, 327. Taylor, *The Gospel According to St. Mark*, 532. Myers, *Binding the Strong Man*, 359.

ships between the haves and have-nots. Upon this foundation, Deuteronomy 15:11 commands, "Open your hand to the poor and needy neighbor in your land." If Jesus has the scriptural text in mind, he obviously knows that the serious problems of the poor cannot be solved simply by selling the perfume.[48]

Then we realize that Jesus' saying contains a bitter irony and an acute challenge thrown to the objectors. They are being asked whether they are ready to commit themselves to the social reconstruction project for which Jesus is going to die. In this sense, his saying is not a harmless and socially undisturbing comment.

Jesus' saying, "She has done what she could," not only expresses his full acceptance of her but affirms her behavior. She devotes her whole life as did the poor widow; she risked her life as did the hemorrhaging woman.

Mark's Addition to the Text

Most scholars ascribe verse 8b, "She has anointed my body beforehand for its burial," to a secondary or Markan redactional addition. The saying makes clear the link between the anointing and the burial.[49] According to Mark, Jesus interprets the woman's action as the anticipatory anointing of his dead body.[50] This may have been added retrospectively in order to compensate for a deficiency in the passion story, because there was no opportunity for anointing after Jesus' death (15:46) and the intention was again frustrated by the resurrection (16:1).

On the other hand, Taylor argues, "Anointing for burial is not the woman's purpose. . . . Neither is it necessary to explain" the absence of anointing at his burial. "On the contrary, if, as is probable, the incident happened shortly before the passion, it is natural that Jesus should have interpreted the woman's action as the anointing of his body."[51] Taylor apparently takes verse 8b as primitive, and the present location of the story in the passion account as historical.

Maunder claims that the prediction that the woman's deed will be told reflects the earliest preaching of the gospel.[52] Witherington believes that the woman's deed was recalled simply as a way of honoring her memory.[53] But Mack claims that the woman as well as the objectors are simply "props" used for characterizing Jesus. What will be preached throughout the world is the account of Jesus' death and not her deed, because Jesus did not even turn to her or address her.[54] This is very male-centered exegesis. The verse

48. Sugirtharajah, " 'For You Always Have the Poor with You,' " 104-5.
49. Maunder, "A Sitz im Leben," 79.
50. Elliot, "The Anointing of Jesus," 106. Witherington, *Women in the Ministry of Jesus,* 113. Belo, *A Materialist Reading of the Gospel of Mark,* 206.
51. Taylor, *The Gospel According to Mark,* 533.
52. Maunder, "A Sitz im Leben," 79.
53. Witherington, *Women in the Ministry of Jesus,* 111.
54. Mack, *Patterns of Persuasion,* 203.

has raised much discussion among scholars. Lastly, if we take the formulary phrase, "Truly, I tell you" (cf. 3:28; 9:41; 10:15, 29), Jesus' saying, "Wherever the good news is proclaimed in the whole world, what she has done will be told in remembrance of her," expresses the world-wide preaching of the gospel. Then it reflects the later point of view.[55]

But we may say that at least for Mark the woman was the very first one to sense that Jesus was sure to die and the significance of that event. This is why he placed the story at the beginning of the passion account and wrote that "what she has done will be told in memory of her." For Mark she was the one to be remembered when Jesus' death and resurrection were recalled. In contrast, most scholars shift the subject to be remembered from the woman to Jesus and his good news.

CONCLUSION

In this story, Mark is apparently pointing to another "discipleship paradigm." It is expressed in the woman's devoting her whole life. Mark apparently sees the power of the gospel activated in the interactional relation between Jesus and the woman and the existential commitment of lives. Mark does not describe Jesus as a solitary or solemn authority, but humanly depicts him as one who identifies himself with the rejected and allows himself to be touched even by those who were called "untouchable." Moltmann-Wendel refers to Mark's special ways of expressing "the corporeality of the experience of joy, well-being and sorrow."[56] The physical proximity Jesus has exemplified (8:20; 7:33; 1:31; 9:36; 10:16) may give confidence to people who are aware of themselves as wretched. The "embarrassing," extravagant anointing could only come out of such confidence. "In a solitude that is becoming increasingly painful,"[57] we may infer, he delights in her gesture that springs from the depths of her heart and body.

As Moltmann-Wendel rightly says, "Every culture has its phobias about touch."[58] In a society such as first-century Palestine, which kept the purity regulations for its social and religious integrity, touching became a most sensitive issue. The human body itself, when it was unclean, leprous, hemorrhaging, or dead, became taboo. Such "unclean" people were absolutely isolated from society so that the "clean" part of society might be secure and holy in a cultic sense. In order not to expose themselves even to a chance contamination, the "clean" would choose to restrain themselves from all unnecessary contacts.

The anointing of the dead was never done by men. It was women's

---

55. Taylor, *The Gospel According to St. Mark,* 533. Witherington, *Women in the Ministry of Jesus,* 114.

56. Moltmann-Wendel, *The Women Around Jesus,* 101.

57. Ibid., 102.

58. Ibid., 103.

responsibility, and therefore women were not allowed to enter the temple, except for the special place set aside for them just as a court was also set aside for foreigners. In such circumstances, the physical proximity of Jesus with the untouchable caused a big stir in the community. He allowed himself to be touched by the hemorrhaging woman. He touched the dead daughter of Jairus. He cured the lepers and ate with them. He allowed the woman to touch his body and anoint him. Jesus broke through the taboo of all the purity laws that were intended to defend political, social, and religious integrity but were in fact often utilized as a device to keep the established power structure safe.

There was all the difference in the world between Jesus' behavior and that accepted by his culture. He moved into a head-on collision with the holy power structure. The anointing woman became a destructive, unacceptable, and irrational barrier-breaker, putting herself into a life-and-death struggle in solidarity with Jesus' struggle.[59] As Brock says, "His dying is a testimony to the powers of oppression," that is, "the brokenheartedness of patriarchy."[60]

Nevertheless, "in body language, a woman towering head and shoulders above Jesus, and performing a masculine, prophetic action on him, did not quite correspond with the Christian ideal of women."[61] Her deed has not been proclaimed and she is forgotten in church history.[62] As women theologians such as Moltmann-Wendel and Schüssler Fiorenza point out, and as we have already seen, the story became personalized and privatized in Luke and associated with the sensitive love of Mary in John. The woman was changed into a humble servant anointing Jesus' feet. Thus, the woman to be remembered in Mark has since that time more and more been kept in the background until she has become completely hidden and forgotten.

59. Brock, *Journey by Heart*, 97. Myers, *Binding the Strong Man*, 359.
60. Brock, *Journey by Heart*, 98.
61. Moltmann-Wendel, *The Women Around Jesus*, 101.
62. E. Schüssler Fiorenza, *In Memory of Her*, xiii.

6

WOMEN DISCIPLES OF JESUS

(15:40-41; 15:47; 16:1)

I owe much to Elisabeth Schüssler Fiorenza's book *In Memory of Her* in formulating my feminist perspective for rereading biblical texts and reconstructing early Christian history. However, when she says in many places that Jesus called forth a discipleship of equals, I could not but ask whether a collaboration between men and women was ever realized even in Jesus' lifetime. It is needless to say that this call is Jesus' essential message, but in Mark's Gospel, at least, there is no explicit description of men and women disciples working together. The Markan narrative records individuals or a group of men or women separately, except on occasions when it refers to a family group or uses the generic expression "the crowd."

As I kept the question in my mind, I came to realize that the question is not just intuitional but is rooted in my own experiences of being born, nurtured, educated, and living and struggling in a patriarchal society, even though Japanese society is said to have broken with patriarchal conventions in the course of its technological development. Men who have enjoyed their privileged relationship with women from generation to generation do not easily break with their androcentric mindset and accept a new praxis of egalitarian community life.

I fully agree with Schüssler Fiorenza that the discipleship of equals still needs to be discovered and realized by women and men today.[1] However, we also need to know how to do this, and she does not give detailed answers. In fact, it is comparatively easy for women who have been trodden down and neglected to accept equal treatment with men and behave as full members of the community. A negative evaluation by others usually lowers one's self-esteem and intimidates a person, but a positive evaluation is energizing. Women need motivation and encouragement to break out of their silence and invisibility and not act as expected. However, it must also be remem-

1. E. Schüssler Fiorenza, *In Memory of Her*, 154.

bered that there are numerous women who even under oppressive circumstances find ways to overcome predicaments and live creatively. They are not always passive and subservient to authority, nor do they always yield to exploitation, especially in everyday life. They are indomitable enough not to be completely tamed by the culture.

For men, on the other hand, the adjustment needed for them to accept the "equality from below" is even more difficult. As a result, men tend to stick to the status quo or become more entrenched when change threatens. I need to look for energy that will enable us to accept each other as equals and to work together.

WOMEN AT JESUS' DEATH AND RESURRECTION

When the passion narrative is nearly at an end, we meet the three women who are introduced by name for the first time: Mary the Magdalene, Mary the mother of James the less and Joses, and Salome (15:40). From the beginning of the Gospel to this place all the women are nameless except Herodias (6:14-29) who conspired to kill John the Baptist, and Mary the mother of Jesus who is mentioned in a pejorative context (6:3). All the women are introduced in relation to someone else: Simon's mother-in-law (1:29), Jesus' mother (3:31), Jesus' sisters (3:32), Jairus' daughter (5:23), and one of the servant-girls of the high priest (14:66); or with some identifying modifiers: a woman who suffered from hemorrhage (5:25), a Gentile woman, of Syrophoenician origin (7:26), a poor widow (12:42), and a woman with an alabaster jar of very costly ointment of nard (14:3). The fact of women being nameless may be expected because of the cultural bias of his androcentric society that influenced Mark, and because of his intention to make the male disciples the main characters in his Gospel. Munro goes further to say that women are intentionally obscured and suppressed by Mark, even though there are actually many active women in his Gospel.[2] The introduction of these three named women seems very abrupt. They are first introduced at Jesus' crucifixion and appear two more times, at Jesus' burial (15:47) and Jesus' resurrection (16:1). It is hard to accept Munro's thesis that women are not visible before 15:40 because they are "embarrassing" or "problematic,"[3] while, after 15:40, though they are active as one might expect of disciples, Mark's androcentric view tends to suppress their appearance even after 15:40.[4]

A careful reading of the three references to women points up a subtle difference in the names. Most scholars take the second Mary at 15:40 (Mary the mother of James the younger and of Joses), 15:47 (Mary [the mother]

2. Winsome Munro, "Women Disciples in Mark?" *The Catholic Biblical Quarterly* 44 (1982), 226.

3. Ibid., 235.

4. Ibid., 239.

of Joses), and 16:1 (Mary [the mother] of James) as the same person, with the inference that the modifiers in 15:47 and 16:1 are abbreviated versions of the reference in 15:40.[5] Some scholars take "Mary the mother of James the younger and of Joses" as referring to two persons, "Mary the wife of James the younger, and the mother of Joses."[6] Thus four women named.

Furthermore, Mary the mother of James the younger and of Joses may be identified with Jesus' mother whose next eldest sons have been named James and Joses (6:3). If she were Jesus' mother, why does Mark not mention her that way? There seems to be a reason. Mark depicts Jesus' family as thinking that Jesus has gone out of his mind (3:21, 31). But if Jesus' mother and her sons and daughters have joined the community of faith after Jesus' death and resurrection, Mark might want to restore their honor in this indirect expression. Or Mark might be cautious about the tendency to heighten the status of Mary in his community. On the other hand, Mark may not be referring to Jesus' mother but be speaking of James the "younger" to distinguish him from James, Jesus' brother.[7] Or the "younger" could be a disparagement of Jesus' brother who in a certain period dominated the Jerusalem church (Gal. 1:19; 2:12; 1 Cor. 9:5), to show that Jesus' family is not special (see also 3:31-35).

From consecutive references to these women in 15:47 and 16:1, in which names are inconsistent though overlapping, we may infer that 16:1-8 belongs to a resurrection narrative independent from the preceding section. Mark combines the two stories and uses 15:40 to adjust the difference between them.[8] At the same time, it is very important for the resurrection narrative to have these women see where Jesus was laid after his death at 15:47, because Mark must confirm through the women's witness that Jesus really died and was buried.

Mark has not referred to these women before in his Gospel narrative. What kind of relationship with Jesus these women have had is not mentioned. What kind of interactions with him they have experienced we cannot identify. Yet it is plausible to say that each must have had experiences similar to those recorded about the nameless women in Mark's Gospel. Mark only says that "these used to follow and served him when he was in Galilee" and notes that there were "many other women who had come up with him to Jerusalem." At the end of Jesus' life when the narrative is coming to a close, all these women appear as "new actants," "a remnant," and "the lifeline of the discipleship narrative."[9]

5. Ibid., 226. Elizabeth Struthers Malbon, "Fallible Followers: Women and Men in the Gospel of Mark," *Semeia* 28 (1983), 43. E. Schüssler Fiorenza, *In Memory of Her*, 321.

6. Schweizer, *Das Evangelium nach Markus*, 486.

7. Ibid., 486-87.

8. Bultmann, *The History of the Synoptic Tradition*, 276, 284-85. Schweizer, *Das Evangelium nach Markus*, 486-87. Arai, *Iesu Kirisuto*, 337.

9. Belo, *A Materialist Reading of the Gospel of Mark*, 229. Myers, *Binding the Strong Man*, 396.

It is a dramatic reversal. Even the androcentrically "biased" Mark has to record that when Jesus was arrested, "all of them [male disciples] deserted him and fled. A certain young man was following him, wearing nothing but a linen cloth. They caught hold of him, but he left the linen cloth and ran off naked" (14:50-52). Then while Jesus was being examined, "Peter had followed him at a distance, right into the courtyard of the high priest," (14:54) and in spite of his promises he "began to curse, and he swore an oath, 'I do not know this man you are talking about'" (14:71). All the males forsook him when he was in the hands of the authorities. The story of Jesus' disciples seems to end disastrously.[10] "The disciples of Jesus had their doctrine crossed out in a way which so threw them off course that they could only flee."[11] Malbon claims that Mark's description here reveals the male disciples to be fallible.[12]

THE THREE NAMED WOMEN AS DISCIPLES (15:40-41)

There are several characteristics of the women "looking on from a distance" at the cross. They are three named women among many anonymous women who continued to follow and serve Jesus when he was in Galilee and who came up with Jesus to Jerusalem.

Does this mean that they are women disciples who form a nucleus of three within an inner circle of many women, as Peter, James and John do in relation to the Twelve (5:37; 9:2; 14:33)? While Mark says that Jesus personally and individually extended an invitation to Simon, Andrew, James, John, and Levi to follow him (1:16-20; 2:13), there is no woman who hears Jesus' personal invitation to follow within the Markan narrative.[13] It is not clear if Mark means the three women to correspond to the three male disciples. Munro argues that they are women "disciples" but Mark intentionally obscured the fact.[14] Malbon uses the term "followers" to depict these women characters.[15] Dewey asks why Jesus did not appoint any women among the Twelve, and says, "Possibly, in order to proclaim his message so that it would be heard at all, Jesus had to make some accommodation to the standards of his own culture."[16] This is plausible if we think of the difficulty people had even accepting Jesus' interacting with women and being followed by them.

But I would like to ask further whether Mark may have been affected

10. Robert C. Tannehill, "Disciples in Mark: The Function of a Narrative Role," *Journal of Religion* 57 (1977), 402-3.

11. Schweizer, *Das Evangelium nach Markus*, 490.

12. Malbon, "Fallible Followers,"32.

13. Selvidge, *Women, Cult, and Miracle Recital*, 105.

14. Munro, "Women Disciples in Mark?", 231.

15. Malbon, "Fallible Followers," 43.

16. Joanna Dewey, *Disciples of the Way*. (Woman's Division Board of Global Ministries: The United Methodist Church, 1976), 132.

by the structural system of the "twelve apostles" in the church which must have been on the way to becoming the establishment when he was writing. He seems to have criticized the disciples easily, because he felt them to be most important. I believe that his concerns for his community made him write this way. I must wonder how strictly and clearly the boundary of the circle of the Twelve was actually set during the days of Jesus, who rejected any hierarchical institution and tried to break down boundaries (2:15-16, 18-22, 23-27; 3:35; 9:34-35; 10:13-16, 42-45).

In any case, Mark portrays women with Jesus right from the beginning of Jesus' ministry to his death, but almost all of their interactions and conversations with Jesus are invisible.[17] We may rightly infer that Markan generic words indicating the wider circle of the followers, such as "those who were around him" (4:10) and "the crowd," must actually be meant to include both male and female.[18] But it is only women that have accompanied Jesus on the way to his death, risking their lives and safety. We may infer from the phrase "and there were many others" that there must have been quite a number of women among the group of disciples.

In Mark the term "disciples" is used forty-six times. Sometimes it is used to designate just the Twelve (e.g., 9:31), but more frequently it is used to refer to Jesus' followers. Therefore a larger group than just the Twelve must be implied.[19]

"Looking Up"

In contrast to the male disciples, who try to deny Jesus' fate by fleeing and not facing up to reality, these women are looking up to Jesus on the cross (15:40) and watching his tomb at the burial (15:47). And further, they see that the stone of the tomb has been rolled back and they see a young man there (16:4-5). Women keep watching Jesus' most critical moments of crucifixion, burial, and resurrection. Those moments are also the main points of the kerygma or tradition: "Christ died for our sins in accordance with the scriptures, and he was buried, and he was raised on the third day in accordance with the scriptures" (1 Cor. 15:3-4). So women are the ones who do not lose sight of who Jesus was.[20] "Watching" also symbolizes their expression of interest, concern, care, and sorrow. Even though they cannot do a thing to reverse this crisis, their relationship to Jesus is not broken.

"From a Distance"

Opinions are divided on the meaning of the expression that the women are watching Jesus on the cross "from a distance." Elisabeth Schüssler

17. Elisabeth Moltmann-Wendel, *A Land Flowing with Milk and Honey: Perspectives on Feminist Theology*, transl. John Bowden (New York: Crossroad, 1988), 109.

18. E. Schüssler Fiorenza, *In Memory of Her*, 320.

19. Ibid., 49-50.

20. Ibid., 319-322.

Fiorenza interprets it in a positive sense that characterizes them as Jesus' true relatives:

> That they are well aware of the danger of being arrested and executed as followers of a political insurrectionist crucified by the Romans is indicated in the remark.[21]

On the other hand, Munro, emphasizing the "distance" that separates them from Jesus on the cross—in comparison with John's Gospel where they are close enough to converse with Jesus—questions whether the women take the place of the Twelve who have forsaken Jesus and fled. She concludes that Mark is not necessarily in favor of the women and they do not effectively replace the male disciples. Further, she says,

> The phrase απο μακρουεν has even stronger import if Mark intends an allusion to the innocent sufferer of the Psalm from whom friends, companions, and kinsfolk stand aloof and far off (Psalm 38:11; 88:8), which is quite explicit in Luke 23:49.[22]

Opposing Munro's interpretation, Selvidge proposes an alternative reading of the text: "women from afar watching" instead of "women watching from afar." Then the phrase only designates the place from which they originated, not the spatial and psychological distance between the women and Jesus on the cross.[23] This reading is attractive for confirming their closeness to Jesus, but it is unlikely. Malbon notes that the same expression is applied to Peter when he followed Jesus " from a distance" as Jesus was arrested and taken to the high priest (14:53-54):

> Presumably a stronger disciple and stronger followers would have drawn nearer to Jesus at these critical moments of trial and crucifixion. To be present at all is a mark of followership, but remaining at a distance is a mark of fallibility—for Peter and for the women.[24]

We cannot say for certain that Mark intends to apply the Psalms' image of the solitary, innocent sufferer to Jesus. It seems more probable that the phrase "from afar" is parallel to Peter's case. Because "from a distance" depicts Peter's spatial and psychological distance in remaining an onlooker and reveals his subconscious desire to act as if he were unrelated to Jesus, the same expression may also suggest the distance between the women and Jesus. At least we can say that Mark is not unreservedly praising the behavior of the women.

21. Ibid., 320.
22. Munro, "Women Disciples in Mark?", 235.
23. Marla J. Selvidge, "And Those Who Followed Feared (Mark 10:32)?" *Catholic Biblical Quarterly* 45 (1983), 399.
24. Malbon, "Fallible Followers," 43.

I suggest that women who are considered almost worthless in society have no need to flee from a dangerous place. Though they do not run the same risk of being seized as men might do, yet it is far more natural for them not to make their appearance in such a public place. They are used to being invisibly modest but are nonetheless ready to be with Jesus, who has given them a completely new and different self-image.

"Kept Following and Serving Jesus"

There are distinctive verbs that describe these women. Mark reports that "they used to follow him and served him when he was in Galilee; there were many other women who had come up with him to Jerusalem" (15:41). Most scholars, seeing in the verbs "follow" and "serve" the key "discipleship" themes described by Mark, recognize the women as model disciples.[25] The verbs used in the imperfect tense express their continual following of Jesus. This kind of relationship created between women and a teacher, which has been engendered as a result of Jesus' ministry, is as far as we know distinctive to Jesus in first-century Palestine. All the rabbis are, of course, male, and since to be a disciple of a rabbi means to become a rabbi sometime, disciples are expected to be all male. The disciples go everywhere with their rabbi and learn all the details of the scriptural texts and the laws so that they may become experts in the traditions.[26] Jesus acts and teaches in completely different ways, even though he is considered a rabbi. Here is another instance of boundary-breaking by Jesus.

The women's discipleship in Mark, specifically their "following" and "serving," can only be understood within his total description of what discipleship means.

MARK'S THREEFOLD TEACHING ON DISCIPLESHIP
(8:34-38; 9:35-37; 10:42-45)

Structural Observation

Mark 8:31 — 10:45 contains the threefold teaching of Jesus on the role of the disciples. The teaching is carefully placed after the three passion

25. Myers, *Binding the Strong Man*, 396. E. Schüssler Fiorenza, *In Memory of Her*, 320. Dewey, *Disciples of the Way*, 51,132. Selvidge, *Woman, Cult, and Miracle Recital*, 107. Malbon, "Fallible Followers," 40, and "Disciples/Crowds/Whoever: Markan Characters and Readers," *Novum Testamentum* xxviii, 2 (1986), 109. G. Kittel, "ακολουθεω," *TDNT* 1, 213. Leonard Swidler, *Biblical Affirmations of Women* (Philadelphia: Westminster Press, 1979), 194-5. Munro, referring to some scholars, says that these women are very rarely recognized as disciples. "By and large their role goes unexplored and unexplained, while some interpret ηκολουθουν in terms of διηκονουν, understood to define their function as that of serving food and attending to domestic chores in general, or as rendering material support for Jesus' mission" "Women Disciples in Mark?" (232).

26. Dewey, *Disciples of the Way,* 48. K. H. Rengstorf, "μαθητη", *TDNT* 4, 416-61.

predictions of Jesus (8:31; 9:31; 10:33-34), each of which is immediately followed by the disciples' negative response (8:32-33) or behavior contrary to that of Jesus (9:33-34; 10:35-41).[27] This arrangement is decisive for the Markan redactional purpose. Teachings on discipleship are located following passion predictions and passion rejections, emphasizing "passion" as the core of discipleship.

All three of Jesus' passion predictions follow the same literary pattern, which basically reflects the form of the kerygma of the early church. He predicts the suffering, crucifixion and resurrection of the Son of Man (8:31; 9:31; and 10:33-34).

To call him Christ as Peter does in 8:29 may refer to the historical situation of the ministry of Jesus, but the terms used here reflect the christological vocabulary of the early church.[28] Peter's refusal to accept Jesus' political fate (8:32-33), the Twelve's argument over who is the greatest (9:32-34), and James and John's petition for the highest ranks (10:35-37) may all indicate that Mark's community does not comprehend who Jesus is and what Jesus wants of them. It is Mark's redactional intention to place the teaching on discipleship right after the prediction of the passion to stress the discrepancy between the way of Jesus and that of his followers. Mark is very conscious of the situation of the community of faith for which he writes his Gospel.

Mark makes us realize the necessity of such teaching as well as the fact that Jesus always goes before his disciples. Discipleship comes only as interaction with Jesus: There is no discipleship separate from Jesus.

The threefold repetition of the passion prediction, its rejection by the disciples and the teaching on discipleship is itself framed by healing-miracle stories of blind men who receive sight (8:22-26 and 10:46-52). In no other place does Mark record two different stories of the healing of the same disability.[29] We may read the symbolic message of these two stories to be that to gain one's sight is one of the first steps for discipleship, but in order to gain one's sight one must get involved with Jesus, as the nameless women already show. Therefore "immediately he regained his sight and followed him on the way" (10:52).

27. Tannehill, "The Disciples in Mark," 400. Werner H. Kelber, *The Kingdom in Mark: A New Place and a New Time* (Philadelphia: Fortress, 1974), 67. Dewey, *Disciples of the Way*, 72. E. Schüssler Fiorenza, *In Memory of Her*, 317. Myers, *Binding the Strong Man*, 237, 405. Andrew T. Lincoln, "The Promise and the Failure: Mark 16:7, 8," *Journal of Biblical Literature* 108/2 (1989), 294.

28. Perrin, *What Is Redaction Criticism?*, 41-42. " 'Jesus' is the Lord addressing his church, 'Peter' represents fallible believers who confess correctly yet go on to interpret their confession incorrectly, and the multitude is the whole church membership for whom the general teaching which follows is designed. . . . It has the form of a story about the historical Jesus and his disciples but a purpose in terms of the risen Lord and his church. It represents Mark's understanding of what the risen Lord has to say to the church of his day."

29. Dewey, *Disciples of the Way*, 72. Myers, *Binding the Strong Man*, 236.

"Follow Me" Means Taking on "Shame" (8:34-38)

In the first section (8:34-38) of the threefold teaching on discipleship we read: "He called the crowd with his disciples, and said to them, 'If any want to become my followers, let them deny themselves and take up their cross and follow me.'" Malbon points out that this is "a pivotal verse concerning disciples, the crowd, and followers,"[30] in the sense that the invitation to follow Jesus is extended to anyone who wishes; therefore anyone can be a disciple. Though Malbon carefully uses "follower," I would use both "follower" and "disciple" with the same meaning. Since this verse links the disciples and the crowd, Malbon argues against Best who makes a definite distinction between the crowd and the disciples.[31]

"Follow" is the key word. To follow Jesus means to deny oneself and take up one's own cross. One cannot follow without getting involved with Jesus, though the reaction shown by Peter after Jesus' first announcement of his passion (8:32) explains how easy it is just to make a confession that "you are the Christ" (8:29) without knowing what it really means. To deny oneself means to renounce the prerogatives that create boundaries around oneself and keep one's life separate from the oppressed.

Crucifixion is the most painful and most shameful method of execution that human beings have ever devised. Thus taking up one's cross means to become the shame of society as Jesus does. It means that when we are in danger of being deprived of our honor we are challenged to face the situation. This seems to be the most serious challenge to face the privileged sector of the contemporary churches in Japan.

Nor should we neglect the fact that at the time of Mark's writing, Christians were already exposed to the danger of persecution by the Roman authorities. To be involved with Jesus is deeply and decisively related to taking the "shame" of the society upon oneself. The verse "Those who are ashamed of me and of my words in this adulterous and sinful generation, of them the Son of Man will also be ashamed when he comes in the glory of his Father with the holy angels" (8:38) also suggests this. Myers explains such circumstances as "a specific kind of political and community practice that takes the disciples/reader into the deepest paradoxes of power."[32] To follow Jesus is to choose between being ashamed of Jesus and his words for the honor of this world and being ashamed of the power of this world for the contrary honor of following Jesus. Once one encounters Jesus, one cannot escape from shame, which is the greatest humiliation reality in the "culture of honor" because it means being excluded from the integrity of the holy. Thus, Jesus is demanding the most paradoxical decision from his followers.

30. Malbon, "Disciples/Crowds/Whoever: Markan Characters and Readers," 109-110.
31. Ibid., 110. See also Ernst Best, "The Role of the Disciples in Mark," *New Testament Studies* 23 (1977), 377.
32. Myers, *Binding the Strong Man*, 235.

Jesus' ministry, concentrated as it is on life-giving miracles and teachings, cannot be without interaction with those who need his life-giving ministry. The essence of this ministry lies in the restoration of those consigned to nonexistence to their wholeness as persons. For that purpose Jesus needs to break down the barriers that exclude the impure in order to preserve the integrity of the pure. In fact, these barriers have destroyed the wholeness of persons on both sides of the barrier. Therefore Jesus' ministry cannot avoid the resistance and rejection that bring on his suffering, execution, and death. Jesus' "suffering is not an end itself, however, but is the outcome of Jesus' life-praxis of solidarity with the social and religious outcasts of his society."[33]

To follow Jesus is to collapse the existing social framework and reverse the world of the "pure" or the "powerful." Suffering and death will also be the outcome of this life-praxis. Elisabeth Schüssler Fiorenza sees here Mark's crucial christological insight.[34] Jesus' teaching points to his suffering as a model for his followers. Jesus himself goes before them. His posture foreshadows the prediction announced in 14:28 and 16:7 that he is going before them to Galilee and they will see him there.

Thus discipleship is not the condition but the outcome of following Jesus.[35] With Malbon, we may say that "discipleship is both open-ended and demanding; followership is neither exclusive nor easy."[36]

"Serving" (9:35-37 and 10:42-45)

In chapters 9 and 10 of Mark, the skillfully designed composition of Jesus' teaching on discipleship deals with the issue of right leadership in the community of faith.

In each case the teachings are preceded by some manifestation of the Twelve's hunger for power or honor. In 9:33-34, the Twelve discuss who is the greatest among them, and in 10:35-41, James and John petition Jesus for the highest ranks and the other ten are incensed about the two. Jesus, responding to their hunger for power and status, discusses the true form of leadership in the community of faith. Thus Mark uncovers a major paradoxical contrast between the desire for power and domination-free service.

Jesus teaches them, "Whoever wants to be first, must be last of all and servant of all" (9:35) and in 10:42-45, he puts the issue in direct contrast to the prevailing power structure. "You know that among the Gentiles those whom they recognize as their rulers lord it over them, and their great ones

33. E. Schüssler Fiorenza, *In Memory of Her*, 317.
34. Ibid., 317.
35. I cannot agree with Dewey's interpretation on this point: "Here, Jesus invites us all to follow him, but we must be willing to pay the cost. For the first saying goes on to list the conditions for following after Jesus; we must deny ourselves, take up our crosses and follow him." (*Disciples of the Way*, 76.)
36. Malbon, "Disciples/Crowds/Whoever," 124.

are tyrants over them. But it is not so among you; but whoever wishes to become great among you must be your servant, and whoever wishes to be first among you must be slave of all. For the Son of Man came not to be served but to serve, and to give his life as a ransom for many." As we read the three consecutive sections on discipleship, we see that the teaching becomes more detailed, the tension is heightened, the emphasis is pointed, and the climax becomes clear.

"Serve" is the key word. Jesus is now talking to those who feel it natural to be served and have never thought of serving others. In the last teaching, a statement about the Son of Man is added to show that Jesus himself stands at the opposite extreme from power by not being served. "Being not served" means that the Son of Man is "not one who holds such a position in the world as to have attendants — the servants of the rich and powerful."[37]

The word "serve" reminds Greek-speaking people of menial work with two basic meanings: first, to wait on table, an activity usually done by male servants; and second, to provide or care for, often in the sense of "women's work," taking care of the home and bringing up children. The word carries the general meaning to serve, especially in the sense of personal service rendered to someone by someone else.[38] People desired to be served, not to serve. They saw no freedom in serving others.[39] It is very interesting that Mark never uses the word "serve" to describe the actions of the Twelve but only those of women and Jesus.[40] If Mark is thinking in an ordinary sense that "serving" can only be applied to activities of the most despised or marginalized in society, he cannot apply the word to male disciples, even if Jesus teaches "serving" as a content of discipleship. If Mark is thinking about how shocking Jesus' teaching of "serving" is, he is commenting on

37. John N. Collins, *Diakonia: Re-interpreting the Ancient Sources* (New York & Oxford: Oxford Univ. Press, 1990), 248, 252. He notes that "to be served" is a "comparatively rare passive," which is "predicated directly of a person in a way that no other passive is" (249). "The passive belongs to the part of usage described as domestic and personal attendance; analysis of that usage has shown that, as in other areas of meaning, the verb looks to the activity rather than to the status of persons, who in this instance are 'attendants'" (252).

38. Hermann W. Beyer, "διακονεω, διακονια, διακονος," *TDNT*, vol. 2, 87, 82. Dewey, *Disciples of the Way*, 85. Luise Schottroff, "Maria Magdalena und die Frauen am Grabe Jesu," *Evangelische Theologie* 42 (1982), 12: "At meals in antiquity there were very strict hierarchical rules according to which the servant was the one who was lowest in the social scale, either the slave or the son or the daughter or the wife." Quoted by Molt-mann-Wendel, *A Land Flowing with Milk and Honey*, who also says: "In terms of social history this serving describes the situation of those whose situation is utterly inferior and who have to do the worst work" (128). Collins argues that "service at table" is not "the so-called fundamental meaning of the words in either Christian or other literature but is one expression of the notion of go-between," which constitutes the root idea (*Diakonia*, 249-50). The basic meaning of the word, according to his study, is "doing messages and being another person's agent" (194). But he also admits that it can occasionally mean menial service, as in some sayings of Jesus (254).

39. Selvidge, *Woman, Cult, and Miracle Recital*, 102.

40. Selvidge, "And Those Who Followed Feared," 398.

how distant male disciples are from what Jesus wants them to be.

The word "serve" is employed so as to present an extreme contrast with the dominant political structure, which seeks for more power at the expense of the subjugated. Jesus is very critical about the Twelve's aspirations to status and power. Actually the Twelve flee from Jesus when they realize that to follow him further is politically dangerous. In such a thoroughly patriarchal sociocultural order, as described in chapter 1, we can see why the Twelve dare not pursue their following to the end. For them it is very hard not to want to seek honor. Their conservativeness vis-à-vis change is shown to contrast strongly with Jesus' sensitive perception and his freedom to crash through the barriers at key moments.

Here we see how Mark reflects the patriarchy of the age. But Mark rejects this alliance with the political and social system of patriarchy and demands that churches not compromise with the dominant trend of that time. Mark may be struggling over the true meaning of messianic politics.[41]

It is not clearly stated whom the Son of Man might be serving or what kind of service he proffers. Collins notes that the second half of the verse, "instead of clarifying the context for an understanding of 'to serve,' has tended to accentuate the word's singularity here because a theology of ransom would not seem to have a natural correlation with the idea of service, especially in a context that is basically ethical."[42] The word "serve" may indicate menial work, and "servant" or "slave" designate those who are considered property without human dignity. One could say that Jesus redefines the meaning of "serving," culminating in suffering and death. The new definition may be more theological and severe, but it gives the absolute assurance of Jesus' solidarity with those who serve. Jesus' solidarity is expressed through giving his own life as a ransom for the benefit of many, thus going before those who choose to follow. If we take "ransom" as a technical term for money paid to liberate slaves and make free citizens,[43] Jesus' life is virtually spent in bringing back to life those who are cast out of society by subjugation, marginalization, humiliation, objectivization, impurification, enslavement, and so on. For that purpose, he breaks down all sorts of artificial barriers essential for the dominant power to keep its exclusive integrity. Thus Jesus' life-giving ministry has to end in his losing his own life. We may say that Jesus' life is itself a new definition of "serving," that is, to use one's life so that all human beings may share wholeness of life.

This following and serving is decided by one's own free will and is not fated or forced as we see in the slavery system. As Jesus' life evidences, life-giving discipleship cannot be without suffering in a patriarchal society. Therefore we are invited to serve "everyone," to practice "life-giving" sol-

41. Myers, *Binding the Strong Man*, 280, 236.
42. Collins, *Diakonia*, 249.
43. E. Schüssler Fiorenza, *In Memory of Her*, 318. Dewey, *Disciples of the Way*, 94.

idarity with the destitute. We see here the climax of Jesus' paradoxical teaching that the way of death is the way of life, that ultimate empowerment of "serving" is found in struggling for "life for all."

Only when we reach this conclusion are we persuaded why Jesus had to use concepts that reflect the hierarchical structure of the serving and the served. To undermine the patriarchal, hierarchical mindset, Jesus needed to start by reversing their value system. Then Jesus redefined the concepts by giving his life on the cross. The cross symbolizes the absolute negation of oppressive power as well as full solidarity with the oppressed. Jesus had to die on the cross because the traditional division between the served and the serving was not destroyed. The division was supported by all sorts of discriminations based on sex, race, handicap, and so on.

In contemporary churches in Japan, the division still exists. And so Jesus' teaching challenges us to overcome the oppressive situation. At the same time, I submit, we are challenged to redefine the concept of "serving" once more so that we all may serve one another, even though we are different physically, sexually and racially.

EXCURSUS: SIMON'S MOTHER-IN-LAW (1:29-31)

Here I will make an excursus on the story of Simon's mother-in-law in relation to one of the central themes of discipleship: "serving." The story is one of the first two miracle stories in Mark, both having taken place on the Sabbath day (1:21). Healings on the Sabbath always provoked major controversy between Jesus and the religious authorities (3:12). After an exorcism at the synagogue, Jesus leaves there immediately and enters the house of Simon and Andrew with James and John. Jesus' first four disciples, to whom he gave personal calls to "follow" (1:16-20), are following him.

"Now Simon's mother-in-law was sick in bed with a fever, and they told him about her at once" (v. 30). They may tell Jesus of her fever to excuse her for being unable to entertain them. For the hosts (Simon and Andrew) or the inferiors (all four disciples), it is a shame not to be able to show proper hospitality to their honorable guest (Jesus). Therefore the words of excuse come first. Luke misses this. Luke's view reflects a later time and either does not understand excuse or does not want the disciples to give it. He responds that they request Jesus to heal her (4:38), while Matthew omits the whole statement and stresses Jesus' initiative as the miracle worker (8:14-15).

The story moves in an unexpected direction. "Jesus came and took her by the hand and lifted her up. Then the fever left her." Jesus goes straight to her and treats her with great care. He does not merely touch or tap her, but takes hold of her hand with his hands and raises her to her wholeness. The lifelike retelling of this encounter suggests that the event was unforgettable, and therefore the story could be very primitive. The encounter shows the impressive physical closeness Jesus has with the woman, express-ing Jesus' deep concern for life. The verb "lift" is the same verb used when Jairus' daughter was raised from her death bed and in 16:6 when Jesus was resurrected. He devotes his life to healing the sick.

The story, although short has stylistic features typical of miracle stories: (1) problem/crisis, (2) act, and (3) response. We can trace these features in this story as follows: (1) the woman is described as fever-ridden; (2) Jesus heals her by taking hold of her hand and the fever leaves her; and (3) she serves them.[44]

Wire, who categorizes miracle stories using the theme of interactions as the organizing key, organizes them into four groups—the exorcism, the exposé, the provision, and the demand—and classifies this as one of the demand stories, although she says this story is anomalous.[45] It is not certain whether the four meant to request healing for her, but they did play the role of interceding for her. There is, however, "no intensifying of the demand to make a true demand story, possibly because the connection to Peter was sufficient reason for its telling."[46] It is apparent that Matthew and Luke heighten the miraculous element in their stories.

We need to ask what Mark's redactional intention is here. Simon's mother-in-law, on being raised from her fever, "served" them. Scholars point out that Mark carefully uses the imperfect tense for the verb "serve" while he uses aorist verbs for the healing process.[47] The "service" offered by Peter's mother-in-law, is not momentary but lasting. Scholars vary on interpreting the meaning of the verb, because Mark does not elaborate on its content.

Taylor says, "The serving at the evening meal is mentioned as the sign of the cure."[48] Waetjen goes a little further and says, "She arises and spends the remainder of the day ministering to them and their needs. Certainly more than the preparation of a meal is implied here. Her service engenders serenity, joy, comfort, well-being, and communion for them all."[49] He sees her gratitude as entailing the celebration of those who are present. Selvidge raises a question: "Would the Markan writer preserve a story about Jesus healing a woman just for the purpose of fixing him dinner or demonstrating her 'village hospitality'?"[50] Referring to the usages of the word in Mark, she reminds us of the connection with the central themes of discipleship in Mark, saying that the verb "is central to the mission of Jesus and to those who claim to be followers of Jesus." So, "in this story the mother-in-

44. Arai, *Iesu Kirisuto*, 244-45. Bultmann, *The History of the Synoptic Tradition*.

45. Wire, "Gospel Miracle Stories and Their Tellers," 83-84.

46. Ibid., 100.

47. Taylor, *The Gospel According to St. Mark*, 180. Howard C. Kee, *Community of the New Age: Studies in Mark's Gospel* (Philadelphia: Westminster Press, 1977), 152.

48. Taylor, *The Gospel According to St. Mark*, 180.

49. Waetjen, *A Reordering of Power*, 83.

50. Selvidge, *Woman, Cult, and Miracle Recital*, 399.

law is carrying out the same mandate that Jesus requires of all followers. It does not necessarily have to be menial tasks."[51] Kee, also referring to the technical use of the word in Mark, says that "she took care of their needs on a regular basis."[52] On the other hand, Malbon raises the question of whether "her service, her ministry, shares — and foreshadows — the theological connotations that the ministry of Mary Magdalene, Mary the mother of James and Joses, and Salome manifests later (15:41)."[53]

If we read this story just as it is, it is possible to say both that she does serve an evening meal as an expression of her gratitude and that she carries out the praxis of discipleship. If the first interpretation is dominant in Mark's telling, it implies another instance of the hospitality expected from women. This interpretation supports the gender role ideology that has been accepted by the church.

The latter interpretation could be justified if we see that the story is located here to provide a hint that is to be developed later and to challenge the readers to think throughout the Gospel narrative. If so, it also explains why Mark does not elaborate its meaning here.

To clarify Mark's intention, I would like to refer to the story of Jesus calling his first four disciples (1:16-20). In the story we can see how Jesus calls male disciples. First, his calling is made verbally. Second, the calling is something that could replace their occupation. Third, the first two followed him and the last two went after him. Both verbs imply one of the themes of discipleship: "following." Fourth, Jesus' calling coincides with forming a community of followers. It should be stressed that Jesus does not practice single-hook fishing of disciples.

Male disciples, responding to Jesus' words calling them to "make them fish for people," started their praxis of following Jesus. Mark does not elaborate here what "following" means. In this story, Mark simply foreshadows the first step in discipleship — "following" — thereby already introducing into the narrative the implicit possibility of their failure. The failure may be reflected in the fact that Mark never uses "to serve" of male disciples. Disciples follow Jesus but do not go further. We can detect that Mark's criticism of the disciples is implicit from the beginning of the Gospel.

Reading together the stories of the calling of the four and the healing of Simon's mother-in-law, I wonder if Mark does not intentionally almost juxtapose the two stories and arrange the two important verbs explaining discipleship, one in each story. At the end of the Gospel, women are referred to as having continuously both followed and served (15:41). Apparently serving cannot be without following, but following can be without serving. If the true praxis of discipleship is found in both following and serving, while the male disciples follow, Simon's mother-in-law is the first

51. Ibid., 398.
52. Kee, *Community of the New Age*, 152.
53. Malbon, "Fallible Followers," 35.

to serve, and she keeps on serving. I see the significance of the imperfect tense of "to serve" in this sense. It is noteworthy that her calling takes place through healing and physical contact, in contrast to the men whose calling is only verbal. It is symbolic to see her raised by the life-giving Jesus to her wholeness and to start following him. The reciprocity of the giving of life and the response works vigorously here again. It entails the community of living interactions.

Therefore, I conclude that the verb "serving" in this context plays a decisive role for the whole Gospel and implies far more than just serving a meal. In these small stories the Markan redactional intention concerning discipleship is beautifully carried out.

WOMEN AS TRUE DISCIPLES?

Many scholars try to evaluate how Mark dealt with disciples. Some interpret "disciples" allegorically. Theodore Weeden, using a redaction criticism method, concludes that the disciples represent Mark's historical opponents and therefore receive negative treatment.[54] We find that adequate evidence is lacking to verify the existence and nature of such opponents. Ernst Best thinks the disciples represent the church and the crowd represents the unevangelized.[55] But it is not Mark's practice to draw such a distinctive line between the two groups, as we have seen already.

Some take a "reader-response" approach. According to Tannehill, the positive portrayals of the disciples are intended to get readers to identify themselves with the disciples and the negative depictions of them are meant to distance readers from the disciples' less acceptable behavior. The total idea is to lead the readers to a new self-understanding and repentance.[56]

Best interprets the disciples both positively and negatively, showing a dynamic interplay of faith and disbelief. The disciples fluctuate between success and failure.[57] John Schmidt sees the disciples' characterization as devastating in contrast with the women, who are viewed positively. "Mark presents all of the inner group as male and as lacking the understanding appropriate to their position. They never are held up as models for Christian imitation." But women, on the other hand, are depicted as positive models of discipleship. "Women are presented as persons who really see who Jesus is and who act on that vision."[58]

54. Theodore Weeden, "The Heresy That Necessitated Mark's Gospel," *Zeitschrift für die neutestamentliche Wissenschaft* 59 (1968), 143-53.
55. Ernst Best, "The Role of the Disciples in Mark," *New Testament Studies* 23 (1977), 377.
56. Tannehill, "The Disciples in Mark," 392-93.
57. Best, "The Role of the Disciples," 390-93.
58. John Schmidt, "Women in Mark's Gospel: An Early Christian View of Women's Role," *The Bible Today* 19 (July 1981), 230-31.

Munro, who uses an historical-critical approach, takes a negative attitude toward the disciples, although she thinks Mark also suppresses a more positive image of women because of the social, political, and cultural context in which he writes.[59]

Malbon suggests a composite view of looking at the different characters in the Gospel with positive and negative features. Discipleship is to be understood from both the failure and the success and from the tension between their success and failure.[60] "The women characters supplement and complement the Markan portrayal of the disciples, together forming, as it were, a composite portrait of the fallible followers of Jesus."[61]

Having studied the verbs linked with discipleship, I conclude that the "following" offered to everyone entails "serving" in the sense of "life-giving" suffering. "Service to everybody" is inclusive and life-giving, while "rule by power" is exclusive and not of any life-giving value in itself. In Mark, "serving" is applied only to women, from the beginning of the story (1:31) to its end (15:41). So, returning to 15:40, we can only conclude that the women depicted by Mark are the true disciples of Jesus in the sense that they are ready for devoting themselves to "life-giving" suffering. Thus, the women disciples keep challenging those who avoid joining the struggles of the oppressed. The women disciples continue to disturb churches that seek patriarchal honor and hierarchical authority. So it should be implied that the discipleship of "following and serving" has the power to regenerate a true community of faith. Women and men are both asked to respond to the challenge of praxis so that we may become a church in its deepest sense.

59. Munro, "Women Disciples in Mark?" 234-35.
60. Malbon, "Fallible Followers," 30.
61. Ibid., 33.

7

THE EMPTY TOMB

(16:1-8)

HOW MARK CONSTRUCTS HIS STORY

The Resurrection

At the end of chapter 15, after Jesus is laid in a tomb in the evening of the day of preparation, that is, the day before the Sabbath, the whole narrative of Jesus' ministry seems to come to a tragic end. Darkness and sorrow cover the whole scene. Two of the names of the three women mentioned in 15:40, Mary the Magdalene and Mary the mother of Joses, are recorded as the witnesses.

However, the narrative starts up again. "When the Sabbath was over, Mary the Magdalene, Mary the mother of James, and Salome bought spices, so that they might go and anoint him."

It is a little odd to repeat the names of the three women after the similar passages in 15:40 and 47 if the story comes from the same cycle of tradition. Mark probably constructed the story based upon the tradition that was circulated apart from the passion narrative.[1]

Based on his textual analysis, Taylor concludes that the story is not historical but dramatic and imaginative.[2] He suggests that Mark had two traditions available to him: the tradition that the women visited the tomb and found it empty, and the kerygma that Christ was buried and raised from the dead on the third day.[3] It is probably true that the resurrection event (Acts 2:24; Rom. 1:4, etc.) and the appearance of Jesus (1 Cor. 15:4-8) are the main interest of Mark's readers. Myers, who calls the story "a carefully crafted apotheosis," affirms that the Gospel narrative "is rescued

---

1. Taylor, *The Gospel According to St. Mark*, 602. Bultmann, *The History of the Synoptic Traditions*, 284.
2. Ibid., 605.
3. Ibid., 603.

from tragic irresolution," though even the last few verses do not "offer a 'happy ending' in which all is resolved." At least "the discipleship narrative is given a new lease to continue."[4]

The story is silent on how and when Jesus was raised and on when and where the resurrected Christ appeared. The fact has led some scholars to suggest that the true ending must have been lost.[5] I would rather follow Myers who thinks "such speculation can now be considered obsolete."[6] I think Mark uses this puzzling ending to suit his redactional purpose.

For Mark, those women also play the important role of witnesses to the fact of Jesus' resurrection. Thus the story resumes on the third day (two nights and a day) since he died on the cross. And it is "very early on the first day of the week, when the sun has risen," that they go to the tomb. The story begins with a new daybreak of a new week. It may symbolize something new and fresh.[7] A new age seems about to dawn.

The threefold reference to the time may explain how earnestly the three women have waited for the very first opportunity to rush to Jesus' tomb for the last rite of anointing the dead. It could be the only available moment and the last opportunity for them to express their love. So far, at least, the women have not failed as the men did. They have not betrayed him, denied him, or fled.[8] The stone that has closed the passion narrative by sealing off the body is thus rolled back.[9]

But Mark would not add another story just for the purpose of pointing out how the women cared for the dead, a service for which women are normally liable and competent. Mark must have a redactional purpose for adding his resurrection story.

All through Mark's passion story, Jesus' community gradually collapses, particularly in Judas' betrayal, the flight of the disciples, and Peter's denial. Mark cannot finish his Gospel without at least an attempt to restore the linkage between the disciples and Jesus, since the community of faith has in fact survived, although it did not experience a triumphal victory or the restored Davidic kingdom. Jesus' defeat and death in utter solitude cannot be the end of the whole narrative. Rather, Mark needs to prepare the way for a Galilean appearance of Jesus, which should lead the disciples to regeneration. For Mark, the fact that Jesus is resurrected is most essential. He is not interested in how and when the resurrection of Jesus occurred. Mark's final emphasis is on the encounter with the resurrected Jesus in Galilee.

4. Myers, *Binding the Strong Man,* 397.
5. Schweizer, *Das Evangelium nach Markus,* 497-98. Taylor, *The Gospel According to St. Mark,* 609.
6. Myers, *Binding the Strong Man,* 399.
7. Waetjen, *A Reordering of Power,* 241.
8. Dewey, *Disciples of the Way,* 133.
9. Belo, *A Materialist Reading of the Gospel of Mark,* 231.

I will follow the proposal supported by most form-critical and redaction-critical analyses that verses 7 and 8b are Markan redactional statements.[10]

The Three Women

These three women, who themselves suffered from pain, disease, oppression, seclusion, and contempt, were healed and made whole by encountering Jesus. They were empowered through their interaction with him to discover themselves and their dignity as persons. Thus they saw hope to live only in following and serving him. Their life-giving encounters with Jesus led them to identify with his suffering and feel true empathy with him at his death. They could not leave him alone, nor find any place to hide from his tragic fate. To accompany him to the end of his life was the only possible expression of their love and faithfulness.

"As they entered the tomb, they saw a young man, dressed in a white robe, sitting on the right side; and they were alarmed. But he said to them, 'Do not be alarmed; you are looking for Jesus of Nazareth, who was crucified. He has been raised; he is not here. Look, there is the place they laid him' " (v. 5-6). "Being alarmed" or "deeply troubled" is a verb with a strong impact, "being shaken to the core and terrified."[11] The verb is used only by Mark. The other two references apply to Jesus in Gethsemane (14:33) and to the people when they saw Jesus again after his transfiguration (9:6).[12] Moltmann-Wendel, noting that sayings about women and about Jesus run parallel in the Markan story, points out that "two different situations which both times confront people with an abyss in their previous experience, the empty tomb and Gethsemane, are associated by the same emotive word. There is something of the same quality about the experience of grief, shock and anxiety for both Jesus and the women."[13] The women may have had no idea that Jesus might be raised, but they are chosen to be the first to receive the news of Jesus' resurrection. Matthew and Luke of course change the emotive expression into a gentler or nonemotive expression.

The verb "see," which has been the key term for expressing the women's behavior throughout Jesus' crucifixion and burial (15:40, 47) is repeated (16:4). This is "more than simply watching. It is perceiving, understanding, knowing, a total comprehension."[14] The verb expresses the special relationships resulting from the previous encounters. It is not just looking on, nor is it intellectual comprehension.

Seen from the perspective of women, Jesus displays a side of his humanity which is hardly seen in christology: his capacity for rela-

---

10. Lincoln, "The Promise and the Failure," 296. Taylor, *The Gospel According to St. Mark*, 608. Bultmann, *The History of the Synoptic Traditions*, 285, 309.

11. Moltmann-Wendel, *A Land Flowing with Milk and Honey*, 129.

12. Dewey, *Disciples of the Way*, 133. Myers, *Binding the Strong Man*, 398.

13. Moltmann-Wendel, *A Land Flowing with Milk and Honey*, 129.

14. Ibid., 130.

tionship, the need to enter into creative dialogue with people, and also the tragedy of failing them. Here it becomes evident that he already practised with others — above all with women — a non-hierarchical ordering of society based on mutuality.

At the same time it is also evident that this mutual life-style was already overpainted during the writing of the Gospels with conceptions of the exalted Son of God, who no longer needed human relationships.[15]

" 'But go, tell his disciples and Peter that he is going before you to Galilee; there you will see him, as he told you.' So they went out and fled from the tomb, for terror and amazement had seized them, and they said nothing to anyone, for they were afraid" (v. 7-8).

If we disregard verses 7 and 8b as Mark's redactional statement, the story goes as follows: the women who come to the tomb in order to anoint the corpse of the crucified Jesus are confronted with a young man who gives them the news of his resurrection. Because the message is far beyond not only their expectation but also their comprehension, they are utterly shocked and flee from there, filled with anxiety.

It seems very natural for them to flee from the tomb, for terror and amazement have seized them. Such a religious and mysterious experience may be called an epiphanic encounter. Considering how unlikely the situation is, the reaction of the women should not be thought unusual. The story conveys well a situation in which they have been completely thrown off balance.

But we may also say that they may sense a more imminent danger of being blamed and arrested as followers of Jesus, since Jesus' corpse has now disappeared from the tomb, which could lead to rumors or riots.[16] The fear of the women can thus be founded either way, though I suggest that the first way is more likely.

Mark's Motives as Editor

Mark, whose Gospel narrative does not end after the account of the flight of the astonished women, adds verses 7 and 8b to suit his redactional purpose. According to Mark, the young man, sitting on the right side and dressed in a white robe, continues: "But go, tell his disciples and Peter that he is going before you to Galilee, there you will see him, as he told you." The women are asked to "go" — as the hemorrhaging woman was told to "go" in peace — and to tell the news to the very disciples who forsook Jesus and fled from him with Peter, who denied Jesus and even cursed, being singled out by name. The women are called to be witnesses to the resurrected Jesus by reporting the news.

15. Ibid., 132.
16. E. Schüssler Fiorenza, *In Memory of Her,* 322.

The words "He is going before you to Galilee" are spoken to remind the failed disciples—and the readers—of Jesus' earlier prediction, "You will all become deserters; for it is written, 'I will strike the shepherd, and the sheep will be scattered.' But after I am raised up, I will go before you to Galilee" (14:27-28). "Go before" is also used in 10:32, where Jesus was actually going ahead of them on the road leading up to Jerusalem, showing that the disciples have already tried to follow without understanding. In Jesus' prediction in 14:28, Mark uses the future form "I will go before," but in 16:7, he changes the tense from future to present, "I go before," and adds a promise that they will see him in Galilee.[17] The present form in this case should not imply a virtual future, but suggests that Jesus is already on the way moving toward Galilee. It assures the disciples that they will surely see him, but only if they also stand up and make the move to follow and serve him.

Galilee designates a local place apart from Jerusalem, which is the center of political power and religious authority. Galilee also symbolizes the marginalized crowd with whom Jesus has identified. Jesus' "going before them" connotes more than its literary meaning. It assures them of Jesus' leadership and protection. Malbon, who studies the significance of space in the Markan narrative using structural analysis, suggests that Jesus' message of "going before them" points to the way, to going before. It designates not so much another place as a way between places, that is, a dynamic process of movement.[18] Thus, the meeting with the resurrected Jesus symbolizes the restoration of the disciples and their renewed activization for mission.

Galilee, as the place where they heard and responded to Jesus' personal call, were sent out, and were taught the discipleship of following and serving by Jesus, is not the end point but the beginning. The key is following Jesus, which gives the possibility to begin life anew. This means that this epilogue to Mark's Gospel is actually its prologue. The command to go back to the beginning gives the hope that the disciples can regenerate. Thus, we, learn that Mark's concern centers around the restoration of the failed disciples.

The women's fear and silence could be caused by the strict instructions of the command. In any case, according to Mark, the women, like the disciples also flee from their mission. Mark thus places the women on an equal level with the disciples in their weakness. "And they said nothing to anyone, for they were afraid." The literal reading of Greek with double negatives shows the reinforced silence of the women. Their silence when commended to tell sounds ironic at the end of a gospel in which the people cannot keep silent when told not to tell. The fact that women have been enjoined to tell the news in an age when people do not give any value to witness by women reinforces the irony. Thus the news of Jesus' resurrection

17. Taylor, *The Gospel According to St. Mark*, 608.
18. Elizabeth Struthers Malbon, *Narrative Space and Mythic Meaning in Mark* (San Francisco: Harper & Row, 1986), 165.

is first handed to women. Here we can note another evidence of a break-down of the important barrier that has separated women from men.

And since the disciples have completed their ministry by Mark's time, the women must, after all, have communicated the news of Jesus' resurrection in some way, and the disciples must have taken the news seriously by going to Galilee and meeting the resurrected Jesus. Otherwise evangelism would not have begun at all.

THE WOMEN'S SILENCE

Mark writes his Gospel with contemporary issues in mind, observing the historical reality of mission carried out by members of his community. Therefore, we should ask why Mark in this context has the women say nothing to anyone. Is he asking that the silence of the women be broken by the readers? The narrative world of the Gospel as a whole seems to urge readers to do that.

"And they said nothing to anyone, for they were afraid." The Gospel ends in a stunning way with a two-word phrase or sentence, "ephobounto gar." Mark does not add any explanation of why they are afraid. This blunt and unusual ending must have evoked a more satisfactory and seemingly more appropriate conclusion in the early stage of transmission. The added text at the end (16:9-20), which is strongly influenced by the kerygmatic dogma of the early Christian church, may be evidence that the people were not satisfied with the odd ending. Many scholars ask why Mark ends his Gospel with a post-positive "gar." Some think that it often happens.[19]

Scholars who render the Greek with the sense that the women did not speak to the general public argue that it does not mean that they did not speak to particular individuals.[20] On the other hand, Lincoln points out that in Mark's Gospel "be afraid" is mostly used to depict a negative response due to lack of faith (ten out of twelve instances); thus verse 16:8 portrays disobedience to a divine command.[21] Both observations explain little about the situation. We should rather ask why Mark wants these particular women to keep silent.

Back to the Beginning

From a viewpoint of redaction criticism, Joachim Gnilka says that Mark intentionally makes the Gospel open-ended, for he wants to direct readers to reread the Gospel narrative from its beginning, discover its intention, and bring it to an end themselves. This point of going back to the beginning

19. Lincoln, "The Promise and the Failure," 284.
20. E. Schüssler Fiorenza, *In Memory of Her*, 322. Selvidge, "And Those Who Followed Feared," 400. Malbon, "Fallible Followers," 45.
21. Lincoln, "The Promise and the Failure," 287.

is based on the content of the young man's message (v. 7) and does not deal with the issue of why the narrative ends with the women's silence.[22]

A Moral for the Story

Drawing attention to the readers' point of view, Norman R. Petersen argues that "the juxtaposition of the expectation introduced in 16:7 with the terminal frustration of it in 16:8 requires the reader to review what he has read in order to comprehend this apparent incongruity and its meaning for the narrator's message. The text ends, but readerly work itself goes on. The end of a text is not the end of the work when the narrator leaves unfinished business for the reader to complete, thoughtfully and imaginatively, not textually."[23] Petersen notes that when "the narrator creates an expectation and then cancels it, . . . the wonderment and incredulity require the reader to solve the puzzle of the narrator's meaning."[24] For Petersen, the reader is meant to identify with the disciples who are expected to fulfill the prediction of Jesus' meeting with them in Galilee. If we hear Petersen strictly, we have to conclude that he makes a clear-cut distinction between disciples and women.

Furthermore, Petersen finds Mark's principal story-telling device to be that of "prediction and fulfillment"[25] and explains the defection in 16:8 which frustrates the Gospel's fulfillment by his conclusive statement that "for Mark the will of God and of his Son override the will of men."[26] He does not refer to the action of the women who, after all, must have reported to the disciples, but chooses to see the women's silence broken only by Jesus' words, which "will not pass away" (13:31). This suggests an ironic reading instead of a literal reading of 16:8. Then 16:8 becomes "a prism through which the reader must re-view what has been read in order to complete the imaginative work required by the narrator."[27] He says correctly that the women's silence is not the terminal event, but he does not adequately explain why Mark keeps them silent.

Standing close to Petersen, Lincoln makes use of retrospective analysis which investigates the appropriateness of the ending and its implications. The failure of the women is to be juxtaposed with Jesus' promise, which is the only means of renewing lapsed discipleship. Verses 7 and 8 refer back to Jesus' words of promise which will never pass away (13:10 and 31).[28] What matters, according to him, is that God's word is fulfilled. And that is

22. Joachim Gnilka, *Das Evangelium nach Markus* (Zürich: Benziger, 1978-79). Quoted by Arai, "Epilogue as Prologue," *Kikan Tetsugaku* (1991), 17.

23. Norman R. Petersen, "When Is the End not the End? Literary Reflections on the Ending of Mark's Narrative," *Interpretation* 34 (1980), 153.

24. Ibid., 154.

25. Ibid., 155.

26. Ibid., 156.

27. Ibid., 162.

28. Lincoln, "The Promise and the Failure," 295-96.

already known to the implied reader because of "the post-resurrection role ascribed to the disciples by Jesus himself in chapter 13" and ascribed to the actual readers because they have heard the Christian message.[29] Therefore there is no need to ask how the message is conveyed or who tells it. Thus we lose any coherent significance of the women in the resurrection story.

Thomas E. Boomershine stresses positive connotations of the women's terror and amazement in verse 8, although he admits that their flight and silence have negative attributes as well. The positive connotations, according to him, challenge the reader to carry out the apostolic commission.[30]

Tannehill, taking the Gospel as a single, unified story narrated by the author, states that its protagonists are Jesus — a single central figure — and a group of companions, or "disciples."[31] In reading it, he suggests the necessity for the reader's active imagination to establish connections among the parts.[32] He stresses the creative activity by which the imagination comprehends events as real even when they are not directly connected with the reader's life and experiences. He depends on Wolfgang Iser's theory,[33] according to which the implied author's viewpoint is made clear through Jesus' behavior and words, while the Markan community is identified with the disciples.[34] Thus the author of the gospel reflects indirectly his perception of the reader's situation and needs, the main point of identification being the male disciples and their relations to other characters. "The author composed his story so as to make use of the initial tendency to identify with the disciples in order to speak indirectly to the reader through the disciples' story."[35] "In doing so, he first reinforces the positive view of the disciples which he anticipated from his readers, thus strengthening the tendency to identify with them. Then he reveals the inadequacy of the disciples' response to Jesus, presents the disciples in conflict with Jesus on important issues, and finally shows the disciples as disastrous failures."[36] For Tannehill, the two phases of the initial identification with the disciples and then the gradual distancing from them are very important to move readers to self-criticism and repentance.

29. Ibid., 292.

30. Thomas E. Boomershine, "Mark 16:8 and the Apostolic Commission," *Journal of Biblical Literature* 100 (1981), 237.

31. Tannehill, "Disciples in Mark: The Function of a Narrative Role," *Journal of Religion* 57 (1977), 388.

32. Ibid., 389.

33. Ibid., 389.

34. Ibid., 391. Wolfgang Iser, *The Implied Reader* (Baltimore: Johns Hopkins Univ. Press, 1974), 278-9: "The literary text activates our own faculties, enabling us to recreate the world it presents. The product of this creative activity is what we might call the virtual dimension of the text, which endows it with its reality. This virtual dimension is not the text itself, nor is it the imagination of the reader; it is the coming together of text and imagination."

35. Tannehill, "Disciples in Mark," 392-3.

36. Ibid., 393.

Tannehill interprets the women's silence as an indication of further failure by Jesus' followers, which explains the fact that even the message of the resurrection does not guarantee a faithful response. It simply reveals the weakness of Jesus' disciples and readers. Women are not alternative models to the disciples, rather both similarly represent failure as Jesus' followers. Furthermore, since the women fail to convey the message, it is possible that the disciples are unaware of the chance for a new beginning after disaster. Therefore the renewal is not a simple and automatic affair. Tannehill concludes that whether the church, including the reader, makes decisions will decide the outcome of the story, because the Gospel is open-ended.

He does not mention on what basis the church should make decisions or what can be the motivations for or the modes of decision-making. He ends with hope for an open future that is, according to him, found in the predictions of 14:27-28 and 16:7 announcing that the resurrected Jesus will go before the faithless disciples to Galilee and see them there.

> The relation between 14:27 and 28 indicates that this anticipated meeting can be a remedy for the scattering of the sheep and the loss of their shepherd, that is, this meeting can restore the relationship between Jesus and disciples, in spite of desertion and denial. So the Gospel holds open the possibility that those who deserted Jesus will again become his followers, reinstating the relationship established by Jesus' call.[37]

Thus we may conclude that both Petersen and Tannehill identify the women with the disciples as those who fail Jesus. They do not see any significance in the women's following Jesus to the end of his life through all the most dangerous occasions, nor in their serving Jesus all through his life by the sorts of servitude that are so familiar to them. Apparently they do not see the distinctive forms of discipleship shown by the women.

A Feminist Perspective

Malbon, using the terms "followers" and "followership" instead of "disciples" and "discipleship," tries to take a wider scope to define the content of following Jesus. Followers include the crowd, women, and certain exceptional individuals like Bartimaeus and Jairus, besides the disciples.[38] Both disciples and the crowd embody the fallible image of following Jesus.[39] For Malbon, "Discipleship is both open-ended and demanding; followership is neither exclusive nor easy."[40] She is critical both of those who justify the

37. Ibid., 403-4.
38. Malbon, "Fallible Followers," 30.
39. Ibid., 32.
40. Ibid., 32.

disciples at each point and of those who depict the disciples only in a negative light and make the women a positive model of discipleship over against them.[41] After observing both positive and negative characteristics of the disciples, she says, "The women characters supplement and complement the Markan portrayal of the disciples, together forming, as it were, a composite portrait of the fallible followers of Jesus."[42]

That the women followers keep following to the end suggests to her the surprising fact that Christian discipleship/followership is open to all people. I appreciate her opinion at this point.

Furthermore, she observes that in Mark's Gospel the historically conditioned expectations concerning women are completely reversed by their following and serving.[43] I do not agree with her on this point. If following means taking the shame of society upon oneself, as I have explained previously, it means to put oneself under others and therefore implies a non-hierarchical power structure. And if serving is to vitalize those who are oppressed, it implies non-patriarchal horizontalization of society. These two qualifications naturally contradict the patriarchal and hierarchical structure of society. In such a structure, nevertheless, the women have gained wisdom and created means to survive. In addition, if they now learn that following and serving does not mean to be subjected to humiliation but to practice true discipleship, because women have been historically conditioned to accepting a lower status in society, it would be easier for them to practice following and serving, even though they might find it difficult to take courage in speaking up or behaving like honor-seeking men. Subjugation and obedience have almost become second nature to them.

The reversal occurred in the value that Jesus' followers put on following and serving, not in society's expectations of women. No one else but the women are in a position to feel comfortable with Jesus' teaching of discipleship. Therefore the women played key roles as disciples, and Mark also, in constructing his Gospel could not deny their positive role. Because these women never deserted him and became witnesses to Jesus' resurrection, Mark could write his Gospel. For Mark, I must say, the story of the women was even convenient as a witness to the reality of Jesus' resurrection.

According to Malbon, since the narrator as well as the reader assumes that the women did tell the disciples about the resurrection, the significance of the women's silence can only be found in the outward movement of the text from narrator to reader. The narrator invites readers to speak now and continue the line of followers.[44] Her explanation is not necessarily clear on what has motivated the narrator to end the narrative with the silence of

41. E.g., Marla Schierling, "Women as Leaders in the Markan Communities," *Listening: A Journal of Religion and Culture* 15 (1980):250-57. John Schmidt, "Women in Mark's Gospel," 228-33.

42. Malbon, "Fallible Followers," 32.

43. Ibid., 42-43.

44. Ibid., 45.

the women and on what will motivate readers to break the silence of the women if they have not yet seen the resurrected Jesus.

She also maintains that both the disciples and the women are fallible, though the women are portrayed as minimally fallible especially in comparison with the disciples. The women are "good" or "positive" in the sense that they exemplify followership. She explains the difference by Mark's tendency to overturn expectations — in this case, to counter the stereotyped concept of Jesus' faithful followers. She is very cautious about idealizing the women as model disciples in relation to Mark's critical attitude toward the male disciples.[45]

However, Malbon has not made clear the relationship between the disciples whom she considers the implied readers and the women who appear at the disciples' flight and act as if they were disciples. Neither has she made clear the relationship between the implied readers and the historical readers for whom Mark writes the Gospel. And she also says that "the relation of the Markan narrative to early Christianity and its relation to contemporary Christianity" is not "given directly and unambiguously within the text."[46]

Dewey sees the implied readers identifying both with the disciples and with Jesus. The reality of the implied readers' situation is that of the disciples, but they wish to live with the values and demands exemplified by Jesus.[47] No one is excluded from failure and everyone needs God's forgiveness. Therefore the invitation to see Jesus in Galilee, which premises forgiveness, remains.[48] Her explanation of the relation between the implied readers and the disciples is very explicit, but she never refers to the women and their relation to discipleship.

Schottroff explains the silence of the women in 16:8 in terms of the uneasy situation in which the Markan community was involved, 16:8 being taken as a Markan redactional statement. Mark makes the women silent because they were afraid. He expects that the community will experience the same dreadful destiny as Jesus did (8:34-36, 13:12), and he takes very seriously the anxiety they are now facing. So he tries by telling stories of the disciples, the women, and Jesus, who have all experienced fear, to encourage members of the community to face their anxiety and continue in the way of following Jesus.

According to Schottroff, when Mark talks about the flight of the disciples and the silence of the women, he challenges the community to see that they have actually overcome their fear and become messengers of the gospel. So 16:8 which is the end of the Gospel, is not the end for Mark and

45. Ibid., 45-46.
46. Ibid., 47.
47. Joanna Dewey, "Point of View and the Disciples in Mark," *1982 Seminar Papers. SBL ASP* 18: Society of Biblical Literature (1982), 103.
48. Ibid., 134.

his community but the beginning of the work of the disciples and women after Jesus' death.[49]

Schottroff's understanding of Mark is that Mark does not see any particular role that is distinctive to the women but sees both the disciples and the women equally fail and equally start proclaiming the gospel. She does not see any difference in the situations or historical experiences of men and women. They live and behave as disciples with equal rights that are realized because of their poverty and through their hope for the Reign of God.[50] Poverty is the common experience for them. Therefore she does not take patriarchy into consideration.

To the extent that she views 16:8 from a Markan redactional point of view, I agree with her, but it is inadequate to deal with men and women so interchangeably. Both men and women may be destitute, but the situations women have experienced are socially, culturally, or religiously far more miserable than those of men.

Moltmann-Wendel interprets the flight of the women as Mark's challenge to women to claim self-identity and not hide themselves in the group. She is not clear on whether 16:7 and 8b are Markan redactional statements or not and how the women are related to the disciples. She seems to take these verses as primitive and interpret them as historical.

Citing Valerie Saiving Goldstein, she says, "In contrast to the male sin of hubris, wanting to be like God, women are alienated from themselves and from God in that they cannot be themselves."

> In Mark they flee (16:8), are weak and suddenly afraid when they no longer find Jesus and are to proclaim the resurrection of Jesus. The sin of women is that they no longer tolerate the risk of "I am," long for continuity and leave the narrow way of autonomy from which our relationships first develop — that they stick in a group, are choked by a bond, lose themselves in some form of solidarity.[51]

As one of those who have long been made to live in and be accustomed to the lifestyle of self-alienation in a group-oriented patriarchal society, her definition of women's "sin" sounds unreasonable. I argue that this comment of hers is only possible for women who have been privileged to live in a so-called Western society in which self-identity is well established for both women and men. Most of the women followers in Mark's Gospel were those who were marginalized and dehumanized in the culture of honor/shame from their birth and who did not even know any other way of life, because the dyadic life-pattern had become almost their second nature. In such a

---

49. Luise Schottroff, "Frauen in den Nachfolge Jesu," *Traditionen der Befreiung: Sozialgeschichtliche Bibelauslegungen*, ed. Willy Schottroff and Wolfgang Stegemann (Japanese edition), 76-77.

50. Ibid., 72.

51. Moltmann-Wendel, *A Land Flowing with Milk and Honey*, 164-65.

society in which not having a self is most virtuous, how can women resist their expected role of being buried in the group-oriented worldview? Should we call this "sin"? Asian women would never call their situation their "sin." It could be called "sin" if the women had already experienced an established self-identity long enough to be able to cope with the temptation of sticking in a group. But the women we have met in Mark do not belong to that category of women. For them to "lose oneself in some form of solidarity" had not been a temptation, but a requirement of life.

Only when they encountered Jesus or he them, and only when they interacted with Jesus, were they liberated from the bond of oppression and able to find the hope to be themselves. That is why the women could be faithful to the last moment of Jesus' life. It was only Jesus who could change their disastrous situations.

When they found that they were no longer able to see Jesus, the unexpected message of Jesus' resurrection came upon them. It was this incredible news that filled them with terror and amazement. So they fled from the tomb. But it does not mean that their lives, which had been empowered by their encounters with Jesus, once again became powerless. As we have already seen, they did, after all, convey the news to others (including the disciples), and if we should take the mission given in v. 7 as primitive, they did carry out their mission. Was it not the women who dared to go through "the narrow way of autonomy" even after such an astounding experience and to be with Jesus ? Moltmann-Wendel does not refer to this fact. She seems to think that the women also failed and kept silence. It is true that women, who had long been "stuck in groups" and "choked by various bonds," would have been tempted to fall back. And it would be possible to read that the women did not "tolerate the risk of 'I am' and kept silent" only if we could ignore Mark's redactional intention in the last two verses.

Challenge to Mark's Community

As we have seen, Jesus was revolutionary in denying any boundary that segregated anyone from the rest of the society. Jesus dealt with women and men on an equal level. Therefore among Jesus' followers we can expect that the traditional hierarchical social order between men and women would have been replaced by an egalitarian community in which people served one another. However, it was women that interacted with Jesus positively, while men quite often interacted negatively. The focus on interaction has revealed the vivid relationship between women and Jesus, and the true discipleship of women. The women, who were marginalized or dehumanized, had nothing to give up or no work to go back to. They could only find their hope and worth in following Jesus. Therefore, living in a non-hierarchical, egalitarian faith community was most encouraging and empowering to them. In addition, acting in harmony, listening to others, caring for others' feelings, and adjusting oneself to circumstances — characteristics taught women in patriarchal society—helped them get involved with Jesus' lifestyle and view of life with deep understanding.[52]

The women already represented and shared the new order, while the disciples had a hard time to adjust themselves to it—to give up their expectations of holding places of honor and to leave behind their work. The disciples showed how difficult it was to leave the old framework of life and how discouraging it was to see the collapse of one's philosophy of life and the breakdown of one's hope. On the other hand, women had had almost nothing to hope for.

When Mark collects, evaluates, and chooses the traditions he wants to use, he has his own intention in writing his Gospel narrative. One of his main purposes, I argue, is to warn his community against falling back into hierarchy. Mark senses the danger that men may stray from true discipleship, which is surely challenging and even threatening to them who are so used to the patriarchal order, while for women the practice of serving is itself quite familiar and comfortable.

From this redactional point of view, we can say that Mark himself composes the negative picture of the disciples in contrast to the positive portrayal of the women. In the Gospel narrative the women are depicted as if performing the role of the disciples, particularly after the latter flee. Furthermore, the women are shown actually practicing the true discipleship of following and serving.

From the observation above, we may conclude that those in the Markan community who need to learn from the negative and positive pictures of the disciples and the women are the men who are in danger of alienating themselves from Jesus' teaching on true discipleship and reverting to the old hierarchical system with which they are comfortable.

However, this conclusion does not solve the puzzle of why Mark says the women keep silence. There are several proposals that try to explain the women's silence in Mark.

Some suggest that the disciples' flight proves their fallibility or failure, while the women's presence at the tomb is a positive sign about the women. Yet, since Mark wants to encourage the disciples, he needs to draw a parallel between them and the women by keeping them silent in the end. Thus he fails to make the women alternative models to the male disciples who have lived in the culture of honor.[53] Others interpret the women's silence as an element that seals the disciples' failure (the disciples never hear the news) or as a parallel to the disciples' fallibility (the women never tell the news). Thus Mark portrays both the disciples and the women as

52. Cf. Carol Gilligan, *In a Different Voice: Psychological Theory and Women's Development* (Cambridge: Harvard Univ. Press, 1982), 62.

53. Shierling, "Women as Leaders," 251-52. Schmidt, "Women in Mark's Gospel," 232-33.

fallible followers.[54] Still others maintain that the fear and silence of the women belong to the structure of epiphany: the silence is both the sign of the proper limits of humanity in the presence of divinity and the sign of human fallibility in being effective followers.[55]

There is not a persuasive reason to explain why the women are kept silent at the very last moment. Since, after all, they convey the message to the disciples, we only need to consider it from the perspective of Mark's redactional or narrative intention. I cannot find any reason except Mark's androcentric mindset. If it were only the women that continued their discipleship of following and serving, he would have to end up recommending the women as the models of discipleship. If we reflect on the long history of women being treated as inferior by men, the reversal of values performed by Jesus should have resulted in a full recommending of the other side. It is necessary to encourage and empower doubly or triply those who have been seriously hampered. Of course this does not mean the reversal of the relation between men and women. But it must appear threatening to men. In order to restore the fallible disciples, who needed to be honored so that Mark's readers could identify with their failure and recovery, Mark depicts the women, too, as fallible and parallels them with the disciples. Otherwise no man would have listened to him. It seems to me that Mark is also a man, who regards the male disciples as the most important in the community and hopes that they will become true leaders by taking up the issues that confront them.

And if it is Mark's serious intention to reinstate the leadership of male disciples in his community of faith, he needs to restore the disciples in the Gospel narrative. To encourage and activate contemporary failed disciples, Mark must provide motivations, energy, and models to follow. Mark could have found these models in the women, but Mark also failed to perceive what the good news had done to women. Patriarchal mentality hindered him from seeing that point.

As a woman, I do not think that, in interpreting Mark, one should make a point of emphasizing that both men and women are equally fallible. Of course that is the reality of life. But Mark should have paid more attention to the beginning of the Gospel, which activated women to accept such a new order. As we have already seen, women restore the wholeness of their lives through interacting with Jesus.

Despite this deficiency in Mark, it is remarkable to notice that he repeats Jesus' prediction that he will go before the disciples in 14:27-28 and in 16:7. The prediction shows that the interaction will continue even after Jesus' death. The meeting in Galilee between the resurrected Jesus and

54. Dewey, "Point of View," 134: "There is no one whose faithfulness does not falter and who does not need God's forgiveness. The invitation to follow Jesus remains." Munro, "Women Disciples in Mark?" 238-39: "Mark discredits both the disciples and the women as opponents."

55. Malbon, "Fallible Followers," 44.

his followers can be the only remedy for the disciples' desertion and denial. The relationship will be re-established by Jesus' call again, just as his personal call established it in the beginning of his ministry. The disciples and the women are invited to stand up and follow Jesus, who is going before them. In this sense, to go to Galilee is not to escape the challenges of life, but to risk their lives in involvement with Jesus in the paradox of power and suffering.

The promise that Jesus is going ahead also calls the women not to allow the hierarchical relationship to be reinstated, but to challenge all disciples, including themselves, toward true discipleship. Thus, the Gospel is asking a response from both women and men by revealing where they stand and showing where to proceed.

Thus Mark is challenging his community, which has been straying from the true concept of discipleship, to connect serving and dying for many with leadership. How we activate this challenge offered by Jesus through Mark in the power politics of our contemporary society is the lasting question for us. We must yet look for its answer, since history shows the church's failure to practice such discipleship.

8

DIVORCE, PROSTITUTION, AND ADULTERY

In previous chapters I have dealt only with stories in which women play significant roles in making Jesus become truly Jesus. The text of the discourse on divorce does not directly treat interactions between women and Jesus. Nevertheless, Jesus' radicalism can be traced in his revolutionary attitude toward sexuality. This is why I have included this interchange of Jesus with the leaders.

LEGAL ASPECTS OF PATRIARCHAL SOCIETY

"Is It Lawful for a Man To Divorce His Wife?"

Jesus' unaffected way of interacting with women is astounding and unexpected. The religious establishment is offended and has to face its own reactions to Jesus' teachings and behavior. Matthew 19:3-12 is almost parallel in context as well as contents, except that Matthew "rearranged the Markan argument to conform to more acceptable scribal reasoning."[1]

The Pharisees, who seek to discredit Jesus by getting him to say something offensive, approach Jesus when "he went to the region of Judea and beyond the Jordan" (10:1). This means, according to the Markan narrative, that Jesus is already on the way to Jerusalem, where his journey is going to culminate in his death on the cross.[2] The issue they raise to plot Jesus' defeat provides him with another opportunity to show his egalitarian spirit. Jesus refuses to be trapped.

"Some Pharisees came, and to test him they asked, 'Is it lawful for a man to divorce his wife?' " (v. 2). They raise a question on another practical issue of life, as they did earlier on washing hands before eating (7:1-23).

1. Myers, *Binding the Strong Man*, 265.
2. Norman Perrin, *What is Redaction Criticism?* (Philadelphia: Fortress Press, 1969), 44. Barbara Green, "Jesus' Teaching on Divorce in the Gospel of Mark," *Journal for the Study of the New Testament* 38 (1990), 72. Myers, *Binding the Strong Man*, 264.

In Matthew, the question raised by the Pharisees is recorded a little differently: "Is it lawful to divorce one's wife for any cause?" (19:3). While in Mark they ask the legitimacy of divorce itself, in Matthew they assume the right to divorce one's wife and merely ask its legitimate grounds.

Jesus first refuses to answer directly, giving a question back to them: "What did Moses command you?" (v. 3). Since the Scriptures and traditions are their canon, it is a good way to keep the discourse fair and square. It also seems to be Jesus' tactic to develop his teaching from the other party's point of view. Their answer is, "Moses allowed a man to write a certificate of divorce, and put her away" (v. 4). The answer refers to Deuteronomy 24:1: "Suppose a man enters into marriage with a woman, but she does not please him because he finds something objectionable about her, and so he writes her a certificate of divorce, puts it in her hand, and sends her out of his house . . . " According to this law, all the initiative is to be taken by the husband. Men could easily divorce their wives at any time, for almost any reason, since it is the husband who defines what is "something objectionable" in his wife. There is no room for wives to appeal. As long as this law binds wives, they can never expect reciprocal relations with their husbands.

If a husband finds something unpleasant in his wife, it could be a legitimate reason to divorce. The question the Pharisees raised in Matthew is in line with this law. At the time of Jesus, the way the Pharisees interpreted the law varied depending on the school. The stand introduced here was taken by Hillel and his school, according to whom burned food or a noisy voice could be a reason for divorce. So the central issue of the question is to make clear what constitutes legitimate grounds for divorce. On the other hand, Shammai and his school, who are more conservative, interpreted the law more restrictively, putting more stress on determining what could be considered "unpleasant" on the woman's part.[3] The question may have been raised with the intention of aligning Jesus with one of the schools,[4] but Jesus shows no interest in it.

In Mark, the legitimacy of unilateral divorce by husbands is questioned directly. The question is not immediately related to a discourse among the Jewish scribes. Here we may see a distinctively Markan understanding of Jesus: Mark does not deem it appropriate for Jesus to be asked the legitimate causes for divorce.

A Woman as One Owned by Others

In the biblical world, women can generally be described as someone's property. Until marriage, a woman is the property of her father, after mar-

---

3. Elaine Pagels, *Adam, Eve, and the Serpent* (New York: Random House, 1988), 13-14. Hauck/Schulz, "πορνη, πορνος, πορνεια, πορνευω, εκπορνευω," *TDNT*, vol. 6, 591. Green, "Jesus' Teaching on Divorce," 73. Myers, *Binding the Strong Man*, 265.

4. Green, "Jesus' Teaching on Divorce," 73.

riage the property of her husband, and as a widow the property of her son. The tradition is very similar to the Confucian teaching of three obediences which has been widely practiced in Japan. It teaches women to obey their fathers while they are unmarried, to obey their husbands when married, and to be under the protection of their sons when old.[5]

Even today our Family Registration Law requires every citizen to register as a member of a certain family. When a baby arrives, parents are obliged to have his or her name enrolled in the family register at the government office within a week after the child's birth. When a man and a woman are about to be married, they delete their names from their own family registers and open a new family register. "Family" is the smallest unit that constitutes Japan as a nation. Because of this family registration system, the government has oversight over every citizen. Based on the registration, the civil office sends all sorts of information and requirements to every member of the nation.

This legal system originated as a part of the emperor system supported by the State Shintoism under the philosophy that Japan as a country constituted one big family. The father of the nationwide family was the emperor, and each family member was required to obey the emperor as the absolute authority. The literal meaning of patriarchy, "the rule of the father," was practiced literally. Shintoism played a very important role when the government aimed at national unity by heightening the spirit of loyalty and patriotic sentiment. Because of the public propaganda of this "one-big-family" state, national unity was hierarchically confirmed under the slogan of homogeneity of the people. This resulted in the establishment of barriers between the insiders and the outsiders, and discrimination against foreigners and people in the outcast villages.

Needless to say, this system of national patriarchy contributed to the strengthening of the patriarchy in each family (the so-called "Ie-system": "Ie" means a household) Nationally the emperor was absolute, and domestically fathers were absolute as the heads of the household. Wives and children were to be subordinate. Thus the discrimination of women and girls became more decisive. Women were recognized only when they gave birth to descendents. Therefore it was long thought unnatural for women not to be married. The Ie-system was abolished in 1945, almost fifty years ago, but its mentality is not yet erased and controls the subconsciousness of the people.

When a woman and man marry and establish a new family, they register their family name. Without doubt, husbands' family names have almost always been registered until recently. For a woman, it means to enter her husband's family and contribute by giving birth to the descendents of his family lineage.[6] It is possible for a family to trace its family line through

5. Sallie B. King, *Passionate Journey*, 171.

6. The Family Registration Law will be amended in 1993, and a new married couple may register both family names, though their child must register only one of the parents' family names.

generations. A wife has been called in Japanese "a woman who serves her husband's family relations," because she cannot concentrate on her relationship with her husband but finds herself wedded to all his relatives.[7] A mother-in-law has been called "a woman who manages his big family" since she has been a matter of grave concern for families, not just a personal relationship between a woman and a man. There has never been a legislative family system, but the Family Registration Law has contributed to support the conventional patriarchal system in our society. We have experienced how difficult it is to do away with such a convention, especially one once supported by the command of a divine emperor. It should be added that the concept of the "one-big-family" state has fostered the sense of group-orientedness with which people have learned to be in harmony with other people and not to disgrace those who are above them in their social groups. A dyadic way of thinking is required, and people are trained willingly to sacrifice themselves for the sake of their authority. So there is little room for the sense of human rights to come up in such a society as this.

In patriarchal societies such as Palestine at the time of Jesus and modern Japan, women's whole lives were defined by their subordination to men. Women could not be freed from this objectification as a possession in such androcentric societies. According to the law, an Israelite woman could be divorced at any time, if she was not a virgin at marriage, did not bear sons, or did not otherwise fit her husband's willful thinking. Divorce could occur very easily and one-sidedly. We can easily see that the question in Jesus' context was based on this typically androcentric mindset, which established the one-sided social practice of divorce legitimated by law.[8] Here patriarchal marriages were presupposed and never questioned.

Perceiving their mindset, Jesus answers, "Because of your hardness of heart he wrote this commandment for you" (v. 5). The commandment itself is the inevitable product of the social system of patriarchy. Jesus attributes the commandment to the husbands' hardness of heart. It reveals how difficult it is for those who have long been privileged and enjoyed their willful lives to recognize their deficiency and transform their way of thinking as well as their conduct. They are simply threatened and become defensive.

One-sided Legal Treatment: Adultery

The one-sidedness that humiliated women is found in the legal treatment of adultery. The biblical writers paid extremely careful attention to setting up detailed laws on adultery with comparatively little restriction on prostitution. Strict control is exercised over adultery.

7. Cherry Kittredge, *Womansword: What Japanese Words Say about Women* (Tokyo and New York: Kodansha International, 1987), 73.

8. E. Schüssler Fiorenza, *In Memory of Her*, 143. Myers, *Binding the Strong Man*, 265.

Adultery is controlled by strict rules and detailed provisions in the Old Testament. Leviticus 20:10 and Deuteronomy 22:22-29 explain in detail the commandment, "You shall not commit adultery" (Exod. 20:14). In Israelite society, adultery came into existence when a man had sexual relationships with either (1) a married woman, (2) an engaged virgin, or (3) a non-engaged virgin. If a man committed adultery, he was to be killed, except in the case that the adultery was with a non-engaged virgin. In this case, he was obliged to marry her himself, and was never allowed to divorce her.

He was convicted on the charge that he infringed the owner's rights over the woman. He was severely punished because he had affected the honor and property of the other male party, not of the woman. The married or engaged woman involved in the sexual relationship was also killed or, if not engaged, obliged to marry the man, because she had insulted her owner. Thus we can define adultery as an insult of honor and an attack on another man's property. It is an infringement of the marital relationship of one man by means of sexual relationships between his woman and another man, or it is an insult of a father's honor and an attack on his property by causing his daughter to lose her virginity. It was essential for a father to keep his daughter a virgin so that he could transfer her from his household to her husband's.

At a glance, the teaching on adultery seems to call for inviolability and purity in marital relationships. However, the teaching was altogether one-sided and given only from a male point of view. Women's dignity or rights were hardly taken into consideration. If the tokens of virginity were not found at her marriage, she would be stoned to death (Deut. 22:13-21), while a man would never be questioned about his virginity. If a husband became jealous that his wife may have defiled herself, he could take her to the priest who administered upon her a number of severe laws to find out the truth (Num. 5:11-31). A woman, however, had no recourse against her husband if he were defiled. Women simply were not taken to be human beings with equal rights to those of husbands or fathers. Women are humiliated as men's property. They are fully objectified.

In Japan between 1899 and 1947, those who committed adultery were sentenced guilty by Civil Law. The Civil Law, abolished at the end of the Second World War, gave all the power to the heads of households to support the patriarchal system and keep a male genealogy. No marriage could take place without the permission of the heads of both families. Once a woman got married, she was considered incompetent and was unable to make any contract without her husband's supervision or to take care of her own property. Her only value was found in giving birth to a boy who succeeds in her husband's lineage. Her experience had much in common with the experiences of women in the biblical world.

In Japan as well as in Israel, adultery was regarded as violation of a man's property. If a wife had sexual relations with another man, the man was guilty to her husband and had to compensate him. A man, even if he had a wife, was free to have sexual relations with any women but other men's wives. Even if he had sexual relations with someone's wife, he was not guilty unless her husband sued him for damages. And it often happened that the husband would not sue the man who had sexual relations with his wife because he was more afraid that his wife's misdeed would be talked about. When a wife committed adultery, she could be divorced with no exception. A wife could be sued for adultery and sentenced to two years imprisonment or a lesser punishment. But a wife had no right to sue her husband for adultery. The law was absolutely one-sided.

No Option Except To Become a Prostitute

It was very hard for divorced women and unmarried women to live in a society where marriage was almost the only way for women to be socially accepted. They might become slaves of male or female owners. In this case, too, they were used as sexual objects as well as substitute childbearers in place of legal wives who were barren. The only possible way for a woman to make a living by herself might be to become a prostitute. The fact that the original Greek term for prostitution as used in the New Testament means "to sell" may indicate that prostitution was already given tacit consent in that society and was popular among the people of the time.[9] As far as the Old Testament is concerned, we cannot find any critique of the society that tolerated the practice of prostitution, although prostitution, along with other practices such as homosexuality, abortion, and infanticide, contradicted Jewish custom and law which confined sexual activity to procreation.[10]

We must be careful not to confuse adultery and prostitution. It should be noted that the term "prostitute" was used for the Israelites when they became unfaithful to their only God, Yahweh, by withdrawing from Yahweh and following other gods. The term designated the Israelites' apostasy from and unfaithfulness toward their God (Exod. 34:15f; Lev. 17:7; 20:5f; Deut. 31:16; Judg. 2:17; 8:27; Isa. 23:17; Jer. 3:1; Ezek. 6:9, etc.). The word might imply "go astray or leave away (from God)."[11]

However, when we learn that the gods they earnestly followed were the Canaanite fertility gods such as Ba'al and Asherah, we see why the term was used to imply their apostasy and how deeply they were influenced and tempted by those gods and their cults. Fertility was believed to be caused by divine power through the reproductive cycle of crops and herds. Life-

9. Georg Fohrer and Evalt Lövestam, "Ehebruch," *Biblisch-Historisches Handwörter-buch*, (Göttingen: Vandenhoeck and Ruprecht, 1963, Japanese translation (Tokyo: Kyo Bun Kwan, 1989), 341.

10. Pagels, *Adam, Eve, and the Serpent*, 11.

11. Athalya Brenner, *The Israelite Woman: Social Role and Literary Type in Biblical Narrative* (Sheffield: JSOT, 1985), 126 in Japanese edition.

bearing functions participated in the activity of divine power.[12] Sexual intercourse was adopted as a part of worship rituals. The worship rituals for Ba'al and Asherah were held on the high places, and in some cases even in the house of Yahweh (2 Kings 23:7f). Sexual relations on the high places were cultic and therefore divine. Such relations were distinguished from secular sexual relations, that is, prostitution. Women who served at the high places of Ba'al and Asherah were called temple prostitutes. This means "those separated and devoted to gods." They prayed for fertility through practicing the cults of divine marriage on the high places. In addition, they collected donations from pilgrims and visitors by engaging in sexual intercourse with them (Deut. 23:18). We see, therefore, that the cult and prostitution had not a few characteristics in common (i.e. sexual intercourse and money). It is probable that the Israelites were for a long time strongly influenced and tempted by the Canaanite fertility cults in which sexual intercourse and sacrificial feasts played important parts (Gen. 38:21ff.; Num. 25:1; Jer. 3:2; Isa. 57:5,7; Hos. 4:14; Ezek. 22:9, etc.).

The Deuteronomic law unconditionally forbids the cult (23:17-18), leaving no room for temple prostitutes. However, we might infer that the Israelite society adjusted to female temple prostitutes, though not to male ones, from the fact that there are quite a few references to the expulsion of male temple prostitutes (1 Kings 14:24; 15:12; 22:47; 2 Kings 23:7), but none to the expulsion of female ones, and that there are occasional references to female prostitutes that suggest their popular acceptance by society.[13] The system by which they collected donations from visitors in return for sexual relations apparently opened the way for women to achieve their economic independence.

It is not strange that the Old Testament has no verb to refer to the acts of sexual intercourse with those cultic devotees. These acts as such were devoted to pagan gods, and therefore recognized as "going astray from Yahweh" in the biblical world. They were subject to harsh criticism. The people were to draw a clear line between Yahweh and other gods. The prophets of Israel often used "to engage in prostitution" as a metaphor for Israelites' apostasy from Yahweh (Hos. 4:12-15; Isa. 1:21; 23:15; Jer. 2:20; 5:7; 13:27; Ezek. 16:15-37; Nah. 3:4, etc.).

It is, however, imaginable that there existed a rather strong tendency to welcome and tolerate the sexual availability of women, and the sanctioning of prostitution was implied within the context of patriarchy in Israelite society.[14] In the course of time, "to engage in prostitution" was used for

12. G. Fohrer and L. Kövestam, "Ehebruch," *Biblisch-Historisches Handwörterbuch,* 70. Hauck/Schulz, "πορνη, πορνος, πορνεια, πορνευω, εκπορνευω," 587.

13. In Genesis 38, for example, the words for prostitute and temple prostitute are both used, and seemingly without distinction between them. See also Hos. 4:14.

14. Genesis 38:15: When Judah saw a woman with her face covered, he took it for granted that she was a prostitute. Joshua 2:1-2: Two spies who went to view the land secretly came into a house that they could identify as the house of a harlot and lodged

prostitution, extramarital relationships, and deviant sexual acts in secular contexts. In addition, the term was applied only to women.

Compared to the severe punishment policy for cases of adultery, prostitution was hardly regulated by law at all. The only law concerning prostitution in the Old Testament is in Leviticus 19:29, which reads: "Do not profane your daughter by making her a prostitute, that the land not become prostituted and full of depravity." Even this law was directed at fathers to impress upon them how important it was to preserve their daughters' virginity. The law was in no way intended to protect women's dignity and rights as human beings. Such a concept could not be expected in a society that protected women as long as they were treated as objects and possessions. Perhaps it would be appropriate to say that prostitutes were women who had lost their owners.

Men were never convicted for having relations with prostitutes. Thus with no legal protection or restriction, prostitution was popularly accepted, and prostitutes were familiar figures in the life of the people, even though prostitutes were shunned socially and religiously and treated with contempt. Therefore, prostitution took on a perjorative connotation.[15]

PROSTITUTION AND ADULTERY IN THE GOSPELS

On Behalf of Prostitutes

Although there are only a few direct references to prostitutes and prostitution in the gospels, all of them are very important. The term "prostitute" is used only twice in Matthew's Gospel (21:31-32) and once in Luke (15:30). In Matthew, Jesus says, "You [the chief priests and elders of the people] did not believe [John the Baptist], but the tax collectors and the prostitutes believed him." Here Matthew contrasts those who insist that they themselves are clean and pure because they fulfill the requirements of the laws with those who cannot fulfill the laws of cleanliness and purity and are thus called sinners. In this way prostitutes become a paradigm of those who hasten to John and probably later to Jesus when they hear the gospel. Mark does not use the term "prostitute," but instead he uses the phrase "tax collectors and sinners." Luke uses the term when the elder brother blames his prodigal brother who squanders his property in loose living, saying to

there as if it were natural for them. 1 Kings 3:16-17: The two harlots began to tell the story of their babies to the king without blaming their other parties. Judges 11:1: Now Jephthah the Gileadite was a mighty warrior, but he was the son of a harlot. Judges 16:1: Samson went to Gaza, and there he saw a harlot and went in to her.

15. Genesis 34:31. The purity code required priests to pay much attention to their cleanness so that the daughter of any priest, if she profanes herself by playing the harlot, profanes her father and she shall be burned with fire (Leviticus 21:9). The priest shall take a wife in her virginity (Leviticus 21:13-14).

their father, "He has devoured your property with prostitutes." From this pejorative expression, one can infer that prostitutes are ranked at the bottom of society, discriminated against, and shunned. According to Matthew, however, Jesus says, "Truly, I tell you, the tax collectors and the prostitutes are going into the kingdom of God ahead of you [the chief priests and the elders of the people]." This statement is also revolutionary because Jesus not only turns upside down the value system of his time, but he completely reverses the standard. Jesus is fully on the side of prostitutes and invites them to the inheritance of God as the first guests of honor.

Both Sexes on an Equal Level

As we have already seen, the expression "to engage in prostitution" has been applied only to women, even though prostitution cannot exist without the lust of men. Jesus seems to be the only "man" who is conscious of both sexes in relation to the question of prostitution.

Both Mark 7:21-23 and Matthew 15:19-20 mention prostitution and adultery together in their list of vices. "For it is from within, from the human heart, that evil intentions come: *fornication,* theft, murder, *adultery,* avarice, wickedness, deceit, licentiousness, envy, slander, pride, folly. All these evil things come from within, and they defile a person" (Mark 7:21-23). Both Mark and Matthew use the term "person" to identify those who practice these evil things.

Both biblical languages (Hebrew and Greek) are languages in which the masculine functions as generic. In such languages, feminine forms are used only when the words definitely designate someone female. Otherwise, male forms are used to indicate male or both genders.[16] Thus, "person" here cannot designate only woman; it designates both man and woman or man only. Therefore, Jesus' saying makes two things clear. First, fornication involves both sexes—a woman selling her sexuality and a man buying it. Second, it is one of the things a person should resolutely avoid. Jesus' rejection of prostitution is radical and allows no exceptions.

The principle established by Jesus is followed in Paul's letters (1 Cor. 6:19; 1 Thess. 4:3-5; Gal. 5:19-21), letters written by Paul's disciples (Eph. 5:5; Col. 3:5) and a pseudo-Pauline letter (1 Tim. 1:9-10).[17] From the fact that adultery and prostitution are mentioned side by side, we can infer that these two connote different sexual relationships.

16. Wire, *The Corinthian Women Prophets,* ix. E. Schüssler Fiorenza, "Text and Reality—Reality as Text, 28.

17. Hauck/Schulz, "πορνη, πορνος, πορνεια, πορνευω, εκπορνευω," 590: "Not without some influence on the part of the moral preaching of Hellenistic philosophy the so-called list of vices developed in the Judaism of the Hellenistic diaspora. If the list is always a variable one, there is still a traditional core which includes adultery and fornication along with idolatry, witchcraft, murder and the like."

"God Made Them Male and Female"

If we recognize that there was "no recognition of reciprocal rights for women in Jewish family law at the time,"[18] we are now ready to go back to the text. In his discourse with the Pharisees Jesus refuses to be confined to a discussion of the Mosaic law, but refers to the creation story (Gen. 1:27 and 2:24). He uses texts from the Bible against opponents who base their authority on it. In Mark 10:6-9 we read, "But from the beginning of creation, 'God made them male and female.' 'For this reason a man shall leave his father and be joined to his wife, and the two shall become one flesh.' Therefore what God has joined together, let no person separate." The phrase "and be joined to his wife" is regarded as disputed. Some important manuscripts such as Sinaiticus and Vaticanus omit it.

Though it is not certain which of the manuscripts of the creation story Jesus relied on, Hebrew or Greek, the Hebrew text we have reads as follows:

Genesis 1:27 "And God created humankind in God's image, in the image of God he created humankind male and female he created them."

Genesis: 2:24 "Therefore a man leaves his father and his mother, and clings to his woman and they become one flesh."

Both Hebrew and Greek texts of 1:27 use the same masculine terms which can designate either gender. But the 2:24, which was written earlier than the text of 1:27, uses a term "a man" that distinctly expresses male, while the Greek text uses a term "a person" that can be used for both genders.

Without the phrase "and be joined to his wife," in Mark's quotation of Genesis 2:24, this whole sentence becomes applicable to both genders. Following this quotation, when we read Jesus' words "Therefore what God has joined together, let no person separate," we may take "a person" as designating both genders. If this is the case, it is possible to infer that Mark intended to put both genders on the same equal balance. Both male and female are responsible for not separating what God has joined together.

On the other hand, in Matthew there seems no textual problem, and the Genesis phrase "be joined to his wife" (19:5) makes it clear that "a person" designates only the male. Therefore, the phrase "let no person separate" can also imply "let no man (husband) separate." If Matthew was fully aware of the illegitimacy of the one-sided right of divorce, we may assume that the evangelist intented to reject male arbitrariness in divorce. If not, his androcentric mindset is still neglecting the female party.

Thus it is clear that Jesus is confronting the situation in which the freedom of divorce is granted only to husbands, their arbitrariness is justified by law, and their guilt is excused by lawful means.

18. Myers, *Binding the Strong Man*, 265.

Therefore, his severe statement prohibiting divorce is aimed at those husbands who practice divorce for selfish reasons. It is the absolute negation of the prerogative unilaterally sanctioned on the side of the husband.

In making this extremely radical statement, Jesus intended to restore women, who had long been regarded as property, to an egalitarian relationship by rejecting the traditional custom. Women regain their dignity as human beings in the sight of Jesus.

Reading his words in their historical and social milieu, we therefore cannot take them as a declaration of the unconditional prohibition of divorce. His words are radical as well as essential, but we must be conscious of the fact that they are also contextual. The most important point is that the ethics that have until now favored only men are made void.

JESUS' REVISION OF THE CONCEPT OF ADULTERY

The concept of adultery[19] is radicalized by Jesus. He revises it by denouncing the one-sided relationship and putting both woman and man on the same level. He makes his position clear in the following dialogue with his disciples. The disciples ask him again about divorce. Mark records two different answers by Jesus: "Whoever divorces his wife and marries another, commits adultery against her," and "if she divorces her husband and marries another, she commits adultery" (10:10-12). It should be noted that Jesus uses exactly the same verbs for both wife and husband. He deals with the wife and her husband on the same level. Undermining the traditional relationship between a possessor and the possessed, Jesus brings wives and their dignity as persons into the foreground. For him, adultery is no longer the injury of a man's property.

A husband can be charged with adultery if he divorces his wife. This means he can no longer enjoy the one-sided privilege of divorcing his wife at his will. On the contrary, he is obliged to be faithful to his marital relationship just as his wife is. Jesus also declares that the charge of adultery can be applied to a wife. It is interesting to note that Jesus' statement is fair to both husbands and wives, and is made on the premise that a wife can carry out her right to divorce her husband. Jesus' idea is fully egalitarian and prescribes that the charge of adultery may be levied against either the wife or the husband if they break their marital relationship. Thus Jesus requires that both sexes be faithful.

19. Originally and traditionally adultery meant to infringe on a man's honor and property through sexual relations with a woman belonging to that man. The meanings of words continually reflect the political, social, and religious circumstances of the age in which they are used. Words used in the Bible are no exception. From the time the oldest source was written in about 1000 B.C.E. until the writings were completed, about 1,200 years had elapsed. During that time, numerous materials were added. It is only natural to assume, therefore, that connotations of the same word may have changed as they appear in the various books of Scripture.

The one-sided and arbitrary execution of divorce is based on the idea that men are allowed to possess women. Jesus breaks with this view completely and rebuilds a new relationship between woman and man as equal partners before God.

Mark is careful to depict how Jesus puts both genders on equal balance. On the other hand, Jesus' answer in the Matthean text — "Whoever divorces his wife, except for unchastity, and marries another, commits adultery" (19:9) — puts more emphasis on the husband's responsibility. Furthermore, we read in Matthew 5:32: "Every one who divorces his wife, except on the ground of unchastity, makes her an adulteress; and whoever marries a divorced woman commits adultery." Matthew does not seem to have a reciprocal view of divorce. In addition, there must have been some change in the meaning of adultery, in which, as we have seen, the honor of the owner of the woman involved was the main issue and both parties to the adultery were punished by being stoned to death. At this point, Luke, who deleted the discourse, reports the same view (16:18).

For Matthew, the wife's unchastity (*porneia*; prostitution) provides one exception to the prohibition of divorce. He probably added this phrase to his source when he wrote his Gospel. If a wife would be found guilty of adultery by unchastity (prostitution), and if she knows she would be killed for adultery, would she willingly engage in prostitution? We are not able to judge from this phrase who would be able to convict the woman of unchastity. Matthew is conservative and conforms to the Pharisaic reasoning. It seems that the distinction between adultery and prostitution is already ambiguous.

However, it should be added that Matthew also records the most pointed and revolutionary expression of Jesus' heart: "But I say to you that everyone who looks at a woman lustfully has already committed adultery with her in his heart" (5:28). Matthew fluctuates.

It is regrettable that the very impact Jesus gives to this concept is not discernible in Japanese translations, which only reflect the mindset of the translators. The Japanese translation is based on the traditional Japanese view of a family-centered marriage structure. In Japanese the text reads as follows: "Whoever divorces his wife and takes another woman for himself and for his family, commits adultery against her, and if she separates herself from her husband (is divorced) and is married to another, she commits adultery." Women here are depicted as thoroughly passive, reflecting the subordinate relationship of women to men in Japan.

We read in Matthew 19:10-12 that the disciples do not comprehend the impact of Jesus' statement and react against him saying, "If such is the case of a man with his wife, it is better not to marry." Their reaction that it is unbearable to be bound by the marital relationship typically reflects their view of women as property. Jesus' response to them focuses on those who cannot be other than single, the eunuchs. "There are eunuchs who have been so from birth, and there are eunuchs who have been made eunuchs by others, and there are eunuchs who have made themselves eunuchs for the sake of the kingdom of heaven." Eunuchs are more severely excluded from the circle of the elect than are prostitutes and tax collectors (Deut. 23:1). They are men who are despised by all and cannot get married even if they wanted to. Thus Matthew describes Jesus as inviting all who are rejected and excluded. He may be speculating about how the true community of faith is to be constituted.

There must be many people who do not marry for the sake of the gospel. Prostitutes also must be invited to be active in the community of faith. Jesus and some of his disciples are also single. The newly born community of faith is supposed to be fully inclusive, according to Matthew. We cannot conclude, however, that Jesus encourages singleness or makes it an ideal way of life.[20]

Jesus rejects any boundary created by the law to separate the clean from the unclean and exclude the latter as sinners. He removes any barrier that forms groups of human beings according to artificial criteria. Jesus intends to accept all as they are. He rejects no one. From what we have seen about Jesus' concern with egalitarian relationships between man and woman, we may plausibly infer that Jesus could never accept prostitution in which women are objectified and deprived of their human rights. Men of authority in first-century Palestine, however, especially those who tried to trap Jesus, did not regard it as a problem. Therefore little reference to it was made in the gospels.

A CONTEMPORARY ISSUE: JAPAN'S INTERNATIONAL SLAVE TRADE

It is remarkable to note that all through biblical history, the issue of prostitution, especially from the viewpoint of the prostitutes, was virtually ignored. As I have already pointed out, prostitution as a vocation must be dealt with in the context of the discriminative social structure of sexism. Women, especially unmarried women, in a patriarchal society could be forced into such a situation. Prostitution is not a private matter.

Japan's history in relation to prostitution is quite similar to the situation in Palestine in biblical times. In Japanese, prostitution has long been defined as "woman's selling her sexuality." The definition makes its reciprocal connotation ambiguous. Even though Jesus tried hard to make it clear that both sexes are involved in prostitution, the Japanese translation tends to blame only the woman involved. It is worse yet when the term is translated by the imprecise word "immorality," with no clear indication of what

20. Cf. Pagels, *Adam, Eve, and the Serpent*, 16: "Even more startling, Jesus endorses — and exemplifies — a new possibility and one he says is even better: rejecting both marriage and procreation in favor of voluntary celibacy, for the sake of following him into the new age."

it actually designates. We see here the Japanese male-controlled view of church history reflecting the structurally patriarchal framework of Japanese society.

In 1956, licensed prostitution was abolished in Japan, due to international pressure from the Treaty Banning Trafficking in Prostitution or Exploiting Others for the Purpose of Prostitution established by the United Nations in 1950. The Law still lacks a provision for punishing men who solicit prostitution.[21]

As the GNP of Japan increased and Japan became one of the major world economic powers, the prostitution issue has once again come to the fore. Japan's wealth has attracted a continuous wave of illegal foreign workers, mainly from Asia, that shows no sign of receding despite tighter immigration regulations than ever. Due to its geographical isolation and cultural insularity, Japan encountered this problem much later than other rich countries that have long been facing the issue of migrant laborers. Therefore, when foreigners started to enter Japan and work illegally because of the rising yen and the abundance of unskilled job vacancies, Japan was unprepared, relying on the weak enforcement of its out-of-date immigration law. As the Syrophoenician woman dared to encounter Jesus, those migrants took the initiative to come into Japan to share its market of labor.

Although in the past Japan only accepted skilled workers from foreign countries when it needed their skills (approximately 200,000 people), it has been forced recently to examine the whole system of the acceptance of migrant laborers to break the deadlock caused by a shortage of labor, world economic trends and the uncontrollable flow of unskilled laborers from Asia.[22]

Foreign laborers with entertainer and tourist visas draw our special attention. In 1989, there were 38,000 people with entertainer visas, most of them women from the Philippines who actually worked as hostesses at bars. People with entertainer visas can acquire more stable positions in Japanese society then those with tourist visas, yet their income tends to be smaller because of the double tax system that requires them to pay tax both in Japan and in their home countries.[23]

Most illegal unskilled workers arrive on three-month tourist visas and are hired by small, uncompetitive businesses. Between 1982 and 1986, the number of foreigners prosecuted as illegal immigrants tripled, and that number continued to increase. In 1990, according to the official estimate, over 100,000 people were illegally working with a tourist visa and only a fraction (22,626) were deported in 1989. Most men with tourist visas come from the Philippines, Bangladesh, Pakistan, and China and work on con-

21. "Migrant Women Workers," *Japan Christian Activity News*, 703 (Sept. 1992), 8.

22. Aiko Utumi, *Migrant Laborers from Asia* (Tokyo: Akashi Shoten, 1988), 16. Karabao no Kai, *Our Fellow Foreign Workers: Report from Sites* (Tokyo: Akashi Shoten, 1988), 168.

23. Karabao no Kai, ibid., 168.

struction sites, in factories, and in other unskilled sectors, while women are mainly from the Philippines, Thailand, and Taiwan.[24] In many cases, women are forced to work in the sex-entertainment industry as hostesses, strippers, or prostitutes, even though they made contracts as waitresses, models, or baby-sitters in their home countries. Coming to this prosperous country of high technology and a strong currency, women are led to believe that they would be paid enough to support their families at home. When they arrive, however, they find a completely different reality, in which the only way they can earn money is by engaging in prostitution. There are, of course, promoters, production groups, and club managers who earn a huge profit through victimizing them. Groups of bullies connected with internationally organized prostitution make use of the weakness of these women for raising funds.[25]

The real issue here is not the women's illegal status as such, but rather the fact that Japan tolerates those who, taking advantage of these women's intention to work, engage in modern slave trading and also those who sanction the existence of prostitutes as a necessary evil. They assume that the women are fully aware of the situation here and do not object to engaging in prostitution, and they proudly say that they are merely cooperating with these women who need to earn money.

We cannot tolerate the victimization of women by Japanese men. We cannot condone Japanese men who violate contracts with these powerless women, pay them no wages, inflict pain and injury by confinement and assault, and most of all deprive them of their human dignity. Many Japanese Christian women have been fighting against such a discriminatory social structure through a variety of movements and institutions.[26] We also challenge the lukewarm attitude taken by churches that work hard to keep clean only the inside of the churches. We also challenge the traditional tendency to regard prostitution as a private matter and to blame prostitutes as sinful and shameful. As we face the global issue of the pressing increase of economic refugees throughout the world today, we need to deal with this issue more seriously.[27]

24. Ibid., 169.

25. Cf. "Migrant Women in Japan, *In God's Image* (Spring 1992), 39-43.

26. HELP (House in Emergency of Love and Peace), which has been accepting many Asian women as they seek refuge fleeing from violence and ill-treatment by their employers, was opened in April 1986 in Tokyo. The shelter was originated as the project commemorating the centenary of the Japan Woman's Christian Temperance Union. Since then, there have been more than ten groups that have started working for such women in various cities in Japan.

27. I owe much of this part to the following book: Shizuko Ohshima and Carolyn Francis, *Japan: Through the Eyes of Women Migrant Workers* (Tokyo: Japan Women's Christian Temperance Union, 1989).

9

CONCLUSION

I have attempted to reread Mark's Gospel from a Japanese feminist perspective. Any feminist perspective must be based on an analysis of experiences of subjugation, marginalization, and oppression, and on the struggle for a discipleship of equals in churches, justice in societies, and peace at home and in the world. As a Japanese woman living in a society that has patriarchal characteristics in common with those in first-century Palestine, my experiences as a woman must have helped me see better the reality of the invisible women behind the texts.

In each chapter I have attempted to come close to the historical reality of interaction between the women and Jesus as depicted in Mark. My interest, of course, is not in pursuing historical factuality. I have taken as my vantage point the interactive dynamics between the women and Jesus. I would like to make an integrative survey of what has emerged from the studies of the individual women.

THE NATURE OF THE INTERACTIONS

Interactions between the women and Jesus were mostly generated through initiative actions on the part of women. The hemorrhaging woman dared to touch his clothing in secret. The Syrophoenician woman broke through Jesus' desire to be alone. The anointing woman invited herself to the house in which the meal fellowship was taking place. If we consider the historical situation that marginalized these women and made them invisible, we see how remarkable and how desperate they were as they dared to take action.

Interactions between the women and Jesus were usually initiated through some boundary-breaking by the woman and then taken up by Jesus. They all surmounted some barriers that constituted the boundaries of honor/shame in the patriarchal society: power, sexual status, and respect for one's superiors. The hemorrhaging woman challenged the purity laws concerning woman's blood and its contamination. The purity code is one of the greatest social barriers that prevented a woman from being an integral part of the society. She was assessed unclean and contagious by the law that created the boundary of sexual status. The Syrophoenician woman overcame the ethnic barrier, while the anointing woman broke down the sex barrier in coming into the closed male fellowship and carrying out the prophetic act of anointing. Jesus also overcame these barriers, but only by responding to their initiative actions. Jesus was challenged by the women when Jesus still intended to behave as a traditional Jewish man.

The women's initiative acts were sometimes motivated by their earnest desire to break through their impasse. The hemorrhaging woman touched Jesus' clothes in the hope that her disease would be cured. Her act of touching was problematic enough, but her situation was more complicated because she suffered not only from the lack of physical health, but also from the disruption between herself and society. She needed both to recover from physical brokenness and to restore the cohesiveness of her life within society. The Syrophoenician woman, hoping her daughter's disease would be cured, dared to break into the house where Jesus secluded himself. The mother caring for a demon-possessed daughter was alienated from the society together with her daughter, who could not hope to pursue the ordinary paths of life that healthy daughters followed.

These women displayed their perceptiveness by understanding who Jesus was, which led them into interaction with Jesus. Both the hemorrhaging woman and the Syrophoenician woman, having heard about Jesus, staked their lives on him. The Syrophoenician woman went further and showed Jesus what he was to be by persistently pressing her case with him. The anointing woman perceived Jesus' fate when nobody except Jesus saw it coming. She anointed him in silence, acting out her confession that Jesus was the lifegiving "Christ." Knowing who Jesus was and what Jesus was to be, she displayed her deep perceptiveness.

The women led Jesus to become a responding "boundary breaker." Having spent his whole life in the culture of honor/shame, which was fully male-oriented and which expected women to bear all the shame, Jesus did not take initiative until the women prepared him by stages to break down the boundaries.

Interactions were reciprocal and both sides received and learned something. The innate power of the life-giving Jesus responded to the hemorrhaging woman's initiating contact, and she was cured. Then he spoke. He invited her to the center of the community of faith from the fringe of the society. Thus the purity code concerning blood, which constituted part of the social and religious taboo, was overridden by Jesus. Facing the Syrophoenician woman, Jesus at first behaved just like his male comrades and tried to keep their collective honor, but quickly changed and became free of gender and ethnic barriers. He cured her daughter's disease. In the case of Peter's mother-in-law, who was cured of the fever, Jesus initiated the action by taking hold of her hand. Then she responded by serving Jesus and the people around. We may infer that Jesus' response to the anointing woman was to determine to go forward to his death at the hands of the authorities.

Interactions often involved issues of life and death. Taboos of contamination and demon-possession tormented the women. The anointing woman prepared Jesus for his death, and the women who followed Jesus through his arrest, crucifixion, burial, and resurrection shared his final moments of suffering.

Interactions often occurred in physical and emotional closeness. The hemorrhaging woman's touching, which was feared to be defiling, was fully accepted by Jesus. The anointing woman touched his head, consoling as well as consecrating. Jesus took hold of Peter's mother-in-law's hand to take care of her.

Interactions were life-communion in which the women concerned and Jesus encountered each other in trust. The women experienced being raised from death to life through life-communion with Jesus that was realized in other ways than only verbally. Our interactional vantage point makes it clear that the good news really became good news once there was a reciprocal commitment of lives.

Interactions with Jesus have led the women to become true disciples.

JESUS REVEALED AS LIFE-GIVING

Thus various interactions between women and Jesus recorded in the Gospel of Mark characterize Jesus as "life-giving." The "life-giving" character is revealed through his full solidarity with those who have lost their wholeness of life: the outcasts of the society. I use the word "outcasts" in its widest sense. The outcasts in Mark's Gospel are characterized as (1) those who are considered a threat to the "integrity" of the elect in society; (2) those who have no means of demanding their right to live in society; and (3) those who are marginalized and afflicted in society. To have solidarity with someone premises an interactional involvement of human lives. It cannot be one-sided or just benevolent. It requires reciprocal life-communion.

To become involved with society's outcasts in a life-giving way does entail social implications. Jesus is a threat to the authorities because he aligns with those who are considered a nuisance to the social order. Such authority is sustained by patriarchy, hierarchy, and monarchy. In Mark authority is often symbolized by the temple-centered religion and state.

As a typical example of the outcasts of Jesus' society, we have met a poor widow. She represents a paradigm of those who are victimized by the temple-centered religion and state. Though she neither interacted with Jesus nor was even aware that Jesus was watching her, she and others like her must have had a strong influence upon Jesus and helped give impetus to his ministry. She challenged the perspective of Jesus. Her life spoke boldly in silence, and Jesus' perceptiveness responded to her. She meant to commit her whole life to God, yet the irony and tragedy is that she is deceived into helping the authorities to maintain the status quo.

As long as women were considered to be men's property, women had to suffer from unequal rights. Unequal rights were one part of the system that supported the patriarchal power structure. Therefore Jesus undermined the unequal relationship between wives and husbands in matters of divorce. The life-giving Jesus who worked to restore the marginalized to the fullness of life is egalitarian in any human relationship.

It must be emphasized that the women who dared out of desperation to initiate an encounter with Jesus sparked his consciousness of being a suffering servant and made Jesus become truly Jesus Christ.

THE GOOD NEWS: LIBERATING OR THREATENING

All these women are considered nonpersons, the property of men whom they must follow and serve. Their self-understanding cannot but be negative. And if they are evaluated only in terms of bearing shame for the sake of men's honor, it is natural that they would find their own subservient behavior virtuous.

Yet their experience of encountering Jesus brought them a revolutionary transformation of their self-understanding. Life-communion with Jesus confirmed for them that they were first-class citizens, equal to anybody else, subjects of history and actors in society. They were empowered to follow Jesus and serve others. Being "protagonists" in following and serving were quite different from following and serving men as despised second-class citizens. These women must have been enthusiastic when they realized that what they used to practice was very close to the essential spirit of discipleship. We have learned from their experiences that what was decisive was how they were identified and accepted. What they did no longer mattered to them. Through their life experiences they had mastered the essence of discipleship: how to live the good news.

On the other hand, the men must have had a hard time. In their particular culture, they were raised to be honorable, to admire power and seek glory. They needed a high sense of mission with high expectations and visible respect. It would have been most difficult for them to accept the overturning of their value system and all the more difficult to accept women as their equal partners. They were the ones that were the most challenged by the good news. Instead of taking on the challenge, they failed Jesus and fled.

The good news liberated women while it threatened men.

Churches in our country have faced this issue, too. Women are called to keep challenging and disturbing churches that otherwise tend to be androcentric.

MARK'S PURPOSE FOR WRITING

"The beginning of the gospel of Christ . . . " (Mark 1:1) is carried through by the women who follow Jesus to the end, but Mark makes the narrative open-ended by the epilogue that circles readers back to the start. The stories of liberated women are suddenly extinguished at the last moment by Mark's statement: "They said nothing to anyone, for they were afraid." Mark has the women remain silent and fail to carry out their mission. This is partly because his main purpose in writing the Gospel is to restore the male disciples in his community of faith to true discipleship. He is criticizing male leaders by depicting women disciples as an alternative paradigm. For that purpose women play important roles in his Gospel narrative. But at the same time, he is challenging the male leaders of the community to respond to Jesus and involve themselves in Jesus' movement. Therefore the epilogue must function as the prologue in Mark's plot.

Mark comes close to depicting women as ideal. However, he does not simply recommend women as ideal disciples: he puts women on the same level as men. This is because he tries to communicate with male members living in the culture of honor/shame. His androcentric mindset also hinders him from fully affirming liberated women.

And so we may infer from Mark's criticism of male disciples that the Markan community of faith is already in the process of repatriarchalization. It is plausible to say that male disciples are seeking their own honor and contending with each other for leadership. Then women may also have become marginalized again. If so, he feels at ease with depicting women as almost ideal.

However, it is difficult to say that Mark has simply made up the stories of women. The male disciples would hardly accept them as evidence of life-giving interaction with Jesus. More likely Mark has collected popular, well-accepted stories. The male disciples might even be acquainted with some of the stories through oral transmission.

Therefore Mark may also mean implicitly to encourage women in his community of faith who have begun to step backward to resist the social pressure to do so. Unless this is the case, Mark's Gospel narrative becomes self-contradictory, because he depicts Jesus as teaching a discipleship of equals.

In either case, it seems that Mark has little interest in collaboration between activities of men and women. Since the urgent issue for Mark is to restore male disciples to true discipleship and to let men be awakened to true leadership, the collaborative community of faith can be expected only implicitly. Here again we see the limited horizon of Mark's male-oriented worldview.

MARKAN DISCIPLESHIP

Jesus' "life-giving" and "boundary-breaking" life inevitably leads him to suffering and death. "He gave his life as ransom for many" (10:45): for the outcasts of society. The praxis of giving his life as a ransom becomes the deepest call to the discipleship of following and serving. This call includes both the oppressors and the oppressed by way of the paradigm found in Jesus' life itself. Therefore the call is to go back to the beginning and to live through the Gospel narrative again.

The paradigm of Markan discipleship implies several things. First, the essence of discipleship may be described as "restoring life to its wholeness." Cohesiveness in life is to be realized with no exception. Second, the motivating energy is found in Jesus' words and praxis: "I go before you." The call has liberated women but threatened men. Third, the only discipleship possible is an inclusive discipleship of equals. Fourth, the traditional concept of leadership that supports the power structure is overturned. To commit oneself to the life-giving enterprise has become the basic task of leaders. Such a revolutionary transformation in the concept of leadership is surely the sociopolitical critique of the age.

Discipleship, while not the sole interest of Mark's Gospel, is nonetheless crucial to it. And his purpose of recording the vital importance to the Gospel of interactions with Jesus has unexpectedly led him to maintain an old strata of traditions about women.

THE CHALLENGE TO WOMEN

What are the women's issues, then? Jesus' movement was not conceivable without Jesus, but it was also inconceivable without women disciples. Women were always following and serving, yet they were not always recognized at the center of activity. They became partners of Jesus. They were called authentic models and told that their names would be remembered wherever the gospel was proclaimed.

Nevertheless, women are even now called to create and to maintain egalitarian, collaborative relationships, to share their experiences of following Jesus and serving others, and to challenge men to be transformed until they commit themselves to solidarity with the powerless by following Jesus who always goes before them.

The privileged concept of the chosen people in Judaism and of the church in Christianity is most dangerous and to be abhorred, because such ideology tends to encourage the chosen to tolerate indifferent attitudes toward the world they live in. Jesus puts everyone on the same level. It seems that the most urgent issue for Jesus is to invite all to make the reality of equality effective in daily life, not in the holy precinct. He does not invite us to be ascetic or single for the sake of God, but asks us who we are and whether we can accept our neighbor as we do ourselves. This question must be taken just as seriously by those who have practiced segregation and subjugation as it is by those who have been their victims.

We may infer that the church from its very beginning was bound by a patriarchal mentality and that Jesus died before he saw egalitarian discipleship in effect. The impact of Jesus' radicalism gave way after his death to more "practical" ethics conformed to society. We read teachings that respond to the demands of the age in many places in Pauline and other letters.

Women's commitment and Jesus' radicalism dismantled the barriers and made them void. We need to locate the barriers that raise up the issues of life and death in our contemporary world. These women in Mark invite us to overcome the barriers from our side so that we may experience life-communion with Jesus. Jesus, who lives radically with the most despised, excluded, and subjugated, and who fights against authoritative patriarchy with all his might, will be on our side. We are invited to discover for ourselves what form our lives may take so that we may live in interaction with Jesus.

We women who live in this patriarchally biased society will continue to disturb churches and our society until we witness the true liberation of the oppressed. We will empower one another so that we do not become discouraged by the actions of the powers-that-be. We will keep engendering our own theology from our experiences and energizing ourselves by it until we see equal discipleship in our churches and society. We can say this because we can confirm that we have been doing our theology in the same ways that have been discovered in the interactions between women and Jesus.

BIBLIOGRAPHY

Achtemeier, Paul J. "The Origin and Function of the Pre-Marcan Miracle Cate-
nae." *Journal of Biblical Literature* 91 (1972): 198-221.
————. "Toward the Isolation of Pre-Markan Miracle Catenae." *Journal of Biblical
Literature* 89 (1970): 265-91.
Anderson, Janice Capel. "Mapping Feminist Biblical Criticism: The American
Scene, 1983-1990." A manuscript. *Critical Review of Books in Religion*. Atlanta:
Scholars Press, 1991:21-44.
Arai, Sasagu. "Prologue tositeno [as] Epilogue." *Kikan Tetsugaku* (1991): 8-31.
————. *Iesu Kirisuto* (Jesus Christ). Tokyo: Kodansha, 1979.
Barta, Karen A. *The Gospel of Mark*. Delaware: Michael Glazier, Inc., 1988.
Beavis, Mary Ann. "Women as Models of Faith in Mark." *Biblical Theology Bulletin*
18 (Jan. 1988): 3-9.
Belo, Fernando. *A Materialist Reading of the Gospel of Mark*. New York: Orbis
Books, 1981.
Benedict, Ruth. *The Chrysanthemum and the Sword*. Cleveland: Meridan Books,
1967.
Best, Ernst. *Disciples and Discipleship: Studies in the Gospel according to Mark*. Edin-
burgh: T&T Clark, 1986.
————. *Following Jesus: Discipleship in the Gospel of Mark*. Sheffield: JSOT, 1981.
————. "Mark's Narrative Technique." *New Testament Studies* 23 (1977): 43-58.
————. "The Role of the Disciples in Mark." *New Testament Studies* 23 (1977):
377-401.
Beyer, Hermann W. "διακονεω, διακονος, διακονια." *Theological Dictionary of the
New Testament*. Vol. 2, 81-93.
Bird, Phyllis. "The Harlot as Heroine: Narrative Art and Social Presupposition in
Three Old Testament Texts." *Semeia* 46 (1989): 119-66.
Boomershine, Thomas E. "Mark 16:8 and the Apostolic Commission." *Journal of
Biblical Literature* 100 (1981): 225-39.
Boomershine, Thomas E., and Bartholomew, Gilbert, "The Narrative Technique
of Mark 16:8." *Journal of Biblical Literature* 100/2 (1981): 213-23.
Borchgrevink, Tordis and Melhuus, Marit. "Text as Reality—Reality as Text."
Semeia 43 (1989): 35-59.
Borsch, Frederick H. "Jesus and Women Exemplars." *Anglican Theological Review*.
Suppl. no. 11 (1990): 29-40.
————. *Power in Weakness: New Hearing for Gospel Stories of Healing and Disciple-
ship*. Philadelphia: Fortress Press, 1983.
Brennan, Irene. "Women in the Gospels." *New Blackfriars* 52 (1971): 291-99.
Brenner, Athalya. *The Israelite Woman: Social Role and Literary Type in Biblical
Narrative*. Sheffield: JSOT Press, 1985.

Brock, Rita Nakashima. *Journey by Heart: A Christology of Erotic Power*. New York: Crossroad, 1988.

Bultmann, Rudolf K. *The History of the Synoptic Tradition*. Translated by John Marsh. Oxford: Basil Blackwell, 1972.

Bundy, Walter Ernst. *Jesus and the First Three Gospels: An Introduction to the Synoptic Tradition*. New York: Cornell Univ. Press, 1972.

Buraku Kaiho Kenkyusho, ed. *Shukyo To Buraku Mondai* (Religions and the Issue of Buraku). Osaka: Kaiho Shuppan, 1990.

Burkill, T.A. "The Historical Development of the Story of the Syrophoenician Woman (Mark 7:24-31): New Light on the Earliest Gospel. *"Novum Testamentum* 9 (1967): 161-77.

———. "Mark 6:31—8:26: The Context of the Story of the Syrophoenician Woman." *The Classical Tradition: Literary and Historical Studies in Honor of H. Caplin*. Edited by L. Wallach. (New York: Cornell Univ. Press, 1966): 329-44.

———. "The Syrophoenician Woman: The Congruence of Mark 7:24-31." *Zeitschrift für die neutestamentliche Wissenschaft* 57 (1966): 23-37.

Christ, Carol P. "Spiritual Quest and Women's Experience." In *Womanspirit Rising: A Feminist Reader in Religion*. Edited by Carol P. Christ and Judith Plaskow. San Francisco: Harper & Row, 1979, 228-45.

Catchpole, David. "The Fearful Silence of the Women at the Tomb." *Journal of Theology for Southern Africa* 18 (1977):3-10.

Coakley, J.F. "The Anointing at Bethany and the Priority of John." *Journal of Biblical Literature* 107/2 (1988): 241-56.

Collins, John N. *Diakonia: Re-interpreting the Ancient Sources*. New York and Oxford: Oxford Univ. Press, 1990.

Corley, Kathleen E. "Were the Women around Jesus Really Prostitutes? Women in the Context of Greco-Roman Meals." *SBL 1989 Seminar Papers*. SBL ASP: Society of Biblical Literature, 487-521.

Crossan, John Dominic. "Empty Tomb and Absent Lord." *The Passion in Mark: Studies on Mark 14—16*. Edited by Werner H. Kelber. Philadelphia: Fortress, 1976.

Derrett, J. Duncan M. " 'Eating up the Houses of Widows': Jesus' Comment on Lawyers?" *Novum Testamentum* 14 (1972): 1-9.

———. *Law in the New Testament*. London: Darton, Longman & Todd, 1970.

———. "Law in the New Testament: The Syro-Phoenician Woman and the Centurion of Capernaum." *Novum Testamentum* 15 (1973): 161-86.

———. "Mark's Technique: The Hemorrhaging Woman and Jairus' Daughter." *Biblica* 63 (1982): 474-505.

Dewey, Joanna. *Disciples of the Way*. Woman's Division Board of Global Ministries: The United Methodist Church, 1976.

———. "Point of View and the Disciples in Mark." *1982 Seminar Papers*. SBL ASP 18: Society of Biblical Literature, 1982.

Dibelius, Martin. *From Tradition to Gospel*. New York: Scribner, 1965.

Doi, Takeo. *'Amae' no Kozo*. Tokyo: Kobundo, 1971.

———. "Amae—a Key Concept for Understanding Japanese Personality Structure." In *Japanese Culture: Its Development and Characteristics*. Edited by R.J. Smith and R.K. Beardsley. Chicago: Aldine Publishing Co., 1962.

Donahue, John. *The Theology and Setting of Discipleship in the Gospel of Mark*. Wisconsin: Marquette Univ., 1983.

Douglas, Mary. *Purity and Danger*. London: Routledge and Kegan Paul, 1966.

Dufton, Francis. "The Syrophoenician Woman and Her Dogs." *The Expository Times* 100 (Aug. 1989): 417.

Elliot, J.K. "The Anointing of Jesus." *The Expository Times* 85 (1974): 105-7.

Fleddermann, Harry. "A Warning about the Scribes (Mark 12:37b-40)." *The Catholic Biblical Quarterly* 44 (1982): 52-67.

Foerster,Werner. "ειρηνη." *Theological Dictionary of the New Testament*. Vol. 2 (1964): 400-420.

———. "Tempeldirne." *Biblisch-Historisches Handwörterbuch*. Göttingen: Vandenhoeck and Ruprecht, 1963. Japanese translation (Tokyo: Kyo Bun Kwan, 1989): 640.

Fohrer, Georg and Lövestam, Evalt. "Ehebruch, Biblisch-Historisches Handwörterbuch. Göttingen: Vandehoeck and Ruprecht, 1963. Japanese translation (Tokyo: Kyo Bun Kwan, 1989): 341.

Francis, Carolyn Bowen, and Nakajima, John Masaaki. *Christians in Japan*. New York: Friendship Press, 1991.

Gavin, William F. "A Lesson from Saint Peter's Mother-in-Law." *Crisis* (March 1989): 42-43.

Gilligan, Carol. *In a Different Voice: Psychological Theory and Women's Development*. Cambridge: Harvard Univ. Press, 1982.

Grassi, Joseph A. "The Secret Heroine of Mark's Drama." *Biblical Theology Bulletin* 18 (January 1988): 10-15.

Green, Barbara. "Jesus' Teaching on Divorce in the Gospel of Mark." *Journal for the Study of the New Testament* 38 (1990): 67-75.

Hauck/Schulz. "πορνη, πορνος, πορνεια, πορνευω, εκπορνευω." *Theological Dictionary of the New Testament*. Vol. 6, 579-95.

Holst, Robert. "The One Anointing of Jesus: Another Application of the Form-Critical Method." *Journal of Biblical Literature* 95/3 (1976): 435-46.

Inoue, Chuji. *'Sekentei' no Kozo* (The Structure of "Keeping One's Appearances"). Tokyo: NHK Books, 1977.

Iser, Wolfgang. *The Implied Reader*. Baltimore: Johns Hopkins University Press, 1974.

Jeremias, Joachim. *Jerusalem in the Time of Jesus*. Philadelphia: Fortress Press, 1969.

Johnson, Luke T. *Sharing Possessions: Mandate and Symbol of Faith*. Philadelphia: Fortress, 1981.

Johnson, S.E. *A Commentary on the Gospel According to St. Mark*. London: Adam and Charles Black, 1960.

Josephus. *Jewish Antiquities*.

Kaji, Nobuyuki. *Jukyo to wa Nanika* (What is Confucianism?). Tokyo: Chuko Shinsho, 1990.

Kan, Sanjung. "Japanese Orientalism—Distortion Lurked in Internationalization of Japan" (in Japanese). *Sekai* (Dec. 1988): 133-39.

Kanamori, Toshie, and Fujii, Hanae. *History of Women's Education for the Last Century* (in Japanese). Tokyo: Sanseido, 1977.

Kanda, Tateo. *New Testament Greek* (in Japanese). Tokyo: Iwanami Zensho, 1956.

Kee, Howard C. *Community of the New Age: Studies in Mark's Gospel*. Philadelphia: Westminster Press, 1977.

Kelber, Werner H. *The Kingdom in Mark: A New Place and a New Time*. Philadelphia: Fortress Press, 1974.

King, Sallie B. (translated and annotated) *Passionate Journey: The Spiritual Auto-biography of Satomi Myodo.* Boston and London: Shambhala, 1987.

Kinukawa, Hisako. "Seisho ni okeru Sei-Baibaishun." (How Selling and Buying Sex is Dealt with in the Bible.) *Fujin Shimpo* 1088 (5, 1991): 22-25.

———. *Seisho no Feminizumu.* (Women in the Bible — To Become Subjects of History.) Tokyo: Yorudan Pub., 1987.

———, and Arai, Sasagu. "Ima Seisho wo Yomu towa." (Series: Contemporary Reading of Biblical Texts.) *The Kyodan Times* 4244 and 4246 (1991): 2-3 and 2-3.

Kittel, G. "ακολουθεω," *Theological Dictionary of the New Testament.* Vol. 1, 213.

Kittredge, Cherry. *Womansword: What Japanese Words Say about Women.* Tokyo and New York: Kodansha International, 1987.

Kopas, Jane, O.S.F. "Jesus and Women in Mark's Gospel." *Review for Religious* 44 (1985): 912-20.

Kuribayashi, Teruo. *Keikan no Shingaku* (A Theology of the Crown of Thorns). Tokyo: Shinkyo Shuppan, 1991.

Kwok, Pui Lan. "Discovering the Bible in the Non-biblical World." *Semeia* 47 (1989): 25-42.

Lee, Eunja. "Together with Our Neighbors" (in Japanese). *Kyokai Hujin Rengo Tayori* 50 (May 26, 1992): 1-3.

Lincoln, Andrew T. "The Promise and the Failure: Mark 16:7, 8." *Journal of Biblical Literature* 108/2 (1989): 283-300.

Lindboe, Inger Marie. "Recent Literature: Development and Perspectives in New Testament Research on Women." *Studia Theologica* 43 (1989): 153-63.

Mack, Burton L., and Robbins, Vernon K. *Patterns of Persuasion in the Gospels.* Sonoma, CA: Polebridge Press, 1988.

Malbon, Elizabeth Struthers. "Disciples/Crowds/Whoever: Markan Characters and Readers." *Novum Testamentum* 28, 2 (1986): 104-30.

———. "Fallible Followers: Women and Men in the Gospel of Mark." *Semeia* 28 (1983): 29-48.

———. "Galilee and Jerusalem: History and Literature in Marcan Interpretation." *Catholic Biblical Quarterly* 44 (1982): 242-55.

———. *Narrative Space and Mythic Meaning in Mark.* San Francisco: Harper and Row, 1986.

Malina, Bruce. "Does Porneia Mean Fornication?" *Novum Testamentum* 45 (1972): 10-17.

———. "Interpreting the Bible with Anthropology: The Case of the Poor and the Rich." *Listening: A Journal of Religion and Culture* 21:2 (1986): 148-59.

———. *The New Testament World: Insights from Cultural Anthropology.* Atlanta: John Knox, 1981.

Maunder C.J. "A Sitz im Leben for Mark 14:9." *The Expository Times* 99 (Dec. 1987): 78-80.

May, David M. "Mark 3:20-35 from the Perspective of Shame/Honor." *Biblical Theology Bulletin* 17 (1987): 83-87.

McKnight, Edgar V. *What Is Form Criticism?* Philadelphia: Fortress Press, 1969.

Meyer, Marvin W. "The Youth in the Secret Gospel of Mark." *Semeia* 49 (1990): 129-53.

Meyers, Carol. *Discovering Eve: Ancient Israelite Women in Context.* New York: Oxford University Press, 1988.

Michaelis, W. "λεπρα, λεπρος." *Theological Dictionary of the New Testament.* Vol. 4, 233-34.

Milgrom, Jacob. "Rationale for Cultic Law: The Case of Impurity." *Semeia* 43 (1989): 103-9.

The Mishnah: Aboth 1:5. Translated by Herbert Danby. Oxford: Clarendon, 1933.

Mizuta, Tamae. *History of Thoughts in Women's Liberation* (in Japanese). Tokyo: Iwanami, 1973.

Moiser, Jeremy. " 'She Was Twelve Years Old' (Mark 5:42): A Note on Jewish-Gentile Controversy in Mark's Gospel." *Irish Biblical Studies* 3 (1981): 179-86.

Moltmann-Wendel, Elisabeth. *A Land Flowing with Milk and Honey: Perspectives on Feminist Theology.* Translated by John Bowden. New York: Crossroad, 1988.

———. *The Women Around Jesus: Reflection on Authentic Personhood.* London: SCM Press, 1980, New York: Crossroad, 1982.

Monma, Yukio. " 'Kegare' to Buraku Sabetu." *Shukyo to Buraku Mondai.* Osaka: Kaiho Shuppansha, 1990.

Moxnes, Halvor. "Introduction: Feminist Reconstruction of Early Christian History." *Studia Theologica* 43 (1989): 1-3.

———. *The Economy of the Kingdom.* Philadelphia: Fortress, 1988.

Munro, Winsome. "Women Disciples in Mark?" *The Catholic Biblical Quarterly* 44 (1982): 225-41.

Myers, Ched. *Binding the Strong Man: A Political Reading of Mark's Story of Jesus.* New York: Orbis Books, 1988.

Namihira, Emiko. *Kurasi no naka no Bunka Jinruigaku* (Cultural Anthropology of Our Daily Life). Tokyo: Hukutake Shoten, 1986.

Noma, Hiroshi, and Okiura, Kazumitu. *Ajia no Sei to Sen: Hisabetumin no Rekishi to Bunka.* (Purity and Impurity in Asia: History and Culture of the Discriminated.) Kyoto: Jinbunshoin, 1983.

O'Collins, Gerald. "The Fearful Silence of Three Women." *Gregorium* 69, 3 (1988): 489-503.

O'Day, Gail R. "Surprised by Faith: Jesus and the Canaanite Woman." *Listening: A Journal of Religion and Culture* 24 (Fall 1989): 290-301.

Oepke, Albrecht. "ιαομαι." *Theological Dictionary of the New Testament.* Vol. 3 (1965): 194-215.

Ohnuki-Tierney, Emiko. *Illness and Healing among the Sakhlin Ainu: A Symbolic Interpretation.* Cambridge: University Press, 1981.

Ohshima, Shizuko, and Francis, Carolyn. *Japan: Through the Eyes of Women Migrant Workers.* Tokyo: Japan Women's Christian Temperance Union, 1989.

Okoshi, Aiko; Minamoto, Junko; and Yamashita, Akiko. *Seisabetu suru Bukkyo* (Sexism in Buddhism). Kyoto: Hozokan, 1990.

Osborne, Grant R. "Women in Jesus' Ministry." *Westminster Theological Review* (1989): 259-91.

Pagels, Elaine. *Adam, Eve, and the Serpent.* New York: Random House, 1988.

Perrin, Norman. *What is Redaction Criticism?* Philadelphia: Fortress Press, 1969.

Petersen, Norman R. "When Is the End Not the End? Literary Reflections on the Ending of Mark's Narrative." *Interpretation* 34 (1980): 151-66.

Pilch, John J. "Healing in Mark: A Social Science Analysis." *Biblical Theology Bulletin* 14 (1985): 142-50.

———. "Biblical Leprosy and Body Symbolism." *Biblical Theology Bulletin* 11 (1981): 103-118.

Platt, Elizabeth E. "The Ministry of Mary of Bethany." *Theology Today* 34 (1977): 29-39.

Plum, Karin Friis. "The Female Metaphor. The Definition of Male and Female — An Unsolved Problem?" *Studia Theologica* 43 (1989): 81-89.

Portefaix, Lilian. "Women and Mission in the New Testament: Some Remarks on the Perspective of Audience. A Research Report." *Studia Theologica* 43 (1989): 141-52.

Quesnell, Quentin. *Mind of Mark: Interpretation and Method through the Exegesis of Mark 6:52,* Rome: Bible Institute, 1969.

Rengstorf, K.H. "μαθητη" *Theological Dictionary of the New Testament.* Vol. 4, 416-61.

Rhoades, David, and Michie, Donald. *Mark as Story: An Introduction to the Narrative of the Gospel.* Philadelphia: Fortress Press, 1982.

Robbins, Vernon K. "Last Meal: Preparation, Betrayal, and Absence (Mark 14: 12-25)." *The Passion in Mark.* Edited by Werner H. Kelber. Philadephia: Fortress Press, 1976.

———. "Using a Socio-Rhetorical Poetics to Develop a Unified Method: The Woman Who Anointed Jesus as a Test Case." *SBL Seminar Papers* (1992): 302-19.

Rogers, Barbara. *Race: No Peace Without Justice.* Geneva: World Council of Churches, 1980.

Ruether, Rosemary Radford. *Sexism and God-Talk: Toward a Feminist Theology.* Boston: Beacon, 1984.

———. *New Woman New Earth: Sexist Ideologies and Human Liberation.* New York: Crossroad, 1975.

Russell, Letty M., ed. *Feminist Interpretation of the Bible.* Philadelphia: Westminster Press, 1985.

Ryan, Rosalie. "Assertive Women in the Gospels." *The Bible Today* 25 (Nov. 1987): 352-57.

Schierling, Marla J. "Women as Leaders in the Marcan Communities." *Listening: A Journal of Religion and Culture* 15 (1980): 250-57.

Schmidt, John J. "Women in Mark's Gospel: An Early Christian View of Women's Role." *The Bible Today* 19 (July 1981): 228-33.

Schottroff, Luise. "Maria Magdalena and die Frauen am Grabe Jesu." *Evangelische Theologie* 42 (1982).

Schottroff, Willy, and Stegemann, Wolfgang, eds. *Frauen in der Bibel.* Munich: Chr. Kaiser, 1980.

———. *Traditionen der Befreiung: Sozialgeschichtliche Bibelauslegungen* (Japanese edition). Tokyo: Shikyo, 1986.

Schüssler Fiorenza, Elisabeth. "Biblical Interpretation and Critical Commitment." *Studia Theologica* 43 (1989): 5-18.

———. *Bread Not Stone: The Challenge of Feminist Biblical Interpretation.* Boston: Beacon Press, 1984.

———. "The Ethics of Biblical Interpretation: Decentering Biblical Scholarship." *Journal of Biblical Literature* 107/1 (1988): 3-17.

———. "Feminist Theology and New Testament Interpretation." *Journal for the Study of the Old Testament* 22 (1982): 32-46.

———. *In Memory of Her: A Feminist Theological Reconstruction of Christian Origins.* New York: Crossroad, 1983.

———. "Rhetorical Situation and Historical Reconstruction in 1 Corinthians." *New Testament Studies* 33 (1987): 386-403.

———. "Text and Reality—Reality as Text: The Problem of a Feminist Historical and Social Reconstruction Based on Texts." *Studia Theologica* 43 (1989): 19-34.

———. " 'You Are Not to Be Called Father': Christian History in a Feminist Perspective." *Cross Currents* 29/3 (1979): 301-23.

Schüssler Fiorenza, Francis. "The Crisis of Scriptural Authority." *Interpretation* 44/4 (1990): 28-54. (Japanese edition translated by Hisako Kinukawa).

Schweizer, Eduard. *Das Evangelium nach Markus* (Japanese edition). Tokyo: NTD, 1976.

Selvidge, Marla J. "And Those Who Followed Feared (Mark 10:32)?" *Catholic Biblical Quarterly* 45 (1983): 396-400.

———. "Mark and Woman: Reflections on Serving." *Explorations* 1 (1982): 23-32.

———. "Mark 5:25-34 and Leviticus 15:19-20: A Reaction to Restrictive Purity Regulations." *Journal of Biblical Literature* 103:4 (1984): 619-623.

———. *Woman, Cult & Miracle Recital: A Redactional Critical Investigation of Mark 5:24-34*. Lewisburg, Penn.: Bucknell University Press, 1990.

Senior, Donald C.P. "Listening to the Voices." *The Bible Today* (Nov. 1990): 358-63.

———. " 'With Swords and Clubs' . . .—The Setting of Mark's Community and His Critique of Abusive Power." *Biblical Theology Bulletin* 17 (1987): 10-19.

Seybold, Klaus, and Mueller, Ulrich B. *Sickness and Healing*. Translated by Douglas W. Scott. Nashville: Abingdon Press, 1981.

Snell, Priscilla. "The Women From Galilee." *Sisters* 60 (Apr. 1989): 483-85.

Sthählin, Gustav. "χηρας." *Theological Dictionary of the New Testament*. Vol. 9, 440-42.

Strack, Hermann L. and Billerbeck, Paul. *Kommentar zum Neuen Testament aus Talmud und Midrasch*. Munich, vol. 2, Verlag C.H. Beck, 1956.

Sugirtharajah, R.S. " 'For You Always Have the Poor with You': An Example of Hermeneutics of Suspicion." *Asia Journal of Theology* 4 (Jan. 1990): 102-7.

Suzuki, Yuko. *History of Japanese Women in the Modern Age*. (In Japanese). Tokyo: Iwanami, 1973.

Swidler, Leonard. *Biblical Affirmations of Women*. Philadelphia: Westminster Press, 1979.

———. "Jesus Was a Feminist." *South East Asia Journal of Theology* 13 (1971): 102-10.

———. *Women in Judaism*. Metuchen, NJ: Scarecrow Press, 1976.

Tannehill, Robert C. "Disciples in Mark: The Function of a Narrative Role." *Journal of Religion* 57 (1977): 386-405.

———. "The Gospel of Mark as Narrative Christology." *Semeia* 16 (1980): 57-95.

———. "Introduction: The Pronouncement Story and Its Types." *Semeia* 20 (1981): 1-13.

———. "Varieties of Synoptic Pronouncement Stories." *Semeia* 20 (1981): 101-19.

Taylor, Vincent. *The Gospel According to St. Mark*. London: Macmillan, 1953.

Theissen, Gerd. *The Miracle Stories of the Early Christian Tradition*. Edinburgh: T & T Clark, 1983.

———. *The Shadow of the Galilean: The Quest for the Historical Jesus in Narrative Form*. Translated by John Bowden. Philadelphia: Fortress Press, 1987.

Thurston, Bonnie Bowman. *The Widows: A Women's Ministry in the Early Church.* Minneapolis: Fortress Press, 1989.

Tolbert, Mary Ann. "Defining the Problem. The Bible and Feminist Hermeneutics." *Semeia* 28 (1983): 113-26.

Tomisaka Kirisutokyo Center. *Tennousei no Singakuteki Hihan.* (Theological Critique on the Emperor System.) Tokyo: Sinkyo Shuppansha, 1990.

Trible, Phyllis. *God and the Rhetoric of Sexuality.* Philadelphia: Fortress Press, 1978.

Twelftree, Graham. "Discipleship in Mark's Gospel." *St. Mark's Review* 141 (1990): 5-11.

Utumi, Aiko. "To Live with Asian People." *Laborers from Asian Countries.* Edited by Aiko Utumi and Yayori Matui. Tokyo: Akasi Shoten, 1988.

Waetjen, Herman C. *A Reordering of Power: A Socio-Political Reading of Mark's Gospel.* Minneapolis: Fortress Press, 1989.

Wahlberg, Rachel Conrad. *Jesus According to a Woman.* New York: Paulist Press, (Revised and enlarged edition) 1986.

Weeden, Theodore. "The Heresy That Necessitated Mark's Gospel." *Zeitschrift für die neutestamentliche Wissenschaft* 59 (1968): 143-53.

Wikan, Unni. "Shame and Honour: A Contestable Pair." *Man* 19 (1984): 635-52.

Wire, Antoinette Clark. *The Corinthian Women Prophets: A Reconstruction through Paul's Rhetoric.* Minneapolis: Fortress Press, 1990.

———. "One God, Two Commands and Many Hearings." Paper read at the AAR/SBL Conference, 1991.

———. "The Structure of the Gospel Miracle Stories and Their Tellers." *Semeia* 11 (1978): 83-113.

Witherington, Ben, III. *Women in the Ministry of Jesus: A Study of Jesus' Attitudes to Women and Their Roles as Reflected in His Earthly Life.* Cambridge: University Press, 1984.

Wright, Addison G. "The Widow's Mites: Praise or Lament? — A Matter of Context." *The Catholic Biblical Quarterly* 44 (1982): 256-65.

Young, Allan. "The Anthropologies of Illness and Sickness." *Annual Review of Anthropology* 11 (1982): 257-85.

———. *Women in the Earliest Churches.* New York: Cambridge University Press, 1988.

Index